MANAGEMENT CONSULTANCY IN SCHOOLS

Management Consultancy in Schools

Edited by
H. L. Gray

CASSELL

Cassell Educational Limited
Artillery House
Artillery Row
London SW1P 1RT

First published 1988

British Library Cataloguing in Publication Data

Management consultancy in schools.
  1. School management and organization
  I. Gray, H. L.
  371.2   LB2805

ISBN: 0–304–31468–4

Phototypesetting by Fakenham Photosetting Limited
Printed and bound in Great Britain by Mackays of Chatham Ltd.

Last digit is print no: 9 8 7 6 5 4 3 2 1

Contents

Notes on the Contributors

John Elliott-Kemp is a former head teacher; he has been a university and polytechnic lecturer with research interests in human potential and cross-cultural psychology. A director of Helios International, he is involved in writing, research and development and fostering a consultancy network specializing in education management. He has worked extensively overseas on programmes in Europe, Africa, India, North America, and the Far East. His teaching and consultancy in the United Kingdom has included work with individual schools, colleges and universities and with local education authorities and the Department of Education and Science.

K. B. (Bertie) Everard is the former Education and Training Manager of Imperial Chemical Industries (ICI), having had responsibility for management training and organization development (OD) from 1966 to 1982. Afterwards he became involved in school management training and consultancy, mainly as a Visiting Fellow of the University of London Institute of Education. His research on problems in schools formed the basis of his book *Developing Management in Schools*.

Harry Gray teaches education management at the University of Lancaster. He has worked as a consultant with a number of schools and written a number of articles and books on matters of related interest. He is currently working with a school in the north-west on a long-term management development project and is engaged with a number of heads on various projects in management development. He has worked outside the United Kingdom as a consultant in Canada, the United States, Australia, South Africa, Germany, Holland and Norway.

Harold Heller is the first Director of the Centre for Adviser and Inspector Development (CAID). He taught in secondary and higher education in London and Jamaica, held administrative and advisory posts in Suffolk and Teesside and became Chief Adviser in Cleveland in 1975. He has particular interests in management education, special educational needs, counselling and group work. He has written widely on educational issues and he has done consultancy work not only in schools and LEAs but also in the National Health Service.

Ian Jamieson lectures in education and industry at the University of Bath. He was formerly Head of Sociology and later Reader in Business and Management Studies at Ealing College of Higher Education. Between these two appointments he was Evaluator and Research Director of the Schools Council Industry Project (SCIP). He has published a number of books on the relation between education and industry and is editor of the *British Journal of Education and Work*. Recent consultancy includes work on the management of curriculum development projects and experiential learning programmes in schools and higher education.

David Keith was a marine engineer for nine years and later an Anglican clergyman. Out of interest in mental and organizational health he read for an MSc in Organization Development at Sheffield Polytechnic and has been a part-time organization development consultant to the Sheffield LEA for 12 years. Freelance practice led to his establishing an organization development unit in the Oldham LEA where work includes training seconded deputy head teachers into an organization development consultancy team.

Mike Lavelle was a secondary school teacher for 12 years before becoming coordinator of the Sheffield Schools/Youth Service curriculum development project in personal and social education. Subsequently he has had substantial experience in training and development in schools and the Youth Service, and since 1983 he and David Keith have worked as co-consultants in the Sheffield LEA's Organization Development Unit. He is also a freelance trainer and consultant in human relations, counselling and organization development.

Mike Milstein is currently professor and chair in the Department of Educational Administration of the University of New Mexico. He has taught in the State University of New York (SUNY) system and lectured in the United Kingdom, China and Israel. In 1974 he spent a year in the United Kingdom helping to set up a new department of education management at the North East London Polytechnic. His consultant work in educational settings is organization development focused. His most recent interests have centred on stress management, plateauing and organizational effectiveness.

Geoffrey Morris spent ten years teaching modern languages and law at the Royal Grammar School, Newcastle upon Tyne, and later became Head of Modern Languages and General Studies at Hampton School, Middlesex. In 1967 he won the support of the CBI (Confederation of British Industries) to organize what was probably the first-ever course in modern management for school teachers in the United Kingdom. Since that time he has played an active role in the development of school management, notably as a visiting lecturer at Brighton Polytechnic and Brunel University. From 1984 to 1986 he was a member of the CNAA Board for Educational Organization and Management and he is co-author, with Bertie Everard, of *Effective School Management*. Since 1981 he has been managing director of EMAS (European Management Advisory Service) Business Consultants Ltd.

Bill Mulford is Dean of Education at the Tasmanian State Institute of Technology, Australia. Starting his career in one-teacher schools, he has held positions in teaching and educational administration in Australia, the United Kingdom, Canada and Papua New Guinea and tertiary positions in Canada and Australia. He has carried out extensive consultancy assignments with schools and educational systems both in Australia and overseas. A pioneer in the use of organization development in Australian schools, he has written extensively in this and related fields.

Stephen Murgatroyd is Dean of Administrative Studies at Athabasca University, Alberta, Canada, where he takes a practical interest in management development. Previously he was a senior counsellor at the Open University based in Wales. Trained as a psychologist, he has worked extensively in counselling and counsellor training. He has consultancy experience with schools, health authorities and industry as both counsellor and consultant. He has published extensively and his books include *Helping the Troubled Child, Helping Families in Distress* and *Counselling and Help*.

Don Musella is currently chairman of the Department of Educational Administration and Head of the Centre for Executive Studies at the Ontario Institute for Studies in Education, Toronto. For five years he was Executive Director of the Ontario Council for Leadership in Educational Administration (OCLEA). Each year he conducts over 15 workshops and seminars on personnel selection and evaluation, implementation of change, organization development and management skills.

Stanley Putnam is head of Brookfield School, Hampshire. An engineer by training, his first job was in the naval dockyards at Portsmouth. As a teacher of technical subjects he taught overseas in the Gilbert and Ellice Islands (now Tuvalu) and Antigua (where he returns from time to time to produce Gilbert and Sullivan). He has always valued education for the opportunities for full personal development that are offered. Quite recently he trained in pastoral counselling and tries to apply counselling principles to the management of the school. He is in regular demand as a management trainer of head teachers throughout the country. He is chairman of NODE (Network for Organization Development in Education).

John Sayer was head of Banbury School in Warwickshire from 1973 to 1984 during an important stage in its development and consolidation. From 1979 to 1980 he was President of the Secondary Heads Association. After retiring from headship he joined the Education Management Unit at the Institute of Education, University of London, where he works with Bertie Everard on programmes for senior managers in schools. He has written books and articles on rethinking the nature of schooling and is much in demand as a speaker and consultant.

Robin Snell lectures in the Department of Management Learning at the University of Lancaster. As a consultant he has run workshops on various aspects of management development among staff in a local education authority (LEA). Current research interests include ethical dilemmas in management development and how individual managers learn and develop through organizational experiences. His papers have appeared in such journals as *Personnel Review* and *Management Education and Development*.

Geoffrey Sworder graduated in chemistry at Oxford in 1950 and joined ICI Ltd, where he worked in a variety of production management positions including five years in Kenya. From 1968 he has been working as an organization development and training consultant, mostly in overseas subsidiary companies of ICI. Retired in 1985 he now operates independently with a variety of client organizations. Of experience in education he says he has not had any 'apart from being educated myself'.

Foreword

This book consists of 15 specially commissioned papers written by individuals who have had direct experience of consulting with schools on matters of management development. The theme of 'management consultancy in schools' has been chosen because it provides a reasonably sharp focus to the consultancy process, raises most of the issues of consultancy in general and has a reasonably coherent pattern of implementation or approach behind it as well as a considerable tradition in commerce, industry and the public service.

The book is intended to be both readable and practical. It is a book for practitioners and users, not an academic treatise on theory and research into the use of consultancy. It has been compiled specifically with the purpose of helping to improve the quality of management in schools. But it is also a compilation of personal viewpoints and perspectives which overall reflect the way some consultants think about working with schools as professionals; that is, as people who have both experience and training in the consultant role.

Each school that engages a consultant does so in a unique and individual way. The needs of every school are different and the relevant processes of consultancy are different but there are some broad general principles that are exemplified throughout the book. One of these is the primacy of the client in determining what is possible and how the consultancy progresses. Another is the concept that the consultant's job is to help the school, not to bring about his own preferred reform.

In the years ahead, because of the new forms of funding for in-service training—the GRIST proposals (grant-related in-service training funding)—more and more use will be made of consultants of various kinds. The use of management consultants is a model for using consultants of any kind in education and how this may be done is shown in the pages of this book.

Although the arrangement of chapters follows a certain logic, most readers will not want to read the book through from cover to cover or all at one go. Dipping into chapters will be the best way of using the book, and for this reason there is some repetition of ideas so that each contribution has its own inherent cohesion. There are four parts in which similar perspectives on the consultancy process are grouped and exemplified. Each is introduced by a short preface that highlights the nature of the perspective in the section.

Thanks are due to the many individuals who have contributed to the volume but who cannot be named because they were client contributors to the process of gaining experience about consultancy. There have been many pioneers in consultancy and their memorial is the betterment of our schools—an undoubted reality despite all criticism from ill-informed quarters.

Lancaster University   *H. L. Gray*
July, 1987

Introduction

I recently became involved in negotiations with a head teacher about acting as consultant for a management development project in his school. We talked over several weeks and eventually agreed on how we would proceed and when to start. He expressed excitement at the prospect of a substantial commitment to school development but wondered whether I was really as enthusiastic as he was; was I still as interested three weeks later after talks had begun? I replied that I was interested and committed, but if I did not seem as excited as he was it was because I had been through the negotiation process many times and often we did not get very far beyond an expression of interest and a desultory sketch of possibilities. In this case, I was able to look forward to something actually happening rather than nurse my disappointment that the school had found the practicalities too daunting.

In many ways one of the most interesting studies would be of why so many contemplated consultancy projects do not get very far. It is not so difficult to chronicle—albeit in an idealized form of recollection—consultancy programmes that have run a good course but it would be helpful to know more about why some of them do not even get started. If we could find out why so many people who contemplate a decent and needed management consultancy give up in the very early stages, we would have the answer to many basic management problems in schools.

Perhaps the most obvious reason why consultancy projects do not progress is the lack of money to pay for them. It is usual before any consultancy commences for there to be a session where negotiation takes place between the principal parties—in schools this will usually be the head and the consultant himself. As with commercial undertakings this will be without cost to the school but at opportunity cost to the consultant. If the consultant is professional the cost may be considerable for even half a day but such use of time is usual because of the potential benefit. But thereafter the school will have to bear costs not only to pay for the consultant but in terms of time and resources reallocated in the school for the project. It cannot be emphasized too much that cost is probably the major factor in preventing—and certainly in reducing the quality of—consultancy in schools over and above anything else. The new GRIST (grant-related in-service training) funding in the United Kingdom is more likely to throw this problem into high profile than make the engagement of consultants for any worthwhile project easier.

But having said that, there are other significant blockages to the progress of consultancy in schools that need to be faced. The first is the lack of a tradition of using external consultants in schools. Over the years schools have been exceedingly resilient in coping with the changes that have been urged upon them by a variety of influences ranging from social needs to government strategies. They have learned to use their internal resources to best advantage with considerable support from the local education authorities, in particular from the advisory services. But state schools have never had to take full responsibility for themselves, with the consequence that senior management has never had to seek the best advice or help in order to cope with major threats or opportunities of a life-saving character. Fee-paying schools have to consider such issues all the time and usually use mechanisms such as a board of governors or trustees, or the proprietary nature of headship, to cope with development matters and crises.

In most schools, head teachers are inexperienced in engaging professional assistance for anything but the briefest term. One effect of this is that they may take a custodial role in protecting the school or a patriarchal role in relating to their colleagues. Consultancy in any of its forms is not yet seen as a means of improving the resourcefulness of the school and of uncovering the wealth of competence so often latent among teaching staff, pupils and parents. Only when heads acknowledge that employing consultants is a positive and enriching process that will support their headship, rather than challenge it, will consultancy become a functionally integrated aspect of school development.

Another serious blockage to introducing consultants is the nature of management structures in most schools. Currently there is no standard form of senior management in UK schools and very few schools have what would be generally considered by management experts to be a satisfactory structure. Of course, each school will have to find its own best formula and that will arise out of an understanding of the relationship between the mission of the school and the talents among its staff. But most schools are weak at the top in a number of ways. The first is usually the absence of good, strong teamwork among the top group—generally the head and the two or three deputies in a secondary school and the head and deputy in a primary school. (For reasons to do with size and the general ethos of primary education, primary schools usually function better collectively than secondary schools and leadership issues are comparatively easier to deal with.)

It would seem essential for secondary schools (and, in a more limited way, primary schools) to identify the top management group and to organize its work—roles, functions, responsibilities—in a truly managerial way. That is, that the management direction of the school should be in the hands of a group of people who have management as their exclusive job. Many schools resist this form of managerialism because individuals are reluctant to give up the teaching role (that is, the class teaching of students) and do not realize that the teaching of students cannot take place properly without the appropriate managerial and pastoral support of staff. The top management group should see itself in the same kind of facilitative relationship to their adult colleagues as class teachers do to their pupils.

The reason why the forming of a coherent top management team is important in my experience is because of another factor that occurs far too often, the separateness that many heads have from their colleagues—frequently managerially and often emotionally (Gray, 1987). Time and time again I go into schools only to find that heads are reluctant to bring in their deputies to join us in the conversation. Often they appear to want to keep their deputies away from contact with an outside professional. I often get the impression that heads (some? many?) either do not trust their deputies or trust some and not others. Sometimes they tell me that one of the deputies is a dead loss, or ready for retirement, or has been in the school too long, or is an unfortunate inheritance. Sometimes they confide that they would hope to appoint a good junior member of staff if the opportunity were to arise but I am left wondering why these good people are kept waiting in the wings while the head prevaricates about doing something for the senior colleagues he cannot work with.

I hope I am not caricaturing the situation but I suppose that an outside management professional is a threat to a head who may feel himself to be in a senior management position but to be untrained for the job. Certainly it is often said that heads receive no proper training for their job (Weindling and Earley, 1987), and it becomes hard to admit after several years in a job that you might be the one who should be first in line for training. I even wonder if it is not a personal characteristic of teachers to find the idea of being 'taught' or 'trained' (an even more horrifying idea) somewhat threatening. Certainly there is some folklore around that teachers make bad pupils.

Time and time again when I talk to heads I am sounded out about management development for colleagues but not for the head him/herself. Of course, this projection of needs onto one's subordinates is not confined to teaching; it is one of the commonest characteristics of senior managers with little experience of management development. But the universality of the belief that 'everyone else but me needs retraining' does not downgrade its significance for schools. My own considered view is that unless management development begins and is sustained at the top of an organization there is little point in trying it elsewhere. Without top managers in on the process the more significant effects are an increase in discontent and frustration, dysfunctional behaviour, and an increased will on the part of those whose insights have developed to move on to better places.

Another problem about consultancy is that it involves commitment to a particular course of action for a very long time. Not many organizations like to be committed to a course of management development that goes on for very long. Most organizations look for short, snappy answers to what they see as simple problems. With schools, such things as periods of examination and holidays get in the way of making long-term arrangements, but the excitement of continual innovation may make a development programme extending into a second and third year seem dull and redundant. Schools work to an unusual time-scale (in organizational terms) in that changes take a long time to happen and be consolidated. It takes several years for a new examination course to be put into place so teachers become wearied by too many long-term strands. Most other organizations have briefer time spans so that projects are constantly being started and finished and the years do not spin out ahead with the same degree of sameness as with schools. There may well be intimations of boredom at the beginning of a long-term school project that militates against its being forcefully embraced.

The contributions to this book are all written by professionals who have had to deal with the conditions I have mentioned in this introduction, though in most cases they are taken for granted and the more positive aspects of bringing about positive change in schools are described. There will undoubtedly be more and more consultancy of all kinds in schools, but in many ways 'management' consultancy presents a good model because it is one that has a long and sustained history in commerce, industry and the public service. Other forms of consultancy can be usefully compared with it and modelled on how the processes are developed and the theories of consultant–client interaction are put into practice (Fullan, 1982). Changes in curriculum require to be managed even though they may appear to be concerned with changing what is taught. For one thing, this involves how things are taught and changing people's behaviour is the most difficult management task of all and the one that raises most ethical issues.

REFERENCES

Fullan, M. (1982) *The Meaning of Educational Change*, New York: Teachers College Press.
Gray, H. L. (1987) 'Problems in helping head teachers to learn about management', *Educational Management and Administration*, **15**.
Weindling, D. and Earley, P. (1987) *Secondary Headship: The First Years*. Windsor: NFER-Nelson.

Part I

First Principles

The chapters in this part of the book provide a general perspective on consultancy in education using a model that sees the consultant as catalyst. For the most part, management consultants try to respect their clients' point of view and see their function most usefully as being to help the clients to decide more effectively what they want to do and to tap the resources available (wherever that may be) so that they can do it. After providing help in this way the consultant withdraws and leaves the 'real work' of running the organization to the members of the organization under the appropriate leadership of the management already established but by now improved and augmented.

In education, the role of 'consultant' has largely been perceived as that of a forceful change agent or reformer—a tradition that was quite strong in the Schools Council and during the period of curriculum reform in the late 1950s and 1960s. On the whole, writers in this collection do not espouse a reformist view of the consultant but a 'facilitative' one. In this perspective the influence of counselling is strong and consultant skills are seen as being strongly akin to the skills of counsellors in other helping professions.

In Chapter 1, I provide a simple introduction to the general principles that apply to using consultants in schools. Because there is so little experience on the ground (that is, in schools themselves) of working with consultants a great deal of caution is called for. Even when schools have used the help of outsiders, they have seldom done so for long periods or with deeply significant problems. I describe the first principles that have to be borne in mind when considering engaging consultants in school and outline the negotiation processes and cost implications.

John Sayer (Chapter 2) writes as a former head teacher of a school generally considered to have been innovative in curriculum and organizational change. He also writes as someone who has had to explain himself to other heads. In many ways, this chapter characterizes the issues as an intelligent and questioning head will see them and exhibits an interesting complexity of vision, conceptualizing and a sense of the practical. It is worth remembering that what at first glance appears to be the most practical is not always the most simple, and that what appear to be clean and neat solutions in theory do not often turn out to be so in practice. Chapter 2 raises issues of school change in the context of the recent history of educational change—those most intent on reform have not always been very clear about what they wanted or how best to do it.

Chapter 3 is a contribution from the antipodes by a writer who introduced organization development forms of consultancy and training into Australian schools. In his chapter, Bill Mulford draws on the extensive literature on school leadership and school effectiveness, and in so doing points the reader to some of the important concepts around in education with which it is necessary to come to terms if the nature and purpose of schools is to be understood—and so provides a basis for considering the basic purpose and functions of consultancy. There is a danger that many schools will undertake consultancy without taking due cognizance of its relationship to an underlying understanding of the nature of schooling. And it is necessary, too, to be clear about what educational change is.

Robin Snell (Chapter 4) writes from the point of view of a consultant with a long experience of research into how people in organizations learn. He shows how difficult it is for consultants to 'know' what clients want or even to understand the full meaning of what they say. Too often the role of the consultant is taken for granted as if he were entirely neutral or benign in his influence on the organization, but it is as important to understand the consultant as a person and practitioner as it is to understand the school where he is engaged and its members. Consultancy is about change and all forms of induced change raise ethical issues. In this chapter Snell reveals a good deal about his own style of working—a kind of insight into how someone works with which schools are not very familiar. Consultants are people and they work in their own personal way. One should not engage any old person but look closely for a compatibility of style and empathy of purpose and values, otherwise consultancy will be at cross purposes with the organization and its dominant cultural and ethical values.

Although writing from Canada, Murgatroyd's chapter (5) is based on a largely British experience. He writes as a practising counsellor and shows how his skills in one helping profession apply directly to another. It is more than likely that in the next few years counselling skills will become more closely allied with consultancy skills though several different models will be employed—the not unlikely material for the next volume on consultancy in schools. The particular model of family therapy used by Murgatroyd is a very powerful one because it brings together a theory of consultancy with a theory of organizations. Increasingly it is being admitted that organizations are not abstractions or 'objectivities' but a complex construct of people and their experiences. We can expect more in this vein in the next few years.

Chapter 1

Management Consultancy in Education: An Introduction to Practice

Harry L. Gray

INTRODUCTION

As was indicated in the Foreword and Introduction, in the context of this book we shall be talking for the most part about what can be termed 'management consultancy' in education. There are other forms of 'consultancy' but they are many and varied, and a book such as this would lose its focus if it did not adhere to a reasonably well-defined subject. In this context 'management' means those systematic and informed activities that help to bring about essential change in organizations. Management is not the process of administration but the creative process of helping the people in organizations to develop for their mutual good. A well-managed school will be one that offers the greatest opportunity for rewards to those who belong to it, consistent with the fulfilling of its social purposes. That 'rewards' and 'social purposes' are open and ambiguous concepts is one of the basic problems of management and reasons why members of the school need help from time to time in working out what might best be done in the school.

CONSULTANCY DEFINED

Consultancy, in the sense used in this collection of contributions, is a helping relationship provided by people who have a particular range of skills for helping managers and others in organizations to understand more clearly what their business is about and how it might become more effective—that is, become more relevant to the social and economic environment in which it functions, from which it draws its resources, and into which it has to return the product of its endeavours. The 'product' is not necessarily, and is seldom solely, a material product but is also a whole range of affective matters such as skills, competences, attitudes, values, understandings and creative insights. It is a mistake to equate management consultancy with the provision of prescriptive advice or the installation of new business systems and procedures though there are approaches to consulting which entail this. A consultant may be most useful as a sounding board or counsellor rather than a giver of advice on technical matters.

Whatever traditions of consultancy exist within the educational system, they are different from those in industry and commerce. For one thing, they are much more casual, more *ad hoc*, less integrated into the system or the institutions. For another, they are differently valued and costed, often being performed entirely without fee and with costs paid reluctantly. There are very few professional consultants within the educational system, except for those who work for international agencies, and none of them will be earning their entire income, in a commercial way, from educational consultancy, at least not without some form of subsidy. There are only a few consultants who are established outside the educational system yet who work within it as management consultants though their number appears to be growing slightly.

CONSULTANTS FROM INDUSTRY

When management consultants who practise in industry etc. are brought in to help with problems in education, they often lack experience of the system and its institutions. Often they have face validity because they bring a useful understanding of how businesses work, but frequently they lack the depth of experience to be as helpful as consultants can be. But education needs consultants no less than other forms of enterprise, and there is every likelihood in the coming years that professional consultancy services will develop perhaps not in great quantity but certainly in improved quality. Already, with the development of national projects like TVEI (Technical and Vocational Education Initiative) and GCSE (General Certificate of Secondary Education) teachers themselves are beginning to learn some of the skills of consultancy and the trend is likely to quicken apace.

INTERNAL AND EXTERNAL CONSULTANTS

We need to distinguish at the outset between external and internal consultants. Internal consultants are employed fully by the organization, or that part of it where they act as consultants, and may have functional positions other than those which require them to offer help and advice. Internal consultants are rare in education in the United Kingdom (the situation varies somewhat in other countries) though it may be considered that LEA (local education authority) inspectors and advisers and HMI (Her Majesty's inspectors of schools) sometimes act in a true consultant role rather than in providing 'mandatory' advice. Other internal consultants may be specialist teachers or teacher advisers who help colleagues with curriculum matters.

External consultants are even rarer in educational systems though they are becoming increasingly thought of as a useful resource. Some field workers engaged on regional or national projects may be considered to be external consultants although it is unlikely that they will be trained as consultants as such. A better way of understanding the nature of external consultancy is to think of someone who is called in to help with a specific problem because he/she has expertise in that kind of problem-solving but from whom any prescriptive advice may be discounted by the client. Sometimes consultants will offer a training or development programme or other structured processes to enable clients to arrive at their own solutions themselves, but they always remain outside the organization, organizationally detached, during the process. The nature of these forms of consultancy will become clear as the book progresses and will be more fully amplified in the specific descriptions of practice.

WHY CONSULTANTS ARE ENGAGED

Consultants are engaged because they have expertise and skills based on their general experience that form a professional basis for helping to solve organizational problems. This is their strength—that they can take (and help others to take) an overview of the presenting problem and problem areas that is broader than the initial perspective of the members of the organization that engages their services. During the process of consultation this general overview will be focused and refined to clarify the particular and specific nature of the client organization's problem. As consultation proceeds, clients will themselves come to a greater and deeper understanding of their problems and the possible solutions, so that by the time the consultant leaves there will be improved competence within the organization itself.

PRESENTING PROBLEMS

Presenting problems usually fall into one of two categories—task and process. Task problems are essentially technical problems to which a material and substantive solution can be offered (even if its adoption is impractical for reasons such as cost). The introduction of record-keeping systems using computer hardware and software would be an example of where a technical consultant would be helpful. In such a case the consultant would advise on materials of various kinds, appropriate machines and relevant software packages. The consultant would probably also offer a training package in the use of the system and perhaps offer some follow-up and evaluation at a later date. In these cases, the client has a reasonably good idea of what his problem is but may be totally uninformed as to the best kinds of solution.

Process consultants will be concerned with identifying the nature of the problem in its personal and interpersonal dimensions: the dynamics of interpersonal problem-solving or blockage. In such cases it is likely that the problem in reality bears only passing resemblance to the problem the client presents. An example of such problems are communication problems which are often presented as technical problems, but which invariably turn out to be matters of interpersonal relationships. In these cases consultants may be able to suggest solutions which are acceptable because they appear to be 'organizational' or 'structural', but they will in fact be dealing with the psychological dimensions of the organization. Successful process consultancy will improve the problem-solving capacity of the organization but task solutions may increase dependency on the consultants who may have to be invited back to provide the next stage of advice.

On the whole people in organizations prefer technical solutions because they appear to be more straightforward, threaten the status quo less, often appear to be complete in themselves and leave the authority structure of the organization either unchanged or reinforced. But eventually all organizations have to resort to process consultancy (although they may resist it), because ultimately problems in organizations are about people and people do not respond well to being subjected to technical solutions. In any case, every problem and every solution has a people dimension.

DO CONSULTANTS SOLVE PROBLEMS?

Consultants are engaged by an organization (or, more correctly, by one or more members of an organization) because the members do not feel that they themselves are fully capable of solving the problem(s) that they identify. Yet, broadly speaking, consultants are cautious about accepting the problem presented to them at its face value. If a client had been able to identify a problem 'correctly', it is unlikely that a consultant would be required; for a properly identified problem other forms of direct assistance may be available. Consultants are invariably invited to offer their services because the client identifies a degree of ambiguity, uncertainty or confusion along with the 'problem'. Clients are too close to their problems to be able to see solutions clearly—at best they see several and require help in making choices.

The critical value of consultants is that they are relatively objective; that is, that they have no vested interest in a particular solution or resolution, they can perceive the problem from a variety of standpoints, have data or experience from other settings, and can assist, at the very least, in a dialogue about the nature of the problem. For this reason, consultants must preserve their independence from the organization and not become too involved with the normal workings of the enterprise. Clients may become very possessive of the consultant and sometimes try (perhaps unwittingly, perhaps not) to subvert the consultants' objectivity so inducing them to accept the organization's view (that is, the view of the most influential individual!) of the most desirable solution. Good consultants resist this, however closely involved with the members they may become. This is not to say that consultants have no values concerning the nature of desirable and undesirable outcomes. These values should be declared where they impinge on the problem because they will affect what work can be carried out and may signal the need for contractual renegotiation or even termination. In any case, the sooner the consultant can leave the organization to carry on alone the better—though hopefully there will be requests for regular return visits to assist with monitoring and evaluation.

THE CONCEPT OF THE 'PRESENTING PROBLEM'

The concept of the 'presenting problem' is crucial to consultancy. Very seldom does a problem turn out to be just what a client perceives it to be and the ramifications often go well beyond client expectations. For one thing, the process implications of any organizational change usually extend to areas of greater consequence than clients anticipate and may have unforeseen challenging implications. Frequently, changes in the organization mean changes in the power structure. This is one reason why consultant reports are often ignored or even rejected—because they open up areas of concern that are unacceptable to the current power and authority structure. Possibly most organizational problems have ramifications that go well beyond original expectations and the analysis of one problem leads, like the unravelling of a piece of string, to several more. The reason for this is the interdependence of the parts of an organization and the nature of interlocking subsystems. Few organizational problems exist in isolation from other considerations, and because consultants are able to view the organization from outside they see relationships that are obscured to the members preoccupied by day-to-day activity.

CHOOSING CONSULTANTS

There are various ways in which a consultant may be chosen. Usually a client will have to make enquiries about the availability of a suitable consultant, especially if he has not used a consultant before. Many consultants are chosen simply by chance the first time round. The best criterion for choice, however, is reputation. The consultant will have performed satisfactorily for a number of clients and information will be obtainable by first of all making enquiries of past clients. Consultants themselves will provide appropriate references to a prospective client who can then ask questions of previous clients before talking with the consultant on matters of detail. Where no consultant is known even by name, professional teacher associations may have a list of names. In all events, extensive enquiries should be made before engaging a particular consultant. In this context, LEA (local education authority) advisers or HMI (Her Majesty's inspectors of schools) would not be considered consultants though they may well be able to give advice on selecting and engaging of external consultants. Colleges, polytechnics and universities may be able to suggest consultants, particularly where there is a management department.

   The requirements of educational consultants are that they should understand the ethos of various educational systems, that they should work from a coherent and academically respectable theoretical base and through a valid intellectual perspective; that they should understand how individuals actually behave in the educational system; that they should have appropriate interpersonal counselling skills; that they should be expert in any technical areas in which they are working. These are essential requirements. It is no use engaging as a consultant an individual or organization who has no experience of consultancy or who has expertise only in non-related fields. Because everyone seems to believe himself/herself to be expert in education, almost all industrial consultants would feel themselves able to help a school to get sorted out and might find an invitation to act as a consultant quite compelling. It would be worth asking such individuals if they would reciprocate and let senior school staff act as consultants to their company on the same terms. On the other hand, a firm of professional consultants may have suitable consultancy skills even if this is their first educational job—though, again, caution is urged as the consultants may have inbuilt prejudices from their own schooldays.

SCHOOLS AS ORGANIZATIONS

While schools and colleges are organizations like any other, and their general similarity cannot be overemphasized, they nevertheless have idiosyncratic characteristics which cannot be understood unless schools themselves have been seriously studied. Experienced consultants will be able to understand special cultural characteristics, but it is fair to say that much time is saved if consultants are experienced in the field. In all consultancy there is a basic need to balance the general and the particular. Indeed, this is essential to the analytical and diagnostic process in all consultancy. The individual ecology of the school influences the characteristics of the problems it has. On the whole, teachers have little knowledge of the generalities of organization theory and so are unable to recognize the particular and peculiar. Teachers acting as internal consultants may, without a proper understanding of underlying theory, mistake the peculiar for the general. While it is true that schools are not manufacturing organizations, have no easily identified customers and therefore conventional service and production models do not apply, it is also true that they are places where people interrelate, and social patterns do not differ in their essential characteristics whatever the kind of organization.

It should be impossible for consultants to stay in business who do not have a thoroughly understood theoretical basis to their work, but sadly such is not always the case. On the whole, teachers use 'administrative' models or 'educational' models to describe organizational behaviour but these are inadequate because they have been learned at too superficial a level. Other consultants, too, may make a similar error of using models that do not work at the required level. Proper diagnosis must be at a deeper level than that at which the problem manifests itself, and only real professional competence will ensure that consultants understand this need for deeper analysis. Even technical consultancy must take place on the basis of an appropriate theory of the organization (organizational theory), or else the organization will be unable to implement and sustain the innovation. Far too many educational innovations fail at this stage of implementation and maintenance.

SKILLS OF CONSULTANTS

Consultants need essential skills in interpersonal relationships and a sense of ethical responsibility. They must see that their clients are not threatened or upset unduly during the consultancy process. By and large, counselling skills are very important because they will be nursing their clients through an examination of current practices and helping them to change to meet the new circumstances. The threat of change for individuals cannot be overestimated for it occurs at all levels and in all parts of the organization. Sometimes the most senior people are threatened, and since they are usually the ones who engage the consultants they may find challenge to their perceptions and assumptions most difficult to bear—especially if they believe that they are being shown up in front of their colleagues and subordinates. A consultant may have to spend a great deal of time with the most vulnerable clients helping them to adjust to changes. The situation will be the same when the innovations are welcomed and desired since no one can guess at the consequences and implications of an innovation. One of the mistakes of technical consultants is that they often miss out the personal and affective areas of change and this is why technological innovations often have destructive effects on organizations. Client organizations themselves have some responsibility in this regard in that they should ensure that the contract always includes some work with people at the emotional level so that the innovation is not destroyed by bad feelings and hostile reactions let alone personal unhappiness and disenchantment.

OBJECTIVITY OF CONSULTANTS

External consultants are engaged because they can provide an objectivity on dimensions that the members of the organization itself cannot supply but there is usually no reason why they should not also work with internal consultants except under special circumstances. Indeed, at some point they will have to provide some training for internal consultants who will carry the innovation through to consolidation and subsequent maintenance. The internal consultants will also be responsible for the recall of the external consultant for monitoring, subsequent problem-solving and training support.

The requirements of external consultants are that they should be specialists in consultancy skills because, as has been described, consultancy is itself a 'professional' and discrete activity; simply being knowledgeable in a technical field is not enough for consultant competence. Yet consultants must also be expert in their own technical field and presumably will have published papers in the professional and specialist literature. They will also have available their own reports, working and occasional papers so that prospective clients can have an insight into their working and theoretical orientation. From this published material the kind of analytical approach they use as well as the kind of help they will give should be readily apparent. However strong they may be at theory they will also need to be practitioners of considerable competence. One of the dilemmas for consultants is that they experience a constant tension between being academics and being practitioners. In many ways they are at the cutting edge of their field so that they are researchers, albeit action researchers. This means that they are also theoreticians but without the leisure of academia to develop fully their theories in all their ramifications. Nevertheless, they should score highly on both theory and practice. If this is a difficult tension for them it is essential to adequate consultancy that an equilibrium be maintained.

THE PROCESS OF ENGAGING CONSULTANTS

Once likely consultants have been identified, there begins the process of engaging them. This usually takes a considerable period of time and should never be done lightly or carelessly. The most important factor in the client–consultant relationship is congruity or compatibility of personal or organizational values. This is not to say that values should be identical, though it is sometimes desirable, but it is essential that they are not at odds or incompatible. It is not easy to discover at first whether this is so or not and considerable time should be spent just talking together to ensure that working together will be as creative and instructive as possible. Inevitably, frustrations and tensions will arise and the conditions for coping with them rely on the ability of the two parties to understand one another, and the trust and confidence mutually given.

Departure from the pattern of events shortly to be described should be a matter of concern and would need clear justification. Before a contract is agreed there must be a period of negotiation which covers what the consultants will do, how they will do it, what the costs will be, and for how long it will be done. This stage of negotiation is usually free of charge and should be as long as the clients believe necessary until they are certain that they do want to engage a particular consultant. Once the contract is signed, time spent with the consultant will cost money or be at the expense of the project. The consultant is normally invited by the client rather than the other way round. Otherwise the nature of the relationship is affected. The consultants are employed by the clients to do the job the clients want albeit in terms of the professional judgement and evaluation of the consultant. His time belongs to the client as does any work that is done, especially 'published' or written-up work. Where the consultant holds a position as a college or university lecturer a clear and explicit agreement should be reached on the vetting of and publishing of ensuing books and articles. Non-academic consultants may also wish to write in order to advance practice in their profession but their clients have claims in terms of confidentiality.

WHO IS THE CLIENT?

During the negotiation period the consultants should meet as many of their potential clients as possible and agreement to hire them should be a shared, real agreement among all parties not just the opinion of the head. In practice, the client is whoever the consultant is working with at the time. The issue of 'who is the client' is very important not only for confidentiality but also because of the nature of the work and the mode of relationships. The negotiation process is continuous, going well beyond the initial contract. As the consultants meet new members of the organization they enter a new process of negotiation and contract building. At no point in time is negotiation ever completed but there is a continuous process of negotiating as events unfold. Trust and confidentiality are of the essence, for the consultant will be privy to a great deal of information that cannot be shared with others. Consultants will work with each individual and group on the problems they mutually agree but they may not wish to reveal these problems to the group and individuals. Whatever information the consultant divulges will be a matter for his professional judgement. It is not always easy for clients who have little consultancy experience to understand this since they may believe that by 'buying in' a consultant they are opening up a new channel to information that would not otherwise exist. Some heads try to extract information from clients that is confidential between the consultant and a member of the school.

MATTERS OF INTEGRITY

Parallel to the issue of confidentiality and the non-identification of members of the client organization, there is also the ethical concern that a consultant may not do the bosses' dirty work for them. Sometimes consultants are brought in to do a job the bosses cannot bring themselves to do. This may well be the reason for the contract, but the consultant will be very cautious about doing just what the boss wants. The consultant will investigate the given problem and make appropriate diagnosis and recommendation but will do so objectively and in professional terms. No consultant can afford to be so partisan as to be just another hatchet man. Even when research leads to conclusions that support the boss's own view, it is more than likely that it will be couched in terms that have much more regard for the interests of subordinates than the boss may like. However, the situation is one that cannot be avoided in consultancy and requires sensitivity on both the clients' and consultants' parts.

CONSULTANCY IS ABOUT CHANGE

It will be understood that the effect, even if not the initial purpose, of consultancy will be change. That is why the word 'innovation' has often been used to describe the consequence of consultancy and because 'innovation' suggests an agreed and generally acceptable change. Change is always unacceptable in some degrees to someone (and sometimes the resisters receive attention out of all proportion to their numbers) but it often comes as a surprise that the initial client must change in ways not anticipated. Change is no respecter of persons and the consultant will have to work with everyone involved if the intervention is to be successful. If it proves impossible to work with key members the work will be impossible or deficient.

The often neglected matter in consultancy is the provision of help to members in coping with change. Much organizational 'reform' faces members with a stark choice of having to accept change as it has been decided by others. The reform is presented as if it were a simple matter of total acceptance but natural change or reform does not happen like this. There is more than the implementation process at stake; there is also the coping process particularly of those whose position has been changed by the reform. The two parallel responses to change are adoption and adaptation and neither can proceed without the other. Adaptation is the personal coping process with which most people need some professional assistance by receiving care and counselling. It may well be that a second group of consultants has to be engaged to deal with the coping processes, and also that this pattern occurs more and more as it is recognized that technological change has deep and functional consequences for people's attitudes and feelings.

PROBLEMS OF TIME

Although a time-scale will have been agreed in the initial contract (albeit a tentative one), it is not always possible nor reasonable to decide on a full-time scale—certainly not a terminal point at the beginning. Unless the matter for consultation is a comparatively simple one the time taken from the commencement or negotiation to the departure of the consultant will probably be longer than anticipated. However, it is usual to indicate some phasing for the consultation with renewal contracting at certain points. Consultation on the theme of general renewal for a school will normally last for a period of from one to five years.

It is just not possible to deal with deep organizational problems in much less than a year, or even work on a small innovation especially if 'follow-up' of even a minimal kind is to take place. But time implies significant costs, and schools and colleges should not be unrealistic about expense. Because consultancy in education is so new, many schools try to make do with a single-day consultancy and consultants agree because they are anxious to make entry into the system. But a day is likely to cause more problems than it solves, however good the consultant may be. In fact all good consultancy creates organizational disturbance of some kind and for brief consultations this is often the most useful thing they can do. Simply by creating disturbance in the situation they open up possibilities of change. Without disturbance there can be no change. Where external consultants cannot be afforded for any significant length of time it will be best to use the consultants to train internal consultants who can then work with them and deal with the periods between the paid visits.

PROBLEMS OF ENTRY

With every kind of consultancy, it is entry that causes most difficulties. Perhaps for schools the current problem is more the lack of funds than anything else, though had there been a consultancy tradition the funds would have gradually become available. Simply obtaining acceptance of the consultant is always a difficulty largely because of the hidden threats to status and esteem of individuals that bringing in a consultant means. The threats may be quite unrecognized and lie entirely in the subconscious. It is virtually impossible to engage a friend or colleague as consultant for obvious psychological reasons and so consultants are—at least initially—strangers to members of the organization.

There is a range of entry problems that always appear even when an organization is accustomed to employing consultants. Often consultants are hired for the wrong reasons which include, paradoxically, the wish to avoid problems. It is often thought that by bringing the consultant in to deal with a specified problem he will divert attention from the 'real' (substantive) to the marginal or irrelevant. Keeping him at work on the 'acceptable' problem means that the organization can avoid its deeper and more critical problems. Often consultants find themselves invited in to solve problems entirely peripheral to major issues, or that the organization just does not have.

An organization may also negotiate by proxy—not just bringing in the consultants to deal with clients other than the inviter, but by allowing a group or individual to negotiate on behalf of others with the consequence that the consultants are not accepted by the wider group. Such a situation might be political—indeed all consultancy is a political act since it involves questions about the power structure—and will lead to a fouling up of the organization because the wrong issues have been presented and the real ones not allowed to surface even though they are part of the dynamics of the situation. In such circumstances there will be little commitment from members and the consultant will be powerless to work with them. He may then become the scapegoat for unresolved conflicts in the organization, while concern over the real issues is displaced by debate about the consultation itself and, possibly, the style of the consultant. It is worth remembering that it is characteristic of organizations (that is, people in organizations) to concern themselves with problems that are not germane to their survival but provide an easy means of avoidance.

CENTRALITY AND MARGINALITY

Although a consultancy project may seem marginal or peripheral to an organization when the decision is taken to undertake it, few problems remain at the margins.

Because many problems are symptoms of deeper problems this is perhaps not surprising, but what is thought of as a trivial or inconsequential issue often turns out to have wide implications perhaps involving a scrutiny and evaluation of values and activities at the centre of organizational life. The consultant will have the job of persuading all the clients that the extra territory is worth entering, and this may be a more difficult problem even than gaining initial entry.

It is usually preferable for a consultant to work with the top management team on the project before working with other members of the organization. One is not often allowed—let alone encouraged—to do this but the soundest advice that can be given to those contemplating employing a consultant is to spend several days working with the consultants themselves before introducing them to other members of the school. This part of the project, however, should be done openly because if the consultants are suddenly introduced in circumstances of familiarity with the top team it will be thought that they are friends of the establishment and their motives and actions will be under considerable suspicion. In fact, however carefully the consultants are introduced they will be objects of suspicion so the more suspicion and anxiety can be reduced the better.

CONSULTANT REPORTS

In general, consultancy projects will lead to a report of some kind, invariably in a written form if only to make certain there are no misunderstandings and misinterpretations. Such reports must be made available to everyone they concern and refer to and not be filed away or released in edited, abridged or bowdlerized form. They certainly should not be shelved even if they contain largely unacceptable news. A series of open discussions will always improve relationships within the organization and the more specific they are the better focused the debate. Who knows but that the debate may lead to a voluntary uncovering of real problems in the organization.

When the report contains important and acceptable recommendations it is essential for it to be followed up systematically, which means a series of meetings, workshops and training activities that lead to action. Sadly, taking action on reports that deal with organizational issues is seldom popular and every effort will be made within the organization to resist organizational and structural change. Often by now this is no longer the consultant's problem; it falls back on the quality of the organization and particularly its leadership.

AFTER THE CONSULTATION

If at all possible, contact should be maintained because almost certainly residual matters will arise and it might be desired to use the consultant's services again. By maintaining contact, channels of communication are kept open that will allow relevant information about the consultant's other work to be fed back to the organization, and ensuing discussion will be worth a good deal for the maintenance of the innovation. If the consultancy project has developed well and become integrated into normal organizational functioning, internal consultants will take over for monitoring and evaluation purposes and they will need help and support. Above all, there will be the opportunity for a reappraisal of management structures and processes and hopefully there will be increased flexibility and a more organic dynamic to the way the organization works. Above all the readiness of the school for future innovation will be secured and the competency in coping with innovation and using change opportunities fruitfully will be increased. By having access to a comparatively inexpensive but specialist resource, the school will have increased its own resourcefulness and potential for renewal.

COSTS AND COMMITMENTS

Because there is no tradition of using external consultants in education, and therefore no bank of knowledge of how to use them or of what are the implications, there has until quite recently been little awareness of the financial costs involved in consultancy. Local and national inspectors and advisers, college and university lecturers have all acted as consultants in one way or another but usually as a part of the service already provided. On these occasions, when fees are paid, they amount to but a small compensation for disturbance and an often unrealistic remuneration for expenses such as travel. Costs and fees are a matter of concern in education anyway because they bear no relationship to real costs; often some form of subsidy is expected from teachers themselves such as giving up their own time or paying for their lunch! Most consultancy currently available is intermittent and casual because there is little awareness on the part of schools of the nature of the relationship that should exist between clients and consultant if the job is to be well done. Current attitudes still derive from a mixture of the voluntary tradition and the charitable works of the industrial expert and benefactor. Fortunately an increasing awareness of the cost implications is now emerging.

WRITTEN CONTRACT

The relationship between client and consultant must always have expression in a written form, however brief, to specify certain essential and material matters. These include the areas of activity of the consultant, boundaries of the client group, the duration of the consultancy, limits on the various costs and expectation for work for the agreed fee, the point of termination and/or renegotiation. There is generally a period of negotiation before a formal contract is agreed, which includes an exploration of the mutual understanding of the nature of the job—do the client and consultant wish to work together and can they agree the general brief? Without such basic understandings the relationship can get out of hand in a variety of ways to no-one's benefit. Agreed professional guidelines are published by various professional bodies and they are observed by commercial consultants. Schools will find the advice of the Local Government Training Board useful in this respect.

   The contract exists between the consultant and whoever has the authority to pay him or his official representative. A payer should not pay on behalf of anyone else unless they have agreed, and it is unprofessional for a consultant to accept a client who has not himself entered into a free and willing contract. In schools there is a tendency for the head to hire in a consultant to sort out a subordinate or subordinate group. While a consultant may well work with a group or individuals apart from the head, the head must be perfectly clear about the guidelines to which the consultant works and the full confidentiality of each client must be preserved. There can be no reporting to the head unless there are clear indications that action would be helpful.

ORGANIZATIONAL SUPPORT

An organization is expected to give full support to a consultant and not to withhold necessary resources. Especially is it important that those members of the organization who are needed for the work should be free to work with the consultant. It is often found that key members are unwilling to work fully with the consultant for any number of reasons. Such situations place the consultant in the impossible position of just being unable to do the agreed job. In some cases the culpable party is a senior member of staff who attends meetings only intermittently, and achieves only the objective of underlining his/her own sense of superiority. Sometimes organizations overlook quite simple forms of support like offering the consultant a base from which to work or expecting him/her to make all his/her own meal arrangements.

HIDDEN COSTS

No form of consultancy comes free. Local authority advisers are all paid salaries and a form of consultancy is the nature of their work. But professional management consultants earn their living by consulting and therefore their time costs money. In addition to attendance on the client consultants have to spend time doing research and preparing reports, all of which takes time that has to be paid for. It is well worth teachers taking some time to work out the nature of costs because they are often quite unrealistic about other people's earnings. A teacher himself earning £10000 ($15000) a year will be earning at the rate of £50 ($75) per day or £210 ($315) per week. However, there are additional costs in employing him which probably double that figure so that he would have to earn £100 ($150) a day in order to be paid that salary. The reasoning is that if he were the sole earner in a business, he would have to earn all the costs of heating, lighting, equipment, caretaking and administration, including some paid secretarial help. Consultants are in this latter situation since they are the income (fee) earners for their companies. Given that a consultant does not earn every day of the week but may be earning on only half of his possible working days, he would need to earn between £250 ($375) and £300 ($450) a day to receive the same salary as a teacher. It is important to acknowledge the true nature of financial costs because often educational institutions tend to offer sums of under £10 ($15) per hour (that is between £50 ($75) and £70 ($105) a day) and consider that they are generous! In addition, of course, to the consultancy fee will be a charge for travel and expenses which may be considerable—especially overnight hotel costs.

Perhaps the least a school should expect to pay for a consultant is £100 ($150) per day (at 1987 rates) plus expenses. Colleges and institutions should expect to pay nearer the market rate of £250–£300 ($375–$450), which is the rate they will be aiming to charge for their own 'full cost' consultancy if they are charging an economic rate. Further education colleges who have embarked on their own marketing of services to outside clients will be seeking to charge over £150 ($225) a day, rising to £300 ($450) or even more. In fact further education colleges are now generally required to make such charges even though there may still be hidden subsidies. A common complaint is that schools do not have this sort of money but it is not actually true. If a local education authority were to free a head teacher to act as a consultant, it would have to pay the salary and provide administrative assistance. If the head were on the full pay roll this would cost in the region of £30 000 ($45 000) per annum irrespective of the number of days that he or she had to work. In commercial terms £30 000 ($45 000) could buy more consultancy than the head teacher consultant could give and payment would only be made for days actually worked. So basically, local education authorities (LEAs) have funds available, albeit locked up in advisory posts or safeguarded salaries.

SOURCES OF FINANCE

There are several sources of finance available to most schools though the pattern will vary from place to place. These include the school or head teacher's fund, a governors' fund, special funds raised by parents associations, Department of Education and Science (DES) money for training, special funding from LEAs or local authority training grants, open courses run by industry, and consultant assistance from industrial firms. Additionally teachers may themselves raise the money for a consultant; often they would do so when they choose independently to attend a course and seek the advice of a lecturer or trainer. The new GRIST funding for LEAs should lead to considerable sums being made available for consultancy and sometimes Manpower Services Commission (MSC) money is available for special projects. The reality is that money is quite often available for schools to commence the use of consultants. Once the need has been established, further moneys can be budgeted for.

Additional hidden costs include the time spent by teachers working with the consultant, extra materials and refreshments consumed during the consultancy, costs of meetings after the consultant has left and printing and distribution costs for reports and feedback. There may be disturbance costs in that routine work is affected, but usually such effects are beneficial since if the consultant has been given the right brief there will be an early improvement in morale. Other subsequent costs may involve more training in or away from the school, additional travel, the purchase of new equipment, and even the employment of more staff in order to introduce cost-effective practices.

One positive effect of proper financial awareness is that consultant help will be better appreciated and more carefully considered. There is some evidence that free or cheap consultant help is little valued and that appreciation increases in proportion to costs.

CONCLUSIONS

In the long run, consultancy provides a relatively cheap resource to assist a school to undertake a process of considerable change and development. The key to success is to undertake it seriously with a commitment to implementing the suggestions that arise from it. Other chapters in this book give examples of how changes have occurred in various school contexts, and it will not be long before there are many more examples.

SELECTED READING

Arends, R. I. and Arends, J. H. (1977) *Systems Change Strategies in Educational Settings*. New York: Human Sciences Press.

Argyris, C. (1965) *Organisation and Innovation*. London: Irwin-Dorsey.

Argyris, C. (1970) *Intervention Theory and Method*. London: Addison-Wesley.

Beckard, R. and Harris, R. T. (1977) *Organisational Transitions: Managing Complex Change*. Reading, Mass.: Addison-Wesley.

Bell, C. R. and Nadler, L. (1979) *The Client–Consultant Handbook*. Houston: Gulf Publishing Co.

Bell, L. A. (1979) 'A discussion of some of the implications of using consultants in schools'. *British Educational Research Journal* 5(1).

Bennis, W. G. (1969) *Organisation Development*. London: Addison-Wesley.

Blake, R. and Mouton, J. S. (1976) *Consultation*. Reading, Mass.: Addison-Wesley.

Bolam, R., Smith, G. and Cantor, H. (1978) *LEA Advisors and the Mechanisms of Innovation*. Slough: NFER.

Boud, D. and McDonald, R. (1981) *Educational Development Through Consultancy*. Guildford, Surrey: Society for Research into Higher Education (SRHE).

Burden, R. (1987) 'Educational psychologists as agents of school organisational development: consultants or reformers'. *Educational Change and Development* 8(1), 19–21.

Cameron, W. G. (1978) 'O.D. consultancy, a model for analysis'. *Educational Change and Development* 1 (2). Crewe: Deanhouse.

Davey, N. G. (1971) *The External Consultant's Role in Organisational Change*. Michigan State University: Graduate School of Business Administration.

Davidson, F. (1972) *Management Consultants*. London: Nelson.

Eraut, M. (1977) 'Some perspectives on consultancy in in-service education'. *British Journal of In-Service Education* 4(1) and (2).

Everard, K. B. (1982) *Management in Comprehensive Schools—What Can Be Learned from Industry*. Goodriche College, University of York: Centre for the Study of Comprehensive Schools.

Everard, K. B. (1986) *Developing Management in Schools*. Oxford: Blackwell.

Fullan, M. (1982) *The Meaning of Educational Change*. New York: Teachers College Press.

Gray, H. L. (1980) *Management in Education*. Driffield: Nafferton Books.

Gray, H. L. (ed.) (1982) *The Management of Educational Institutions*. Lewes: Falmer Press.

Gray, H. L. (1987) 'Management consultancy and training for professional business partnerships'. *Journal of European Industrial Training* 11(1).

Gray, H. L. and Coulson, A. A. (1982) 'Teacher education, management and the facilitation of change'. *Educational Change and Development* 4(1). Crewe: Deanhouse.

Gray, H. L. and Heller, H. (1982) *Problems in Helping Schools*. Crewe: Deanhouse Occasional Papers.

Handy, C. B. (1984) *Taken for Granted: Looking at Schools as Organisations*. Harlow: Longman.

Kakabadse, A. (1983) 'How to use consultants'. *International Journal of Manpower* 5(1).

Keith, L. M. and Keith, P. M. (1971) *Anatomy of Educational Innovation*. New York: John Wiley.

Kubr, M. (ed.) (1976) *Management Consultancy, A Guide to the Profession*. Geneva: ILO.

Lippitt, G. and Lippitt, R. (1978) *The Consulting Process in Action*. La Jolla, Cal.: University Associates.

Local Government Training Board (1984) *The Selection and Use of Management Development Consultants*. Luton: Local Government Training Board.

Mangham, I. L. (1978) *Interaction and Intervention in Organisations*. Chichester: John Wiley.

Mangham, I. L. (1979) *The Politics of Organisational Change*. Westpoint, Conn.: Greenwood Press.

McLean, A. (1983) 'Myths, magic and gobbledegook (rational aspects of the consultant's role)', in Kakabadse, A. and Parker, C. (eds) *Politics and Organisation*. Chichester: John Wiley.

McLean, A. J., Sims, D. B. P., Mangham, I. L. and Tuffield, D. (1982) *Organisation Development in Transition*. Chichester: John Wiley.

Ottoway, R. (ed.) (1979) *Change Agents at Work*. London: Associated Business Press.

Pilon, D. and Bergquist, W. H. (1979) *Consultation in Higher Education, Handbook for Practitioners and Clients*. Washington DC: Council for the Advancement of Small Colleges.

Richardson, E. (1973) *The Teacher, the School and the Task of Management*. London: Heinemann.

Schein, E. H. (1969) *Process Consultation: Its Role in Organisation Development*. Reading, Mass.: Addison-Wesley.

Schmuck, R., Runkel, P., Arends, J. and Arends, R. (1977) *The Second Handbook of Organisation Development in Schools*. Palo Alto, Cal.: Mayfield.

Shay, P. W. (1981) *How to Get the Best Results from Management Consultants*. New York: Association of Management Consulting Firms (ACME).

Chapter 2

Identifying the Issues
John Sayer

INTRODUCTION

It has not been the habit of schools to draw on or to draw in consultants. Secondary schools in particular, with their traditions of other-worldly distinctiveness, their specialized professional structures and their greater internal diversity of resource, have had less permeable boundaries than some other services, and have been both less accessible and less able to derive benefit from insights beyond the institution. That has now changed or is changing. However, the openness to shared governance, to cooperative resource models across organizations and services, to new habits of personal and organizational review and appraisal, have not been part of the training or experience of most teachers. This chapter sketches a background and context from which schools may be able to approach the issues of consultancy and to clarify for themselves what are the situations in which forms of consultancy may be valuable, and how they might best be used. Let us first pick up from the previous chapter some of the meaning of the very word consultancy, this time as it may be seen from the school.

WHAT'S IN THE WORD?

The word is beguiling. Like so many cloaks and vestments, it is reversible. We are still not sure whether education is about putting in or drawing out, whether curriculum is the course set or the race people run, whether with the French *apprendre* we are to teach or to learn. Undoubtedly, the consultant should mean the person who consults; yet we have turned it into the person consulted rather than talk of a consultee. In medical practice, similarly, a consulted physician is described as a consulting physician, whereas in reality it is the general practitioner or the patient who is doing the consulting.

So the first point has to be that consultancy depends on the position and disposition of those who are seeking to consult or are consulting. Once we have settled what the word may or may not mean, this chapter will focus, therefore, on the consulting party. What prompts the desire for consultation? And as that desire becomes a decision, what is the frame of reference, what kind of consultancy is being sought and for what purpose? The first responsibility of those of us who have experience and skills of being brought into consultancy is to share such questions—not to take them over—and to assist in determining whether or not we are right for the situation or any part of it. That happens all too rarely in consultancy; we are all looking for a livelihood, or for opportunities to influence, or for confirmation of the importance and universal applicability of our skills and insights. The responsibility for answering those questions must remain with those who are seeking to consult. They must realize that; and if they do not, we have the responsibility of making that clear. By being drawn into consultation we may well enable others to clarify their own needs and intentions; but if we take over the thinking and clarifying for them, we have become arbiters and have dispossessed them of decision-making responsibility.

I am trying not to use the word *client* because that, too, has suffered a sea change. Its original meaning was that of a plebeian under the protection of a noble, and it has retained the flavour of dependency. The clients of a lawyer are placed in the lawyer's hands, and expect a legal problem to be taken off theirs. Whatever else consultancy does, it must not create a dependency. John Harvey-Smith, of ICI fame, recently challenged the indiscriminate practice of drawing on outside consultancy to improve management practice in industry; he suggested to the British Institute of Management that they should not buy a watch and then hire someone to tell the time. There are many instances of education authorities turning to outside consultants to do their thinking for them and to make recommendations for acceptance or rejection. Usually the motivation has to do with no more than improved efficiency and cost-effectiveness. Rejection makes the education authority as client or customer look politically foolish for having spent money to buy in consultancy; acceptance is a device for ducking responsibility by bowing to expertise. I am not suggesting it is wrong for a client to consult the oracle, the stars or the weatherman, to purchase and bow to expertise; but I do suggest that this is a different use of the word *consultancy* and it should not be confused with the topic of this book.

Let us explore the word further. Its earliest meanings included careful, experienced, weighty deliberation, with the intention of coming to a decision and announcing a plan. It is important to keep that in mind, despite the later trivialization. So we are not in the business of consulting the timetable, which is simply checking a supposed fact. Nor are we in the business of 'being consulted', which is about the right or expectation of a particular office, or about not being neglected or bypassed, or about expected forms of management behaviour. Consultancy, as used here, is likely to be about a fundamental issue of human organization; about rethinking from first principles or even discovering what these are. It is not likely to stop at diagnosis of the nature of transactions, of strengths or weaknesses, of what could be improved or what went wrong; it is in the nature of consultancy that those responsible for an organization are enabled to formulate plans for development and improvement. The root meaning of the word has to do with leaping together; and the leap forward together remains the aim of consultancy and the criterion for its success.

WHAT CONSULTANCY IS NOT

We are still not past the word itself. To understand what *is* the intended meaning, it is helpful to eliminate what consultancy is *not*. It is not advice, although it may start from a desire to take advice. An adviser, whether or not vested with that title, requires a particular kind of credibility, and must be believed to know from recognizably good experience about the particular field of responsibility. Advisers appointed by an education authority are there primarily to advise the employer on what is and should be happening, or to spread through the schools the kind of advice which the employing authority has agreed should be given. That does not debar them from a relationship akin to consultancy, but they have to be able to distinguish one rôle from the others, and be recognized as doing so. It may seem that an adviser is acting as a consultant in attending selection interviews as an observer. That depends on whether the adviser has been asked to attend by the interviewing panel, whether the adviser's presence is expected pro forma, whether the adviser is attending to represent the education authority to recommend that the panel's recommendations should or should not be endorsed. The advisory rôle is fraught with ambiguity unless each activity is carefully defined and agreed.

Perhaps more obviously, consultancy is not the same as inspection. Inspectors may also be drawn into limited forms of consultancy, at the request of schools, although the confidentiality they can offer is also somewhat limited by their responsibilities to their own colleagues and service, and that has to be clear to those making an approach. They may also be approached for particular reasons by an education authority, and their formal powers of school inspection used by the authority in much the same way as a consultant's report. On the other hand, an education authority which has itself undergone formal inspection may approach an independent management consultancy for a second opinion, for vindication, or as a means of doing something about the inspectors' report. If so, those approached have to consider very carefully what is the nature of their task; they may be expected to perform an alternative inspection.

Consultancy is akin to but not the same as counselling, which usually has to do with individual and interpersonal decision-making. Peer-counselling is a particularly valuable resource for those like head teachers and chief education officers whose rôle in any one organization is by definition unique and is therefore isolating; but it is likely to be about personal transactions and pressures, not about the long-term health of the organization. The same applies to the informal counselling of friends and partners, the sensitive listening for false notes and discrepancies, knowing that it is the listening which enables the problem-holder to articulate the real issues. Consultancy, however, is about a whole organization and its development. It may well involve counselling, not least in enabling people to come to terms with modes of consultancy. It will involve many of the issues and trained skills associated with counselling. There is a professional ethic which is similar, if not identical. But the canvas is one of significant organizational development, of strategic change.

Consultancy also involves research and investigation, and must subsume the skills, disciplines and expectations of educational research. It is likely to relate more closely to action research and illuminative procedure than to quantified findings based on statistical method. It will not, however, be confined to the ethnographic recapture of a society experienced from within, or to recounting that experience; shared evaluation will be intended to lead to a development plan. Consultancy is about using evaluation in the management of improvement or change.

Consultancy may be envisaged as a form of management training. Instead of sending individuals away as representatives of an organization, giving time off the job to prepare for a development, the organization as a whole invites in a trainer or group of trainers as catalysts for development on the spot. It does not follow that those who are skilled in running training courses offsite are going to be the best people to involve in the school. It is likely, however, that consultancy and offsite courses will be combined in development programmes, and that trainers will be expected to adapt flexibly across different training modes.

MANAGEMENT NEEDS OF SCHOOLS

Edward de Bono once distinguished quite elegantly between four modes of management: being a train-driver, a doctor, a farmer, or a fisherman. He was wishing to draw out the point that British industry was not bad at training for the first three, but needed to find its way to promote the fourth. The train-driver has to manage the predetermined task of moving a train from A to B in a scheduled time; the doctor is called upon to solve crises, repairing health and restoring the status quo; the farmer has a patch of land from which to extract a maximum yield given the available alternatives and resources. The fisherman, on the other hand, will cast a line speculatively, acting on the interplay of experience, instinct and intuition, not bound by time or targets.

We do not have to agree with either the categories or the caricatures to find some truth transferable to schools. The train-driver functions, executing predetermined tasks according to predetermined schedules already tested as workable, may in moments of self-indulgent gloom be seen as the possible outcome of recent political trends towards central planning and control, taking responsibility and initiative from the teaching profession; or, more realistically, we may identify certain aspects of school management which are like that and should be. The kind of training required to do something the way it has always been done is on the surface straightforward. It does not appear to require consultancy. There is a question of improved efficiency: how to do the existing job better.

But what happens if drivers come forward with different approaches: driving back to front, combining driving and inspection, driving on to the track which will be used for the return journey, combining passenger and freight traffic, linking with road traction, making more frequent journeys with a smaller train? Are they to be told that is the job of others in the system and not their business? It would be rather like the captain of the sinking ship telling the anxious passengers they have nothing to worry about because it is not their ship. So one question for the organization of a school is how to manage suggestions and ideas which are somebody else's or perhaps nobody's business but everyone's concern. Another is how to develop into an organization which by the way it operates will promote and encourage innovation over and above improved efficiency at doing the existing job, will actively encourage everyone to mind other people's business, and will encourage interchange of rôles and responsibilities. A third question is how to maintain or retrieve that 'thinking school' corporate mentality despite external or internal difficulties which may incline people to creep back into burrows.

Those three questions may be of the kind which would involve some form of consultancy.

Similarly, in the picture of the doctor as the crisis-solver, under pressure to solve each crisis within 20 minutes, there may be one approach to improving the capacity to solve crises; but consultancy is more likely to be appropriate in order to draw people out of the shell of pressure-habit, in order to engage on improving health and preventive medicine so that the crises become less frequent or acute. Or take the farmer image. There may be ways to help people to maximize resources and improve cost-effectiveness. But that is a far cry from identifying the product which will be most needed or could best be developed in a future context and planning to change the whole farm accordingly.

The danger of the images we have been borrowing is that they might lead us to suppose that some are called to be drivers, some on call to be doctors, some to be called farmers, leaving a breed of neo-Jansenists, endowed with efficacious grace, super-intelligence and leisure, to be fishermen. Whether that is the image of the head ('I'm the one who does the reading', declared one leading head in the 1970s) or of the consultant, it must change or perish. On the other hand, we have little need in schools for consultancy to improve efficiency and cost-effectiveness alone. School management is about putting together in a common purpose the driving, curing, farming and fishing capacities in each one of us and in our working groups.

SCHOOL-FOCUSED DEVELOPMENT

Over the last two decades, there has been a growing awareness world wide of the professional development needs of teachers, not just as individuals but in the working context of teams and school organizations. In some countries this has been combined at least in phases with a school focus for curriculum development. Britain in the 1960s and early 1970s had the opportunity of new secondary school structures and the liberation of primary schools from terminal examining. These coincided with expansion associated with the raising of the school-leaving age, with a liberal consensus of positive encouragement towards schools carried over from the postwar reconstruction, and with the pre-pill baby boom. In England and Wales, the Schools Council was probably more important for what it stood for than for what it did, but its stimulus of school-based projects for curriculum development and action research was nevertheless considerable for those who were looking for opportunity. The strength of the drive for curriculum development preceded and in some measure may have engendered the moves in the 1970s towards in-service education and training, and contributed in particular to its focus on schools. France, on the other hand, with an equal concern for professional development, has moved its aspiration only much more recently to a school or local focus for curriculum development, and any school focus for in-service education may be expected to follow.

Action research, involving teachers in schools, was in the Schools Council era most clearly identified with curriculum development. It was largely free from government constraints or concerns. This was the period when a Secretary of State for Education could declare without complaint that his powers were confined to the removal of derelict air-raid shelters from school premises. The Stenhouse Humanities Programme represented some of the finest aspirations of that generation. In that programme, as in the development during the mid-1960s, of the new examination, the Certificate of Secondary Education (CSE), there was a somewhat conspiratorial awareness that teachers' involvement in curricular development was the most likely means of in-service education; but it was not translated into staffing organization or across to the in-service budget. In schools, we were less aware of the significance of other work being funded by the Schools Council which went beyond its brief. I am thinking in particular of the example of Elizabeth Richardson at Nailsea, perceiving herself as a mirror for staff experience and very much concerned with the management of the school as an organization.

The Schools Council, having been set up to develop curriculum and examinations, was organizationally distinct from national bodies working towards a policy for professional development. The body to pick up the James Committee recommendations and continue to develop guidelines and to seek clear funding for professional development was born of the Weaver Report on the General Teaching Council, and was set up as an advisory body, the Advisory Committee on the Supply and Training of Teachers (ACSTT), serviced by the Department of Education. Its successor body (ACSET) had in common with the Schools Council only the fact that it was disbanded for the crime of being both representative and workable. There was no cross-referencing between the two bodies. This artificial distinction was reflected more locally, with advisers and inspectors appointed across curriculum areas and unsure of their relationship with local teachers' centres, with area training organizations, and with training institutions.

The same uncertainty was reflected in schools. In the climate of the James Committee report, professional tutors or teacher-tutors were recommended and sometimes established in schools as catalysts for the school contribution to initial training, to induction, and to in-service education and training. How their rôle related to the curriculum development responsibilities of subject departments and directors of studies or to the 'pastoral' responsibilities of heads of house or year, or indeed to the responsibilities of headteachers, was a question explored and resolved in very different ways in different schools and local authorities. There were examples of professional tutors expected or expecting to take over direct responsibility for staff development; equally, there were many examples of a relationship more akin to in-house consultancy. Either way, the professional tutor was caught in a trap if the rôle became permanent. Anything more than three years in a full-time teacher-tutor rôle appeared to de-skill or bring on obsolescence for other management rôles in schools. The problem was akin to that of local authority subject-advisers.

The James Committee concern for the teacher's personal professional renewal and refreshment was shifted by the British government's 'Great Debate' towards a policy focused on the needs of schools. In many ways, this could be seen as potentially the most positive outcome of that confusion of conference rhetoric and underlying social malaise. From the papers of the Bournemouth follow-up conference, mounted by the Department of Education to the tune of a declaration of government intent (of course, later honoured in the breach) to project into estimates the James Committee 3 per cent investment in professional development, we can trace a line of documents and advices which attempted to combine the personal professional aspiration with the identified needs of schools, local authorities and a national society.

At all levels, however, there remained a gap of organization and awareness between curriculum development and professional needs. The awareness-gap in schools has been bridged, perhaps, by two major influences, one of them positive and strengthened by practice elsewhere, the other negative at first, and derived from internal distress.

ORGANIZATIONAL DEVELOPMENT

Perceptions of curricular and professional development were both, though separately, articulated in relation to a whole process greater than either. First curriculum, offering into the 1960s a scraggy assemblage of traditional subjects in search of coherence, came to be discussed as a whole learning experience. The whole curriculum, thought about at first in terms of formal teaching programmes, was extended to the informal, to the hidden curriculum, the curriculum implied by the way school organizations were conducted or relationships in school were experienced.

Concurrently, from the mid-1970s, in-service education and training was being thought through in context. The needs of the individual teacher were not discarded, but were being seen as inextricably related to the context of school groups, the school's purposes, and the school as an organization. The 'thinking school' was one in which all teachers were engaged in curriculum review and development. That very activity, presumably related to the prime objectives of any school, was also seen as one of the most powerful instruments of professional improvement, to the extent that it was difficult to distinguish between means and ends. The curricular development activity of local authority advisers was increasingly through the medium of courses for teachers.

The organization of schools, however, has not reflected that marriage of interests. Head teachers are responsible to governors for the curriculum of the school, whatever that now means. But they are much more likely to have distributed that curriculum responsibility than to have distributed responsibility for the staff. And if they retain direct responsibility for staff, it is not easy to envisage another person having real responsibility for the school's contribution to professional development. For we cannot continue to envisage in-service education and training as something discrete, something added on (like the 3 per cent) and semidetached from the management of schools. If it is not an integral part of the organization, part of the language of change and development, part of the resource planning, then it will continue to be abused and viewed with abuse.

The context in management thinking has been the vogue for organization development (OD). Emerging in the United States business schools of the 1940s, organization development has become part of the school scene in Britain 40 years later. The Inner London Education Authority's lead in 1977 in providing a checklist for school self-review has been slowly adopted, and after a decade some local authorities have negotiated periodic school self-review procedures, and many schools have developed their own schemes. This seems to me to be the point of entry for consultancy in its most useful sense.

The other influence, which I suggested is negative or protective in its origins, has been the demand to put a price on development. In the 1960s and early 1970s, teachers were creating their own momentum, conscious of a general will in society to support change, and happy to devote themselves to new curricula and new school organizations, also knowing that their own opportunities for self-fulfilment and career development were high as schools expanded to meet the population bulge and to add a year to the statutory period of schooling. In first-generation comprehensive schools, there was nowhere in a local authority to go for advice; we raided the minds and mistakes of precursors, innovators or parallel developers in Anglesey, London, Coventry, Yorkshire or Bristol, and took it for granted that we were creating new schools in our own time and with our own ingenuity, over and above the business of running existing schools. It was the amateur tradition of public service in its best sense. In England and Wales in the 1960s, it was in a very hidebound further education sector that teachers protected themselves by tying government to a conditions of service contract, not in schools, which ran on voluntary commitment and goodwill, making huge strides and huge mistakes.

Nowadays everyone, teachers included, is putting a price on everything. Reforms of examination or curriculum have to be costed out before they are agreed, and the cost includes the necessary element of in-service training, not as a pious hope but as a negotiated precondition. No more reports like that of the Warnock Committee, expressing the faith that a government that wills the ends would will the means. Ironically, it is not teachers who are seen to have insisted on clearly defined contracts and conditions of service, which they have long wanted; central and local government, despite having paid the price in further education, are made to appear to be the driving forces; so formal staff appraisal will come in at a price, with time allocated to it, rather than continue to be informal and unrecognized. Government is still making the mistake of throwing money at specific priority initiatives—any one school may be bombarded with a dozen of them, unrelated to each other unless the school itself takes a grip on the whole lot together and relates them to its own priorities and initiatives.

What is happening is that the accumulating tasks of a school are being more precisely defined and negotiated, and that the school organization is therefore being adjusted to accommodate them. Curriculum development is being costed in terms of resource, time and training; teacher-training is being set against the priority needs of schools; and the two separate strands of curriculum and professional development are being brought together in a context of organizational review. It is that adjustment of organization which I believe should be the focus of consultancy. In particular, schools as whole organisms and entities will need to get out of their own skins in order to rediscover the creativity for which the apparently dulling impositions of accountability must become a firm and invisible foundation rather than a replacement. Once that is realized, there will be a desire and demand for access to consultancy as a resource for regular and required school review, well beyond the scope of the do-it-yourself kits which are currently on offer.

THE CONTINUOUS SCHOOL REVIEW

There are now examples of consultants being invited into schools in order to help identify the way forward to regular and systematic organizational review and development planning. The background of the consultant is less important than consultancy style; a team of consultants from different backgrounds but with a visibly common approach is sometimes particularly appropriate. Techniques of mirroring, of enabling individuals and groups to interpret their own language, intentions and behaviour, giving confidence within a defined area of confidentiality, are required with a discipline of consistency. Nothing could undermine confidence more than listening in commuter trains to that new breed of accountancy firm management consultant bragging to each other of their prowess and the failings of firms they are putting right.

It is particularly important that consultants brought into a school should have the effect of reducing dependency on them. Just as it is the vocation of a teacher to become redundant, in the sense of enabling young people to stand on their own feet, so too it must be a test of successful consultancy that the school is able to take forward shared perceptions of change and development, without dependency. Formal and regular organizational review, like formal and regular staff appraisal or formal and regular discussion with parents, may be a way forward to a modification of attitude which will be reflected in continuous review, appraisal and discussion. A consultant or team of consultants brought in to assist in identifying the best ways to introduce a development of this kind must have on the agenda the best ways of continuing the development without needing assistance. This is not to suggest that schools should be encouraged, after the first flip into a more open transaction, to sit with Nellie because Nellie has once used a consultant. What is more likely is that a school will take ownership of the development and will explore further and previously unidentified challenges, for which a different form of consultancy may be appropriate. What we are considering is a form of school organization whose only stability is that it will keep on changing in order to arouse and respond to the constantly changing educational needs of a community.

MANAGING OUTWARDS

This brings us to a dimension of school management which is most likely to make demands on consultancy in the future. It is the interface of school and community. Internal school management, efficiency models, putting things back in order, getting the most out of the available resource—the train-driver, doctor and farmer images—may be the first thought of employing authorities in calling in consultants, but are the areas where consultancy is least likely to be of use, once a few obvious skills and devices have been unpacked and sold. It is in the uncharted and unfathomed waters, the obscure and grey areas, where schools can most benefit from listening interpretation. These, too, are the areas which are most likely to cause organizational stress and therefore to reduce the confidence of an organization in managing activities in which it has proven competence.

Schools are now having to look beyond their own organization to the community of which they are a part, not just in order to identify the market and to be able to project more effectively, but in order to identify their own reasons for existing. Schools, no longer the totality of learning experience, have to latch on to the learning experience and learning opportunities available to young people through new mobility and new media. The relationship with parents is not one of consultation but of shared responsibility for education. Parents and others in the community are now growing into a shared management of schools. Schools with limited resources are having to identify ways to share them with other parts of the education service—special services, youth and community, careers officers, further education—and with other public services. Secondary schools in particular have always had an uneasy relationship with local authority departments, and it is becoming worse because of the pressures upon both. Surveys of job satisfaction show the local authority relationship among the unhappiest parts of headship. There is an interorganizational exercise as well as a transformation of management priorities. Managing outwards is more than a slogan; if heads are not careful, they will be doing that all the time, and never be seen again inside the organization. Boundary management is a seriously neglected part of training for headship and of school organization.

One perplexing problem here is that local authorities, whether viewed as the elected members or those employed to run their departments, are a part of the grey area. It is not easy for a local authority to identify itself as a problem area, or to agree to and pay for independent consultancy as a means to improve the relationship with schools. New funding arrangements may well encourage the practice of bringing consultants into schools to work with the whole senior management team there. It remains to be seen whether the areas of uncertainty between the school organization and others beyond its control, including the local authority itself, can be accepted as the ones in which free-standing consultancy may be most valuable.

CONCLUSIONS

To be effective, consultancy requires a relationship and disposition towards a listening climate which may be further developed in the consultancy process. Unlike bought-in 'knowhow', consultancy does not remove responsibility for decision-making from the organization; it may well extend to shared action-planning, but not to the extent of creating dependency on the person being consulted.

Consultancy in schools is of a different order to professional advice, to inspection or quality control. It goes beyond the personal counselling transaction. It may involve collaborative research, but it has a development as its outcome, rather than a description or conclusion. It is a useful form of context-embedded management training, promoting shared perceptions of the whole school context in the 'thinking school'.

Curriculum development and professional development have previously been organized and funded in artificial separation from each other. The opportunity now exists to bring them together within the general thrust towards organizational development, and to include them in the way schools are organized rather than have them seen as external adjuncts. Continuous review as part of schools' capability of constant change will bring with it the capacity to identify new needs for consultancy, particularly in uncharted areas of growing importance, such as the school's relationship with other services and with the community.

Chapter 3

A Need for Priorities: Drawing on the Research Literature

Bill Mulford

INTRODUCTION

In this chapter I will argue for an emphasis on leadership training as a major concern for consultant help, especially that training which involves staff development. It will be further argued that successful staff development needs to focus on the two major issues related to implementation, that is, the development of an awareness of and skills in group and organizational processes and an enforcement of the symbolic and cultural aspects of the school.

EDUCATIONAL LEADERSHIP: NEW DEMANDS BUT AN UNSATISFACTORY RESPONSE?

There is now a new set of leadership demands for those in educational organizations. More than ever before we face a confusion of goals and crises in the availability of resources. The 'back-to-basics' trend, for example, demands a return to the teaching of traditional skills and values in traditional ways, yet this is within a social milieu where almost all traditions are under assault. At the same time, schools are expected to do more than just teach basics—witness the large allocation of funds to 'vocational' type education. The message is clearly mixed: 'Go back–go forward. Do more–do less'.

Declining enrolments have also made it politically feasible to reduce resources to education. In addition to being asked to do more with less, educational organizations are being asked to do better. They are increasingly being held accountable for outcomes. Schools are caught in a squeeze between rising expectations and declining resources. Schools are expected to solve an increasing array of social problems, but enrolments, money, and public support for education are dwindling. Those who feel the squeeze most are the men and women who decide to take leadership roles—the educational managers and administrators.

The contemporary educational administrator's position can be likened to being between a rock and a hard place. On the one hand, messages from those who study change in schools describes educational leadership (particularly the role of principal) as the key around which all improvements pivot. On the other hand, practitioners themselves often describe educational leaders as powerless functionaries caught in the middle of a myriad of internal and external demands and unable to influence the direction of events in any significant way. They say that most hierarchies, like those in education systems, are nowadays so encumbered with rules and traditions, and so bound in by public laws, that even their leaders do not have to lead anyone anywhere, in the sense of pointing out the direction and setting the pace. They simply follow precedents, obey regulations, and move at the head of the crowd. Campbell *et al.* (1979) focused on what it was like to be a teacher in Australian government schools. Results from data gathered from all Australian states enables the authors to conclude (Campbell *et al.*, 1979) that school principals 'are revealed as very versatile dissatisfiers with their staffs accusing them of low-level involvement in work-force activities, an absence of displays of personal interest and concern, and infrequent bestowal of recognition and appreciation'.

An impression Campbell *et al.* (1979) gained was that teachers were 'not questioning the good-will of their principals, but their priorities'. Other Australian literature (see, for example, McRae, 1975; O'Dempsey, 1976; and Willis, 1980) based on research which attempts to answer the question 'What do principals do in schools?' by actually following them around and reporting on their every movement, suggests the image of the carved wooden figurehead leading the ship—one bobbing and weaving on turbulent waters. This latter set of studies paints a picture of the principal's world as one consisting of variety, brevity, fragmentation, uncertainty, ambiguity, superficiality, control of action by others, a hectic pace, preference for the verbal, and a lack of overt feedback on, or appreciation of, their actions.

By way of illustration, these studies found that:

(a)   the average duration of each principal's activity is about seven minutes with two-thirds of the activities being from one to five minutes;

(b)   just over one-fifth of activities are interrupted with many (one-quarter) never being resumed;

(c)   unscheduled meetings occupy almost one-half of the principal's time with scheduled meetings (20 per cent), desk work (23 per cent) and 'tours' (5 per cent) taking up most of the rest;

(d)   three-quarters of time during the school day is spent in contacts with other people, half of these contacts being on a one-to-one basis.

This literature should concern all educators, including consultants. However, any description of what is the role of the educational leader does not necessarily address what some would consider the more important issue of what ought to be his or her role. Further, it is not difficult for educational administrators to convince themselves that resolving crises, being involved in a whirling carnival of activity, is what the top men or women in a school are paid to do. Crisis management, for all the hazards involved, can have a certain titillating excitement. A crisis a day keeps boredom away. With a crisis successfully resolved one has done something tangible. Motion in itself can be a source of satisfaction. But as the school effectiveness literature demonstrates, solving a crisis a day may keep boredom away for the educational 'leader' but this is certainly not enough to make a difference.

What ought the educational administrator be doing in order to make a difference? In attempting to form an answer to this seemingly simple question, I want to examine three areas:

(a)   research on indicators of school effectiveness;

(b)   research on the links between school administration and student outcomes which reinforces the crucial role of administrators in school effectiveness; and

(c)   suggestions for action.

INDICATORS OF SCHOOL EFFECTIVENESS

It is clear from the literature on indicators of school effectiveness that no one factor accounts for effectiveness. There appears to be a critical mass of positive factors which, when put together, make the difference. What constitutes this critical mass of interdependent factors?

Tables 3.1 and 3.2 summarize a great deal of overseas and Australian literature on the criteria for effective schools. Table 3.1 outlines the results of seven representative overseas studies. The summary work by Renihan and Renihan (1984) in Canada is used as a means of organizing the remaining studies with additions contained in square brackets in the table. (The reader may wish to criticize my placement or grouping of items.)

Other summary studies (that is, studies that compile their indicators from the research of others) in Table 3.1 are those by Austin (1979), Edmonds (1981) and Duckett *et al.* (1980) in the United States. Murphy and Hollinger's (1984) research examined instructionally effective high schools in California, and Rutter *et al.* (1979) spent five years studying 12 unusually effective London (England) high schools. Finally, Brookover *et al.* (1979, 1981) used as their research base 91 Michigan elementary schools.

Table 3.2 summarizes three recent Australian research studies of effective schools. In 1979 Mellor and Chapman (1984) had senior officials of the Department of Education in Victoria nominate nine secondary schools in Melbourne as 'effective'. They included inner city, suburban and outlying (or rural fringe) schools with student populations from 658 to 1020, both coeducational and single-sex, including predominantly Anglo-Saxon backgrounds in five and 'multiethnic' in four, with seven regarded as comprehensive and the remainder selective. A team of researchers was sent to look for the factors which might account for these schools being considered effective. From the detailed individual observational and interview data the research team were able to isolate 14 general factors. Caldwell and Misko (1984) employed a modification of the reputational approach to identify effective Tasmanian schools.

From 1982 to 1984, Hyde and Werner (1984) studied eleven primary schools in the metropolitan south-east region of Western Australia that had been declared to be Priority Schools (originally referred to as Disadvantaged Schools). Particular note was made of the schools that were successful in a variety of areas related to their Priority School Program and school improvement in general. Three common features of effective schools were found to be:

(a)   a shared consensus on values and goals;

Table 3.1 *Representative overseas studies on the criteria of school effectiveness.*

Factors: Based on Renihan and Renihan	Murphy and Hollinger (1984)	Austin (1979)	Rutter et al. (1979)	Edmonds (1981)	Duckett et al. (1980)	Brookover and Lezotte (1979, 1981)
(1) Sense of mission Consistent philosophy and a sense of mission Shared, agreed-upon, accepted as important and clearly stated	A clear sense of purpose	Principal runs school for a purpose rather than from force of habit	School functions as a coherent whole, with agreed ways of doing things that are consistent throughout the school and have the general support of all staff		Clearly stated curricular goals and objectives	
(2) Great expectations For student performance and that they *can* achieve Monitored Teachers and administrators hold for each other	High expectations A commitment to educate each student as completely as possible	Principal holds high expectations for both teachers and students Teachers expect children to show high achievement and display good citizenship	Teachers expect children to achieve well	A climate of expectation in which no children are permitted to fall below minimum but efficacious levels of achievement	High leader expectations—as reflected both in attitudes and behaviour	Staff and principal believe all students can master the basic skills objectives Staff expect students will go on with their education
(3) Academic focus Emphasis on basic academic skills	A core set of standards within a rich curriculum			Clarity that pupil acquisition of the basic school skills takes precedence over all other school activities		The importance of basic skills mastery as prime goal emphasized Staff do not make excuses: they assume responsibility for teaching basic skills and are committed to do so Staff spend more time on achieving basic skills objectives

(4) *Feedback on academic performance* Consistent and continuous Tied to monitoring of teaching performance appropriateness of curriculum level		A means is present by which pupil progress can be frequently monitored	Employment of individualized instruction and structured learning environments There is cooperative team learning	Principal assumes responsibility for the evaluation of the achievement of basic skills objectives
(5) *Positive motivational strategies* Conscious reliance on praise rather than blame A special reason for each student to go to school Designed to enhance student self-image and foster a friendly and supportive atmosphere	Teachers warm and responsive to children Students have positive self-concepts and a feeling of controlling their own destiny Immediate direct praise and approval the prevalent means of classroom feedback A high proportion of children hold some kind of position of responsibility in the school			
(6) *Conscious attention to [a positive, safe ordered community] climate* A safe, orderly learning environment Specific rules, regulations, and guidelines laid down and clearly understood by all A sense of community	Pleasant working conditions for pupils Teachers present themselves as positive role models demonstrating punctuality, concern for physical well-being of school building, concern for emotional well-being of pupils, and restraint in the use of physical punishment Teachers readily available to be consulted by children about problems	There is an atmosphere that is orderly without being rigid, quiet without being oppressive, and generally conducive to the instructional business at hand		

Factors: Based on Renihan and Renihan	Murphy and Hollinger (1984)	Austin (1979)	Rutter et al. (1979)	Edmonds (1981)	Duckett et al. (1980)	Brookover and Lezotte (1979, 1981)
(7) *[Administrative] leadership* Assertive Instructional Assumption of responsibility High standards Personal vision	Instructional leadership from principal (strong leadership and systematic staff development that provide continuing help to teachers committed to instructional improvement) Develop resiliency and a problem-solving attitude in school	Principal participates strongly in classroom instructional programme		Administrative leadership is strong and without it the disparate elements of good schooling can be neither brought together nor kept together	Frequent use of staff development to realize school objectives—the greater the specificity or focus the better	Principal is an assertive instructional leader and disciplinarian
(8) *[Other]* [Teachers take responsibility]		Teachers have freedom to choose teaching techniques				Teachers are not very satisfied or complacent about the status quo Staff accept and are involved in developing the concept of accountability
[Parental involvement]					High levels of parental involvement with school activities	There is parent-initiated contact and involvement at improving the school
[System support]					Support from special project funds from federal, state and local sources Reductions in adult/child ratios Resource and facility manipulations alone are insufficient to affect	

Table 3.2 *Three Australian studies on the criteria of school effectiveness*

Factors	Mellor and Chapman (1984)	Caldwell and Misko (1984)	Hyde and Werner (1984)
(1) Sense of mission	Clarity of purpose—clear well formulated objectives, strong task orientation	A set of objectives it hopes to attain High involvement of staff in the development of these objectives High commitment and loyalty to school goals and values by principal, teachers and students A set of values it considers important Participatory decision-making	A planned emphasis on goal-focused activities that were directed towards clear, attainable and relevant objectives Shared consensus on values and goals Total staff involvement with activities/ programme directed towards improvement of learning outcomes
(2) Great expectations	Expectations and standards—academic, personal, social expectations are clearly enunciated and student progress in all areas is carefully monitored Recognition of achievement—an emphasis is placed on achievement and success commensurate with ability	Students, principal and teachers with high expectations for academic achievement Expectations that all students will do well	
(3) Academic focus	Stable well-defined curriculum—an orderly, structured programme designed to cater for a diversity of student ability and interest Co-curricular activities—rich, varied and appropriate to the interests and future life paths of students	A well-planned, balanced and organized programme which provides for continuity of child's development A programme which provides students with required skills Objectives related to the elimination of prejudice	An integrated school-wide emphasis upon skills relating to the intellectual, social, personal and physical development of individual pupils
(4) Feedback on academic performance			Clear, understandable short- and long-range planning, and the coordination of these through effective monitoring/evaluation activities Observable evidence that there was a flexibility in programmes which facilitated implementation, adaptation and refinement, supported by effective monitoring and evaluation practices

Factors	Mellor and Chapman (1984)	Caldwell and Misko (1984)	Hyde and Werner (1984)
(5) *Positive motivational strategies*	Positive student response—to the curriculum, to staff competence, effort, approachability	A climate of trust and openness of communication High student morale High teacher morale	A commitment to the forging of positive relationships A high degree of teacher empathy, rapport and personal interaction with pupils and parents A positive school climate, with high levels of supportiveness, social cohesiveness and low levels of disaffiliation Well-structured teaching programmes and classroom activities
(6) *Conscious attention to [a positive, safe ordered community] climate*	Cooperative interpersonal relationships Underlying value of concern for people Emphasis on the importance of mutual respect, teamwork, trust, tolerance, consideration Commitment and cohesiveness—a spirit of cohesion and, among staff, enthusiasm, acceptance of schools' purpose and values by staff, students, parents Sense of continuity—tradition. sequence	A climate of respect, mutual trust and appreciation between teachers and students Value system which includes students' respect for themselves, others and the property of others Good discipline, including few occasions where senior administrators need to be directly involved with discipline High levels of cohesiveness and team spirit among teachers Pleasant, exciting and challenging environment for students and teachers	
(7) *[Administrative] leadership*	Leadership—administrators display commitment to clear, well-formulated objectives; display initiatives, are highly supportive of staff, encourage others to accept responsibility	Principal who: is responsible to and supportive of the needs of teachers is aware of and involved with what is going on in classrooms enables the sharing of duties and resources to occur in the most efficient manner has a flexible administrative style sees that a continued review of the programme occurs and that progress towards goals is evaluated provides appropriate feedback allocates resources to meet school needs establishes effective relationships with education department, community, parents, teachers and students is willing to take risks is concerned with own professional development encourages staff involvement in professional development programmes and makes use of the skills teachers acquire in these programmes	Well-developed systems of school level teacher development A visible system of 'rewards' and acknowledgement for individual teachers' efforts that included recognition by the principal and colleagues—and, in some instances, parents The effective management of time and resources within those constraints that existed for the school A total staff involvement with activities/ programmes directed towards improvement of learning outcomes Well-managed school-level decision-making processes which include the use of key teachers, outside experts and a variety of data

(8) *[Other]* [Teachers take responsibility]	Staff stability—minimal turnover, maturity, professionalism, acceptance of delegated responsibility	Strong commitment to learning	Stability and continuity of key staff An acceptance by principals and teachers of a positive accountability, and the acknowledgement of personal and collective responsibility for learning outcomes Principals and teachers who were confident of their own abilities and perceived no threat to themselves in proposed changes
[Parental involvement]	Positive community relationships—community support of the school fostered through the provision of a school programme which conforms to parental expectations, frequent and thorough interaction with parents, encouragement of community use of school facilities	High levels of parental involvement in the educational activities of their children High levels of parent involvement in decision-making	
[System support]	Sufficiency of resources—human, material, financial resources adequate to meet needs	Adequate resources Motivated, talented and capable teachers	An emphasis upon teaching strategies rather than only instructional resources Principals and teachers who accepted that they had some autonomy in devising solutions to local problems, but felt confident that these could be shared with the regional administration

(b) evidence of clear understandable short-range and long-range planning, and the coordination of these through effective monitoring/evaluation activities;

(c) the stability and continuity of key staff.

These three common features developed into eleven additional indicators which more closely related to principal leadership and are also listed in Table 3.2.

It is interesting to note that the criteria selected most frequently by the 'reputable' panel in the Caldwell and Misko (1984) study were as follows (in rank order):

(a) a set of objectives it hopes to obtain;

(b) the principal is responsible to and supportive of the needs of teachers;

(c) the principal establishes effective relationships with education department, community, parents, teachers and students;

(d) the principal allocates resources to meet school needs;

(e) the principal enables the sharing of duties and resources to occur in the most efficient way;

(f) the principal is aware of and involved with what is going on in classrooms;

(g) the principal encourages staff involvement in professional development programmes and makes use of skills teachers acquire in these programmes;

(h) high commitment and loyalty to school goals and values by the principal, teachers and students;

(i) the principal is concerned about his/her own professional development;

(j) the principal sees that a continued review of the programme occurs and that progress towards goals is evaluated;

(k) a value system which includes students' respect for themselves, others and the property of others.

The Caldwell and Misko (1984) study also had a number of outcome criteria which are not included in Table 3.2. These criteria were:

(a) scores on achievement tests which reflect excellence;

(b) low student dropout;

(c) low absentee rate among teachers;

(d) low absentee rate among students;

(e) low student suspension rate;

(f) low delinquency rate;

(g) few applications for teacher transfer;

(h) high success in the placement of students in colleges, universities or jobs.

It is relevant to note that criteria chosen least often by raters included all but the last two. As Caldwell and Misko (1984, p. 45) conclude: 'It is evident that criteria related to leadership and climate were strongly associated with school effectiveness in the minds of raters and that criteria related to outcomes were relatively weakly so associated'. It is also interesting to note the great deal of similarity in the indicators of school effectiveness originating from overseas and Australian studies as it is to be aware of the differences. These differences include:

(a) less of an emphasis on basic academic skills and more of an emphasis on a programme designed to cater for a diversity of student ability and interest in Australian research;

(b)   more of an emphasis on teacher stability and continuity, parental involvement and system support in the Australian material.

LINK BETWEEN SCHOOL ADMINISTRATION AND STUDENT OUTCOMES

Another direction to turn for an answer to the question of what ought the educational administrator be doing in order to make a difference is the plethora of literature in the well-known school climate and leadership studies. Studies in this tradition focus on the general quality, ethos, climate or innovativeness of schools. That is, there is a concentration on the leader/teacher relationship. We should agree that as schools are for teachers as well as for children—teachers spend a great deal of their life in school—it is important that their work environment be a positive one. We should also agree that teachers and school administrators are at schools primarily because of, and for, the children.

If this position is accepted, then we are led to ask a more searching question in relation to the leader's influence on schools. Does the leader have a direct effect on the students, or can we assume that if the relationship between leader and teachers is a positive one then the relationship between teacher and students as well as student outcomes are also positive? For answers to this question we need to turn to North American studies. Even then we will find a dearth of relevant material. Those studies that I was able to uncover are summarized elsewhere (Mulford, 1982b, 1984a, 1984b). In this chapter I just want to provide the flavour of the findings by giving the summary chart from my review (Table 3.3 below) and outlining one of the secondary school studies mentioned in it.

Anderson (1971) collected data from 3792 grade ten students and 806 teachers during the 1968–69 school year in 18 secondary schools in Ontario. The schools represented a selected sample stratified on the basis of school size, school district size, and school type. Results from the study showed that there was a relationship between student alienation and school bureaucratization. The latter was measured through the use of items such as the following (the scale within which each item is found is indicated in brackets):

(a)   'Officials in this school act like little gods, always ordering me about and telling me what to do.'
      (Hierarchy of authority)
(b)   'My relationships with school authorities are very formal and impersonal.'
      (Impersonality)
(c)   'I obey a lot of rules regarding my personal behaviour in and around school.'
      (Rules and regulations)
(d)   'I can take a little action until my decisions are approved by a school official.'
      (Centralization of control)

Increased presence of bureaucratic structure was found to be associated with increased alienation from school. Anderson (1971, p. 11) details the implications of these and other results in the following way:

> Since this study suggests that student alienation from school is related to school bureaucratization, and since research has shown that school bureaucratization is related to the way in which school principals behave, there is a strong possibility that principals who choose to do

Table 3.3   *Summary of studies that examine principal behaviour/values and student outcomes (from Mulford, 1984)*

Author(s) of study	Principal behaviour/values*	School/student outcome
Studies that focus at the school level (illustrative set only)		
Thomas (1973)	+ 'Supportiveness' − 'Operation emphasis'	More innovative primary school
Lieberman and Miller (1981)	+ Teachers given positive support and believe their efforts count + Encourages cooperative effort + Leads change efforts	School improvement
Rutter *et al.* (1979)	+ Strong positive leadership + High expectations + Consistency + Feedback	Positive school ethos (as it relates to high school student attendance, behaviour, delinquency, and public exam results)
Studies that focus at the student level (more comprehensive set)		
Lieberman (1973)	− 'Authority' (keeps decision-making power to him or herself)	Primary students delegated authority by teachers
Seeman and Seeman (1976)	+ Fosters participation in 'dialogue'. 'decision-making' and 'action' + 'Expert' and 'referrent' (not 'punishment', 'reward' or 'legitimate') bases of power	Positive 6th grade student attitudes to self, learning and school
Anderson (1971) McKay (1964)	− 'Bureaucratic structures' − 'Hierarchical authority'	Grade 10 student alienation Grade 9 student achievement on standard external exams (academic aptitude statistically controlled
Capelle (1971)	+ 'Tolerance of uncertainty' + 'Tolerance of freedom' − 'Production emphasis' − 'Aloofness'	High school student 'self-actualization'
Harkham and McCauley (1978)	+ 'Consultative' + 'Participative'	Positive high school teacher and student 'self-actualization'
Office of Education (1974)	+ Positive principal/teacher interaction + Supportive learning climate fostered + A set of school wide practices and support for reading developed	Higher primary reading achievement
Gibson (1974)	+ Participative, goal directed model of administration	Grade 6 boys higher achievement test scores in relation to intelligence test scores
Webber (1971)	+ High expectations + Instructional leadership + Develops a climate characterized by order, a sense of purpose, relative quiet, and pleasure in learning	Reading achievement in early grades of inner-city schools
Austin (1978)	+ Participates in instruction + High expectations of themselves and others	High achievement
Brookover and Lezotte (1979)	+ Provides instructional leadership + Disciplinarian + Evaluates achievement of basic objectives	Improvement in achievement
Venezky and Winfield (1980)	+ 'Achievement oriented'	Schools that succeed beyond expectations in teaching reading

Author(s) of study	Principal behaviour/values*	School/student outcome
Kean *et al.* (1979)	+ Being a reading specialist + Observes 4th grade reading classes	Grade 4 reading growth
Murnane (1975)	+ High teacher ratings	Growth in black student achievement
Coulson (1977)	+ Feels strongly about instruction + Effectively communicates this feeling + Dominant role in decisions about selection of instructional material and in programme planning and evaluation + Emphasizes academic standards	Improved achievement of minority students

* − negative or, + positive relationship with school/student outcome indicated.

so could reduce student alienation from school by modifying the organizational structure of their schools and classroom.

The findings of this study, taken together with those on the association between student feelings of power with achievement, suggest that school administrators may be able to manipulate variables related to pupil achievement. Less bureaucratic modes of school organization may produce higher levels of pupil achievement.

An article by Shoemaker and Fraser (1981) reviews additional studies that help us to provide answers to the issue of principal influence on their schools. Although none of these studies sets out to study the role of principals or specifically secondary principals, most conclude that principals were important in determining the effectiveness of schools, including improved student performance. Shoemaker and Fraser (1981, p. 180) summarize the results of all the studies they reviewed as follows:

What can principals do? Four key themes emerge from our survey of research:

1) assertive, achievement-oriented leadership;
2) orderly, purposeful, and peaceful climate;
3) high expectations for staff and pupils; and
4) well-designed instructional objectives and evaluation system.

Emphasis in the studies of school effectiveness is clearly on interpersonal skills (for example, the need to be supportive, foster participation, and tolerate uncertainty and freedom) and on strong instructional leadership (for example, the need to be involved, help develop school goals and a supportive learning climate, and have high expectations). The similarities with the literature on indicators of school effectiveness are striking.

SUGGESTIONS FOR ACTION

The reviews of literature on how principals make a difference to their schools and students, and which stress the need for interpersonal skills and strong instructional leadership, are a start. The literature on indicators of school effectiveness provides another complementary source of assistance arguing as it does such factors as: a sense of mission; great expectations; positive motivational strategies; conscious attention to a positive, safe, ordered community climate; and administrative leadership. However, it is vastly easier to describe effectiveness than to achieve it. A number of articles contain clear suggestions for action. Four such articles are those by Lieberman and Miller (1981), Leithwood and Fullan (1984), Hyde and Werner (1984), and Miles (1983).

Leiberman and Miller (1981) argue that school improvement occurs on two concurrent levels—the teacher and school organization—and involves staff development, networking and problem-centred activities. These approaches are seen to share the four common features of linkage, developmentalism, systematic ad hocism, and local adaption.

Leithwood and Fullan (1984) start with seven propositions about change in schools which suggests that problems associated with implementation stem from school and school system characteristics that are usually labelled 'capacity'. The propositions include the positions that change is time-consuming, will create anxiety and uncertainty, requires support and positive organizational relationships, and involves development, knowing the rationale and gradually acquired not imposed pressure. Six strategies are seen as increasing the chances of successful change by focusing on improving a school's capacity to cope with improvements on a continuous basis. These strategies are: providing continuous professional development; increasing principal effectiveness; school planning; developing educational policies with a view to their implementation; using standard operating procedures; and, most important, building systematic problem-solving procedures. Hyde and Werner (1984) add the importance for successful implementation of factors such as lead-in time, honest realization of personal limitations, careful selection of key staff members, careful establishment of credibilities, roles and territories of concerned, and constant reminders of resource limits. Miles (1983) points out that institutionalization of change needs to be approached by providing supports and by warding off threats. Supports include such factors as administrative commitment, support, assistance and pressure, and teacher mastery, commitment and stabilization of use. Threats needing to be warded off include environmental turbulence, career advancement motivation, instability of programme staff and leadership, and the vulnerability of the change. Organizational change is seen as critical both to reinforce the supports and to act as a buffer against the threats.

My own position on what makes for successful implementation has been enunciated elsewhere (Mulford, 1979, 1982a, 1982b, 1983; Mulford *et al.*, 1977) but can be summarized as follows. I believe that this future depends on the formulation of new kinds of staff development activities and programmes. Based on an understanding of the realities of schools and of teaching, as well as an appreciation of the demands that are being placed on schools and teachers, new and varied perspectives must be developed to guide school improvement efforts that focus on teachers. I choose the term 'staff development' instead of in-service, or teacher education training, because it suggests a different approach to improvement, one that considers the effects of the whole school (the staff or the organization) on the individual teacher and community member, and the necessity for long-term growth possibility (or development). Because of this position, I tend to be critical of the idea of giving one-shot courses and workshops to individual teachers in isolation from their peers and the school and its community. The crux of my argument is that for more successful staff development in schools there is a need to give greater emphasis to implementation and that the most important aspect of effective implementation is obtaining cooperation among teachers (and between teachers and community).

That gaining cooperative effort, and thus more effective implementation, is difficult should not deter us. One writer (Glaser, 1977), for example, has likened attempted change in schools to the punching of warm jelly: if you hit it hard and often enough, you can splatter some of it, but it soon takes the form of the bowl as it cools and then congeals. Perhaps the most important point to remember is that planning and developing changes are not the same as implementing them.

Many of the unsuccessful attempts to effect change in schools may have had potential. The problem has been, however, that those involved in pushing these changes, often educational consultants themselves, have basically had a content orientation. In other words, their underlying assumption has been that if they could agree on new goals in terms of curriculum, teacher inputs, evaluation, and so on (that is, if they could develop superior content) somehow the schools would respond positively. This does not necessarily follow. In fact school people have been badly disillusioned by the galloping hoofbeats of those itinerant educational pedlars who ride in and out again exhorting the latest elixir.

A common argument is that schools should tackle their problem immediately and directly (for example, through a school-based curriculum development, school evaluation, or clinical supervision), and that effective group functioning and cooperation will somehow result from the spirit of working together for what is superficially agreed to be in the best interests of the school. This is another content emphasis and does not make very much sense. One cannot assume that group effectiveness is just a matter of pushing people in at the deep end of the profusely propounded pool of participation. We must learn how to lose time in order to gain time.

Awareness of, and skill development in, group and organizational processes must be a first step in any effective change. Instead of others trying to insert something into a school's culture, the school leadership should first be trying to help that culture develop an awareness of and a responsiveness to itself. In other words, I am strongly arguing that the way forward towards school improvement is to first focus on developing group and organizational processes, or what is termed 'effective processes to manage change' by Hyde and Werner (1984), 'building systematic problem-solving procedures' by Leithwood and Fullan (1984), 'problem-centred activities' by Lieberman and Miller (1981), and 'organizational change' by Miles (1983).

So my position is that effective cooperation processes first need to be developed by means of which schools and the people in them might have some reasonable prospect of self-renewal, of decisively answering the new set of leadership demands. Fullan (1985) has very recently implied the same point in *Elementary School Journal*. He talks about eight common organizational variables of effective schools as:

(a)   instructionally focused leadership at the school level;
(b)   district support;
(c)   emphasis on curriculum and instruction (for example, maximizing academic learning);
(d)   clear goals and high expectations for students;
(e)   a system for monitoring performance and achievement;
(f)   ongoing staff development;
(g)   parental involvement and support;
(h)   orderly and secure environment.

But he then argues (1985, p. 400) that such a list of organizational variables represent the tip of an iceberg. They say nothing about the dynamics of the organization. To comprehend what successful schools are really like in practice, we have to turn to additional factors that infuse some meaning and life into the process of improvement within a school.

He believes there are four fundamental factors that underlie successful improvement processes, the first two of which closely parallel my position:

(a)   intense interaction and communication;
(b)   collaborative planning and implementation.

The other two factors are:

(c)   a guiding value system (coming up next in this chapter); and
(d)   a feel for the improvement process on the part of leadership.

But, where to next? I would suggest it *is* to the strategic, educational, symbolic, and cultural aspects of leadership—the sense of mission, great expectations, and positive, safe, ordered community climate aspects of school effectiveness.

I agree with Sergiovanni's position that much of the literature on educational leadership relies 'too much on what leaders actually do and how they behave and not enough on the more symbolic aspect of leadership—the meanings they communicate to others'. Sergiovanni (1982, p. 330) distinguishes between the *tactical* and *strategic* aspects of leadership.

> [A strategy involves] enlisting and employing support for certain policies and purposes and for devising plans towards goals. Tactics, by contrast, involve actions or means of less magnitude: they are small-scale actions serving a large purpose. They represent short-term and highly focussed administrative expression that characterize day-to-day leadership activity . . .
>
> In part, the emphasis on tactical requirements of leadership reflects the broader management culture of western society. Such values as efficiency, specificity, rationality, measurability, and objectivity combined with beliefs that good management is tough minded are part of this culture. Metaphors of the battlefields are often used to remind us that one must be hard-nosed, and that the going is tough (in the trenches, on the firing line, bite the bullet, take command, winning and losing).

Given the new leadership demands faced by educational administrators, it is no wonder the tactical requirements of leadership are emphasized. But Sergiovanni (1982) points out:

> Missing from these tactical issues, however, are holistic values of purposes, goodness, and importance. Missing also is an emphasis on long-term quality schooling . . . Often attention is given to the tactical requirements because they are easy to teach and learn, specific, easily measured, can be readily packaged for workshops, and are otherwise accessible. Emphasizing the tactical, because they are accessible, reminds me of the drunk looking under the lamp post for an object lost a block away. . . . For a proper balance [and as the next step for school administrators in achieving school effectiveness] tactical requirements should be clearly linked to and dependent upon the strategic. They represent short-term and highly focused managerial expressions that characterize day-by-day leadership activity. Separated from the strategic, they are ends in themselves devoid of the purpose and meanings needed for quality leadership and quality schooling.

Sergiovanni's (1984) more recent article on leadership and excellence in schooling helps to summarize the different emphases facing an educational administrator looking

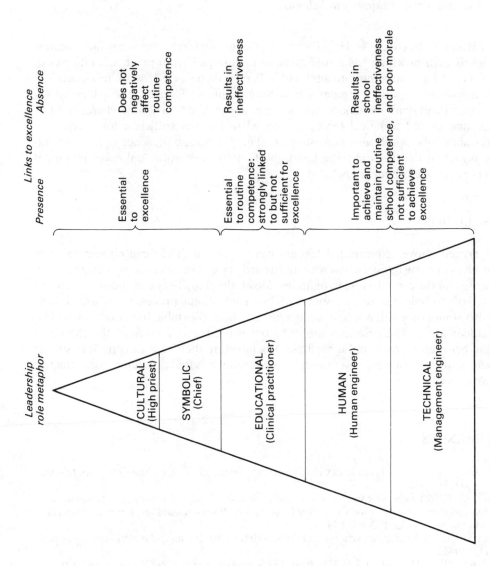

Figure 3.1. Sergiovanni's leadership forces hierarchy.

Examples

Articulate school mission, socialize new members, tell stories and maintain reinforcing myths, define uniqueness, develop and display a reinforcing symbol system, reward those who reflect the culture

Tour school, visit classes, know students, preside over ceremonies and rituals, provide a unified vision

Develop curriculum, provide inservice, supervision and evaluation, diagnose educational problems

Support, encourage, build and maintain morale, use participatory decision-making

Plan, organize, co-ordinate, schedule

Leadership role metaphor

CULTURAL (High priest)

SYMBOLIC (Chief)

EDUCATIONAL (Clinical practitioner)

HUMAN (Human engineer)

TECHNICAL (Management engineer)

Links to excellence
Presence   Absence

Essential to excellence   Does not negatively affect routine competence

Essential to routine competence: strongly linked to but not sufficient for excellence   Results in ineffectiveness

Important to achieve and maintain routine school competence, not sufficient to achieve excellence   Results in school ineffectiveness, and poor morale towards school effectiveness. He talks about a leadership forces' hierarchy that contains five levels each of which has a role metaphor, examples from practice, and links to excellence. I have attempted to summarize Sergiovanni's (1984) work in Figure 3.1.

The important argument to emerge from Sergiovanni's (1984) leadership hierarchy is that cultural and symbolic aspects are essential to excellence in school whereas educational, human and technical forces are linked to but not sufficient for excellence. Sergiovanni (1984, p. 9) also suggests that, 'The greater the presence of a leadership force higher in the hierarchy the less important (beyond some unknown minimum presence) are the others below'.

CONCLUSIONS

As I argued above, educational leaders have a choice. They can choose to liken themselves to being between that rock and a hard place. They can choose to lead only in the sense that the carved wooden figurehead leads the ship. They can choose to venture into today's turbulent waters without skills in organizational processes and a keel. But, as I also argue, they will not only be increasingly uncomfortable but education will be the sadder for it. The priorities are clear but will education consultancy choose to remain between its rock and a hard place bemoaning their lack of consultants/time/resources/support, or will it use research literature such as that presented in this chapter to move forward?

REFERENCES

Anderson, B. D. (1971) 'Bureaucracy in schools and student alienation', *The Canadian Administrator*, **11**(3), 9–12.

Austin, G. (1978) *Process Evaluation: A Comprehensive Study of Outliners*. Maryland State Department of Education and Centre for Educational Research and Development, University of Maryland. (ERIC: ED 160 644.)

Austin, G. (1979) 'Exemplary schools and the search for effectiveness', *Educational Leadership*, **37**(1), 10–12.

Brookover, W. and Lezotte, L. (1979) *Changes in School Characteristics Coincident with Changes in Students' Achievement*. Institute for Research on Teaching, Michigan State University.

Brookover, W. and Lezotte, L. *et al.* (1979, 1981), cited in D'Amico (1982).

Caldwell, B. and Misko, J. (1984) 'School-based budgetting: a financial strategy for meeting the needs of students', *Educational Administration Review*, **2**, 1.

Campbell, W. J. *et al.* (1979) 'Being a teacher in Australian State Government schools'. Canberra: AGP, AACRDE Report No. 5.

Capelle, R. *et al.* (1971) 'Student self-actualization and organization actualization in Manitoba high schools'. A paper presented at the joint CAPE-CCRE-CERA Conference on Educational Research, St John's, Newfoundland, June 1971.

Coulson, J. E. (1977) *Overview of the National Evaluation of the Emergency School Aid Act*. Santa Monica, CA: System Development Corporation.

D'Amico, J. (1982) 'Each effective school may be one of a kind', *Educational Leadership*, December, 61–2.

Duckett, C. *et al.* (1980), cited in D'Amico (1982).

Edmonds, R. (1981) *The Characteristics of Effective Schools, Research and Implementation*, unpublished. Michigan State University.

Fullan, M. (1985) 'Change processes and strategies at the local level', *Elementary School Journal*, **85**(3), 391–421.

Gibson, A. K. (1974) 'The Achievement of Sixth Grade Students in a Mid-Western City', Unpublished doctoral dissertation, The University of Michigan. (University Micro Films, No. 70–15, 729, 1974.)

Glaser, E. (1977) 'Facilitation of knowledge utilisation by institutions for child development', *Journal of Applied Behavioural Science*, **13**(2), 89–109.

Harkham, L. and McCauley, V. (1978) 'Effects of school management systems upon the self-actualization of students and teachers', A paper presented at the Annual Meeting of AERA, Toronto, March 28.

Hyde, N. and Werner, T. (1984) *The Context for School Improvement in Western Australian Primary Schools*, OECD/CERI (unpublished).

Kean, M. H. *et al.* (1979) *What Works in Reading?* Office of Research and Evaluation, Philadelphia School District.

Leithwood, K. and Fullan, M. (1984) 'Fostering long-term growth in school system effectiveness', *Canadian Administrator*, **24**(3), 6–13.

Lieberman, A. (1973) 'The power of the principal: research findings', in C. M. Culver and G. J. Hoban (eds) *The Power to Change*. New York: McGraw-Hill.

Lieberman, A. and Miller, L. (1981) 'Synthesis of research on improving schools', *Educational Leadership*, **38**, 7.

McKay, D. A. (1964) 'Should schools be bureaucratic?' *Canadian Administrator*, **4**(2), 5–8.

McRae, K. (1975) 'Observing a principal at work', in Mulford, B. *et al.* (eds) *Papers on ACT Education 1974–75*. Canberra: CAE, School of Education.

Mellor, W. and Chapman, J. (1984) 'Organisational effectiveness in schools', *Educational Administration Review*, **2**, 2.

Miles, M. (1983) 'Unravelling the mystery of institutionalisation', *Educational Leadership*, **41**, 3.

Mulford, W. (1979) 'Organisation development in schools: an octet of dilemmas', *Educational Change and Development*, **1**, 3, and *ACEA Bulletin*, **12**.

Mulford, W. (1982a) 'Consulting with educational systems is about the facilitation of coordinated effort', in H. L. Gray (ed.) *The Management of Educational Institutions: Theory, Research and Consultancy*. Brighton: Falmer Press.

Mulford, W. (1982b) 'Do principals make a difference?' *ACEA Bulletin*, **24**.

Mulford, W. (1983) 'The first step for school leaders; attain cooperative effort', *Educational Administration Review*, **1**, 1.

Mulford, W. (1984a) 'Principal training: how do we decide the content?', *Educational Change and Development*, **5**, 2.

Mulford, W. (1984b) 'Secondary school principalship: a crisis a day may keep boredom away but is it enough to make a difference?', *Secondary Administrator*, **2**, 2.

Mulford, W. *et al.* (1977) 'Organisational development in schools: early data on the Australian experience', *Journal of Educational Administration*, **15**, 2.

Murnane, R. (1975) *The Impact of School Resources on the Learning of Inter-city Children*. Cambridge, MA: Ballinger.

Murphy, J. and Hollinger, P. (1984) 'An exploratory analysis of instructionally effective high schools in California', *NASSP Bulletin* (in press) (as reported in *The Practitioner*, **51**, 1, 1984).

O'Dempsey, K. (1976) 'Time analysis of activities, work patterns and roles of high school principals'. Unpublished M.Ed.Admin. thesis, University of Queensland, Australia.

Office of Education (1974) *School Factors Influencing Reading Achievement: A Case Study of Two Inner City Schools*. New York State Office of Evaluation. Performance Review.

Renihan, F. and Renihan, P. (1984) 'Effective schools, effective administration, and institutional image', *Canadian Administrator*, **24**(3), 1–6.

Rutter, M. *et al.* (1979) *Fifteen Thousand Hours*. Cambridge Mass.: Harvard University Press.

Seeman, A. Z. and Seeman, M. (1976) 'Staff process and pupil attitudes', *Human Relations*, **29**, 1.

Sergiovanni, T. (1982) 'Leadership and excellence in schooling', *Educational Leadership*, **39**, 5.

Sergiovanni, T. (1984) 'Leadership and excellence in schooling', *Educational Leadership*, **41**, 5.

Shoemaker, J. and Fraser, H. W. (1981) 'What principals can do: some implications from studies of effective schooling', *Phi Delta Kappan*, **63**, 3.

Thomas, A. R. (1973) 'The innovative school: some organisational characteristics', *Australian Journal of Education*, **17**(2), 113–30.

Venezky, R. L. and Winfield, L. (1980) *Schools That Succeed Beyond Expectations in Teaching Reading*. Newark, DE: University of Delaware Studies on Education, Technical Report No. 1.

Webber, G. (1971) *Inner-City Children Can Be Taught To Read: Four Successful Schools*. Washington, DC: Council for Basic Education.

Willis, O. (1980) 'The work activity of school principals: an observational study', *Journal of Educational Administration*, **18**, 1.

Chapter 4

The Ethics of Consultancy in Education

Robin Snell

INTRODUCTION

Consultancy usually involves entering an alien culture and coming across expectations about objectives, methods and relationships which differ from those of the consultant. This results in ethical dilemmas for which consultants are best prepared by examining their own starting assumptions about ethics. Trying to follow prescribed codes of practice is difficult because the assumptions on which these are based are not usually made explicit.

So I will begin by examining how the starting assumptions of consultants govern the conditions under which they prefer to work in education. I then describe my own starting assumptions and preferences and discuss my experience of ethical issues in consultancy. The issues I mention are of general concern for consultants but I do not advocate a regulatory code of ethics. Such codes may help to raise the status of an occupation but my concern is to help the individual consultant to work out his/her own standards and means of resolving ethical dilemmas. Therefore I conclude by suggesting how consultants can clarify their own ethical positions.

THE INFLUENCE OF ETHICAL PERSPECTIVES ON CONSULTANCY MISSIONS

Pupils, students, parents, teachers, educational administrators and managers, politicians and employers all have a direct stake in education and all assume value positions about education. Even those consultants who do not belong to these interest groups will be attracted to education by ideology rather than by the small fees which education offers. I will therefore examine eight ethical perspectives in turn and the kinds of mission that would suit consultants holding them.

Transcendent authority

From this perspective (Ross, 1930), certain actions are fundamentally right and other actions are fundamentally wrong. One source of such knowledge is sometimes claimed to be religious texts or doctrines. Another is a person's own intuition. Most emphasis is placed on the judgements of particular authority figures who are considered to be trustworthy and beyond reproach.

An ideal for the education system would be the promotion of a clear sense of what is right and what is wrong. With this view, the consultant would concentrate on the development of leadership skills for heads, especially those of laying down firm principles, maintaining discipline among staff and establishing clear lines of authority.

Cultural tradition

This is the desire to preserve the traditions, symbols and meanings of one's own region or nation. Most people with this desire also acknowledge that their cultural tradition is simply one among many which all have equal value and demand respect (Berry and Marshall, 1986). A favourite consultancy mission would be to help the school or college to adopt to changing circumstances while preserving the loyalties of members and partners. Staff would be helped to clarify the image of their school or college and how it meets the needs of the local community with its cultural traditions. The consultant would encourage multicultural education wherever the local community was not in a state of monoculture, and would try to establish an appropriate staff recruitment policy.

Only rarely will people hold to their own cultural traditions and also claim transcendent authority. Worries have been expressed (Crews and Cunningham, 1986) about people wanting their own values to prevail over all others in a programme of cultural change. Multicultural education would be an anathema to them. A consultant with such views would prefer education to spread certain cultural values and to stamp out alien ones. Some consultants may have an unconscious tendency to act in such a manner by giving positive feedback on whatever matches their predilections and negative feedback on whatever is different.

Altruistic utilitarianism

The concern in altruism is for the well-being of others, the prevention of hardship and the satisfaction of basic human needs rather than spiritual enlightenment (Nagel, 1970). This concern can extend to the aim of widespread well-being: for as many people as possible to be happy and free of pain.

The consultant would see the aim of education as bringing out the diverse talents in young people so that these can be enjoyed and used for the benefit of all. A favoured consultancy mission would encourage mutual care, trust and support in working relationships and opportunities for self-actualisation among staff (Lippitt and Lippitt, 1978, Chapter 5).

Typical interventions would involve team building among staff, along with the encouragement of 'holistic' curricula to evolve along with the teamwork. The consultant may be deterred from working with an establishment that is riddled with insularity, suspicion and a lack of desire among staff to collaborate with one another.

Egoistic utilitarianism

This is the aim of creating a situation in which each individual vigorously pursues his or her own self-interest and expects others to pursue theirs (Rand, 1964). Someone believing this would encourage others to determine and satisfy their own needs, which means them 'getting on' and striving to 'get off the bottom and up to the top'.

The consultant would see education as instilling the will to compete for positions of reward, and a respect for the virtues of competition and self-assertion. The prevalence of grading and competitive sports in schools would be seen as formative of good self-discipline.

Such consultants would see their role as helping to further the careers of staff who have ambition. Another possibility would be to help heads to think entrepreneurially about fund-raising and to treat the school as a business.

Nihilism

This is not simply a licence to follow one's own urges and biases. It involves instead scepticism about any particular ethical rule. The nihilist would regard such rules as dogma or prejudice and would refrain from taking a firm view on any issue. Given a job of work to do, the nihilist would simply strive for technical and professional excellence.

A consultant adopting a nihilist perspective would not think about the purposes of education other than the need for young people to keep up with technical change and social developments. Favourite consultancy missions would entail being a skilled crafts-person (Beeby, Broussine and Guerrier, 1986), using techniques, training methods and material that caused the consultant the most fascination. Long and protracted periods of contractual negotiations before settling a brief would be avoided unless the negotiating process itself was something that the consultant found fascinating.

Existentialism

Existential perspectives emphasize the obligation to choose one's own standards, meanings and actions and to achieve consistency among them (Green, 1973). From an existentialist standpoint, it would be wrong to be oblivious to questions of value and purpose.

The aim of education would be to help young people to examine future career and lifestyle possibilities. Education would allow a wide range of ideas to be explored, expressed and judged. Unquestioned routine, regime and rule-boundedness in schools and colleges would be frowned upon.

The consultant therefore would set out to help people to question the values behind everyday routine at their school or college. Through biography and life planning, he or she would help individuals to identify what they believed in, what they wanted to achieve and how to achieve it.

The consultant would avoid settings where educators held strongly to the image of the professional as a prescriptive role model for young people to follow and where heads were regarded as the one model for other staff to follow.

Emancipatory radicalism

Radical and emancipatory perspectives emphasize the need to correct unjust inequalities of wealth, power, choice and well-being. The relatively privileged would have a duty to accede to and even facilitate moves towards equal patterns of distribution (Kelly and Llewelyn, 1978).

The way education is organized would be seen as serving élites. Independent schools, and the need for state schools to seek financial contributions from parents to supplement income would be features to eradicate. An aim of the education system would be to build political awareness in young people and respect for social justice. Education would be seen as a means through which the basic rights of minority groups could be secured.

The radical consultant working with an educational organization would confront racism, sexism, heterosexism, prejudicial treatment of non-teaching staff and other discrimination in staff recruitment and staff relations, in the classroom and in educational materials.

In some cases the consultant would have the support of the local authority but would encounter resistance from professional educators. In other cases, staff would be responsive but local and national politicians would complain about what they would call propaganda and political interference in education.

Pluralism

This entails respect for a wide constituency of ethical viewpoints and a desire for these to be fairly negotiated (Mackie, 1977). From a pluralist perspective education should satisfy the diverse wishes of direct stakeholders such as parents, teachers, employers, and administrators. The consultant would seek a brief to help develop methods of open consultation between such stakeholders. These might include student or pupil representative forums. There would be training in open systems thinking and help in role analysis.

Those claiming sole right to manage their school or college would be the least promising clients for such consultants.

My own perspective

It seems to me that living and working in an ethical manner involves doing what one believes in and what one is committed to. This is more difficult than conforming to the demands of others, narrowly pursuing financial incentives or failing to question the workings of our established institutions (Snell, 1986).

For the successful assertion of one's ethics as a consultant, a number of conditions need to be met. First, the consultant needs to have examined his or her own beliefs and feelings about the use of power. Although some consultants are worried by the notion that they bring about change in the workings of organizations and in people's patterns of thought and action, I do not share their concern. The consultant is either an agent for change or an agent for stasis. Either way, the consultant has an impact and the consultant unable to face up to this power would be well advised to seek a different position.

Second, consultants need to sustain in themselves an attitude of mind that is open to the persuasive force of new insights. This includes the expectation that one's own ethics will be continually refined and improved as a wider (but never complete) understanding of the social world is built up.

Third, one needs skills of non-manipulative influencing. The ability to persuade rationally, assert firmly and find some common ground when facing disagreement are necessary for an atmosphere of openness.

I do not believe that there are any absolutely *de facto* ethical or unethical acts. Whether something is right or wrong depends on the actual or intended consequences. Actions should be judged on whether they increase individual freedom of choice and reduce suffering. Thus if someone increases his or her own range of choice at the expense of others who had much less scope to start with, then that person has behaved unethically. Also, if what someone does results in an overall increase in suffering, squalor, misery, deprivation or degradation, then that person has behaved unethically and his/her action cannot be excused by the happiness, if any, that very same act has caused other people.

In relation to bringing about change, I have most difficulty when I think about my work as helping a few people to cultivate powers that they can choose to use in whatever way and to whatever ends they may determine. I feel rather uneasy about working exclusively with comfortable, middle-class professionals. We work in pleasant surroundings and are well looked after by ancillary staff. I enjoy their company and regard my work as helping them to reach more widely informed choices. My worry is that they are not my entire ethical universe. I concern myself politically with the unrecognized and unset rights of people who are not there, the casualties and alienated bystanders of our economic system and its associated institutions.

So it is not that I bring about change in the world that bothers me. I am concerned instead with the *direction* of that change (Kelly and Llewelyn, 1978). Management development has begun to awaken to the injustices of sexism and racism, perhaps assisted by world opinion on apartheid. I believe that management development should set out to be a positive force for change in these areas and to foster respect for the lives and needs of all people at work, managers and non-managers alike.

As with all of us, there have been occasions when I have been wronged and from them I have induced one of the principles important to me: an equitable distribution of informed choice. I have sometimes had my scope for choice encroached upon by someone who already had far more than I did, and I have also been misled so as to reduce the validity of my choices. I have met people who have told me about suffering and from their experiences I am sure that it is right to aim to minimize suffering.

I think therefore that education should promote basic democracy and compassion and should build the necessary understanding for people to resist the forces that threaten and impair such principles. I do not think that schools offer much in this respect, and ideally I would welcome the advent of a de-schooled society run on the lines suggested by Ivan Illich (1973). Since I cannot see how to change the system from the way it is now to that particular configuration, I am in sympathy with consultancy interventions aimed at making the education system run along more democratic (upholding the rights of non-élites and non-majorities) and more compassionate lines than they are today.

The ethical perspective that I favour the most is radical and emancipatory. I sympathize with altruistic utilitarianism but I think it should be based on recognition of a person's rights to a minimum of pain (Popper, 1966; Keeley, 1978) rather than a certain level of pleasure. Because I think there are some fundamental standards of ethics I cannot go totally along with an existential perspective on ethics. There are some basic human rights but beyond these basic minima I would agree with existentialists that ethics are a matter of personal choice-making and meaning-making.

I like to work with people whom I trust to be in sympathy with these principles. I find that I am generally not invited to work in settings where this is not the case. Perhaps I have found my own ethical market. Or maybe people widely ascribe to radical and emancipatory ethics without buying into politics which flow logically from them. They have instead to cope with what they see as the day-to-day realities of organizational life.

ISSUES AND DIMENSIONS OF ETHICS IN CONSULTANCY INTERVENTIONS

Having discussed consultancy missions, I will now deal with ethics in consultancy interventions. There is a general consensus that the consultant should not impair freedom of action and thought among clients and participants and should prevent suffering. There are differences in how consultants apply these fundamental ethical principles to their practice. I therefore discuss my views on, and experiences with, some ethical issues which relate to these fundamental principles. For other viewpoints on similar issues see Pfeiffer and Jones (1977), British Psychological Society (1985), Lippitt and Lippitt (1978), Newby (1982), Phillips and Fraser (1982, Chapter 3), Walter (1984), Walton and Warwick (1973) and Wooten and White (1983).

Honouring individuals' trust

Relevant principles here include maintaining confidentiality and making interventions aimed exclusively at training and development and not covertly for some other purpose. These issues relate to freedom of thought and action among participants, since they enhance their psychological safety and extend the choices open to them during interventions. An agreement about confidentiality need not entail a total ban on sharing information about what has been said or done. A confidentiality agreement will usually specify what, if anything, may be revealed to other parties who may be specified (Bromley, 1981).

'Purity', the avoidance of covert agendas such as staff appraisal or selection for promotion, relates to confidentiality since information can only be passed on covertly if it goes against the spirit of confidentiality agreements.

I once found myself under pressure to break confidentiality. I was halfway through a series of interviews with staff at a district office in a local education authority. A senior manager suggested that before I do the remaining interviews I reveal to him what I had found out about specific individuals. I declined the request and suggested that he ask them directly. I prefer to agree to reveal no information at all that can be linked with specific individuals. During the same study I came under pressure sometimes from interviewees to name them as holding particular opinions very strongly. I suggested that if they wanted to go public on an issue that they should do so in a direct manner rather than through me, and declined their request.

I can only promise to keep my own part in a confidentiality agreement. I make no guarantees about the extent to which participants maintain confidences with one another although I encourage them to do so.

I had an uncomfortable experience when I met a senior manager to go through the draft of a report I had written concerning the careers of office juniors. I had used short anonymous quotes in my report to illustrate general findings. To my horror and embarrassment, the senior manager said he could recognize certain individuals from the style and content of the quotes (even though these were restricted to one line each). At that point, I felt that I had gone near to the edge of a breach of confidentiality and explained to the manager concerned that this made my position difficult. I knew he could not be certain that he knew who had said what, but I now feared that people would feel that their quotes were too conspicuous.

I therefore proposed to the senior manager that I would delete the quotes. My main instinct at the time was one of self-preservation rather than of ethics. I am unhappy now to have colluded in a little cover-up, and I have learned to be especially careful about the use of direct quotes in reports. Confidentiality-related issues tend to dominate the ethical worries of consultants and trainers whom I meet. One of the difficulties I discussed recently is analogous to the following situation.

A deputy headmistress attending a course confides in a small group setting that the conduct of her headmaster is causing her some distress. The head has been drinking heavily during the day and has been making administrative errors, some of which the deputy had had to sort out. Although the trainer is deeply concerned about the possible professional malpractice of the head, she does not know whether to alert someone in the local authority to the need to investigate.

One option would be to explore with the deputy the possibility of raising the matter with an adviser or line manager at County Hall. Another option would be for the trainer to agree to make the contact personally, not revealing how the information has arisen. If the matter is treated as a problem owned by the deputy head, then the principle of confidentiality is preserved and the trainer role is not compromised.

In the future, the purity and confidentiality of development may be threatened by the misuse of 'self-insight assessment centres'. These may become popular in training for heads since there is a widely acknowledged difference between the professional qualities required in teaching and those needed for the managerial, administrative and micropolitical tasks of headship. In order to assess their suitability for headship, potential heads may attend assessment centres for critical feedback about their performance on simulated tasks.

If truly confined to self-insight, assessment centres would preserve purity and confidentiality. Trainers may come under pressure to reveal secret information to promotion or selection panels. If the trainer intends to disclose information, this fact and the purpose served by disclosure need to be announced in the publicity material for the assessment centre and at the beginning of the assessment centre workshop (Rochester, 1985; *Standards and Ethical Considerations for Assessment Center Operations*, 1975).

I regard the level of confidentiality to be subject to strict contractual agreement between consultant and participant, regardless of the demands from a sponsoring organization. Any change in this contract should be initiated only by the participants, such as a request for a character reference or for a reference about attainment. This is very different from the rights of pupils, who have no choice about being the subjects of school reports.

Integrity and flexibility

Relevant principles here include honesty about one's intentions and expectations about what will happen; helping participants to arrive at well-informed decisions about participation; treating participants as agents of their own training and development needs; and having a clear and explicit brief. These issues interrelate with the previous ones and follow from the underlying principle of allowing freedom of thought and action. Providing full and adequate advance information about a consultancy intervention to participants gives them freedom to withdraw in good grace. If there is deception, partial disclosure (manipulative persuasion) or coercion, then people are not in a position to take charge of their own destinies.

The principles are good ones but are impossible to achieve fully in practice. For example, if the consultant treats participants as agents in the intervention, then the consultant cannot determine what will transpire and hence cannot inform participants of this in advance. It is possible, however, to indicate the likely processes and outcomes based on past experience, giving sufficient 'flavour' to enable potential participants to judge the possible risks and benefits of taking part before agreeing to do so.

Because many process interventions are indeterminate, it is advisable to make clear at times of tension the right of people to withdraw from situations that they had not anticipated. At a recent workshop for a partnership of male and female educators and trainers, my own position on this point was clarified. The workshop resulted from the men wishing to explore the implications of working more closely with the women and vice versa. It transpired that some of the women had small but significant grievances about the behaviour of the men which they wanted to clear up early in the workshop so as to proceed freshly and optimistically. The men were uneasy about this so I suggested that if the time available to share the grievances was limited to 45 minutes would everyone agree to remain in the room for that period? Some felt unable to agree to this contract but said they would stay as long as they felt able. This gave them freedom to withdraw gracefully, and in the event everyone stayed to give, receive and listen to the feedback.

Attendance on the event had been voluntary although one participant told me he would put a 'three-line whip' on some of his male colleagues who were of equal status to him in the organization. No matter how ethically necessary the subject matter of an intervention (for example, directed at the challenging of racism, sexism and other discrimination) I prefer the participants to be encouraged rather than compelled to take part. I took the participant's quip to mean that he would be encouraging his colleagues to come. My reason for preferring encouragement to compulsion is that for development to be possible participants must bring an open mind to a workshop and be willing to be challenged and confronted. Compulsion all too often brings with it a desire to defend oneself against criticism and not even *hear* criticism. The person might just as well not be there. If the person is not there it is *known* that he or she has chosen not to attend, whereas if the person is there but chooses not to pay attention it will not be widely known that he/she had closed their mind on important issues.

Widening awareness and resourcefulness

Relevant principles include disclosure of information relevant to participants' careers; openness about organizational power relations; consciousness raising (making people aware of social forces governing their working lives); promoting democracy and collaboration during training and afterwards at work; building creativity, not domestication; providing lasting value to people rather than short-term palliatives. Most of these principles follow from the need to allow participants freedom of will during and after consultancy interventions. Freedom can be eroded through a 'hidden curriculum' in a consultancy intervention. A hidden curriculum prescribes what is right and wrong for an organization, especially about its power structure, but does so by implication rather than through straightforward discussion and debate.

 If a consultant to an educational institution does not explicitly address differences in interest and power between various groups of participants, he or she is colluding to cover up the darker side of educational life. In work within a local educational authority I made no attempt to cover up the power struggle between people working in district offices and those at headquarters, nor did I fail to raise as an issue the difference in power and status between administrators who held a teacher's qualification and those who did not hold one. I was asked by those at headquarters to side with them against the districts, and to recommend an administrative qualification for non-teachers which would have kept the education service busy but which would have given no help to non-teachers in competition for promotion to senior jobs. My failure to collude with such pressures but rather to stick with the issues of democracy and equity made me few friends because people wanted an easy solution to what I saw as a problem endemic in hierarchical departmental structures and attitudes (Snell, 1985). I think I should have been much more explicit about what was happening but I was too immersed in the situation to be sufficiently analytical and could not clearly articulate my perceptions.

 I would like to have reported more articulately my emerging horror at the repetitive routines through which junior administrative staff were expected to go, and at my discovery of many well-intentioned administrators who were striving to be considered for promotion to managerial positions through taking on more and more routine work in an attempt to be seen as widely competent. I regret that only now do I see in perspective the lives of the people I met there, the delusions which kept some going and the disillusionment which others suffered. With a clearer understanding of this I would have made a more concerted effort to encourage wider creativity and democracy in the department.

 I am happy about the other training work I did during that time, which made explicit the power relations among counsellors and various levels of management in the local authority, and between staff on the workshops and participants. The training attempted to make managers more creative in their handling of people and of problems. But unfortunately this training was not widely available in the education department at the time.

Accessibility and support

Relevant principles here include encouraging open access to development opportunities; not unduly restricting the right to act as consultant to holders of particular qualifications; general evenhandedness and fairness in one's interventions; and choosing clients, purposes and courses of action in accordance with one's values. These principles have in common the underlying aim of not allowing consultancy to become a tool of some groups to restrict the level of freedom of other groups.

There have been efforts, through the production of distance teaching materials, to widen opportunities for vocational education: open access learning (Hodgson, 1985). Opening access for staff in education to competent consultancy interventions would reflect their right not to have restrictions on necessary learning opportunities, and so relates to the dimension of freedom. There are two problems in meeting this need. First, consultancy interventions to improve management skills and teamwork are labour-intensive, so responsible consultants will not package up an intervention and sell it cheaply for use at a distance. Second, because the fees offered by the education service to consultants are so low, the availability of good consultants is limited. The consultant wishing to encourage open access may do a certain amount of 'charitable' work in education. Influencing the level of resources set aside for staff development in education is a matter of local and national politics.

I am sceptical about moves to 'professionalize', management consultancy. I would encourage some aspects of professional association, such as the dissemination of sound concepts; the techniques and research methods to novices; the sharing of latest developments among experienced practitioners; and the clarification and identification of irresponsible practice.

At its worst, professionalization entails restricting rights of practice to those with specific qualifications which are of little relevance to the work itself. Some professionals also dismiss as misguided, naive and uninformed any criticisms from lay people. Professionalism can be disabling (Illich, 1978; Johnson, 1984). Consultants need appropriate preparation and development but should not be judged on whether they possess a particular professional qualification. As an alternative I suggest that the suitability of consultants for a particular assignment is judged through references, testimonials, whether they listen to and take an interest in the unique problems of the client organization and whether their perception of the mission is compatible with the wishes of clients.

Issues of evenhandedness and fairness arise in how the consultant deals with conflict among participant groups. Being fair *can* involve 'taking sides' (Strien, 1976). Allowing an unevenly matched battle to take place without intervening is very unfair if the consultant has the power to redress the balance and ensure that negotiation takes place between equally powerful stakeholder groups. This calls for political judgement and where some consultants would see a fair balance of power, others would judge one group to have an unfair advantage. Time is needed to fathom out undercurrents of power and so a period of *laissez-faire* is necessary before the consultant can assess what might be fair or unfair (Gray and Snell, 1986).

It is important for me to work for a balance of freedom. Consultants are often called in by someone to remove obstacles to their own plans, and going along with this will often entail infringing the rights of others. What I see as a balance of power may differ from someone else's view. But I would not willingly serve someone else's plans if I thought they were unfair. Hence there are many briefs that I would not undertake, however large the inducement or moral pressure that potential clients might think they were exerting.

Well-being

Relevant principles here include promoting genuine happiness and growth rather than pain; offering criticism out of a desire to promote development not punishment; looking after one's own well-being. The principle behind these issues is the reduction of misery and the promotion of welfare.

One dilemma in consultancy is how 'cruel' one has to be sometimes in order to enable development to take place. Since the harsh world of experience, the 'school of hard knocks', is often mentioned as the major source of learning and development by educational administrators, I am surprised at how alarmed some consultants are about causing upsets in their work. Ideally, consultancy interventions would enable individual and team development to take place in a totally painless manner, but I do not believe that pain can be totally prevented in learning. Some of the feedback necessarily shared for the common good will be painful no matter how sensitively it is given.

This is different from putting down participants through ridicule, or causing them deliberate embarrassment. A consultant who sets out to expose someone's weakness in front of colleagues is unlikely to contribute to general well-being. One director of education who was set up to look silly in a meeting with colleagues withdrew active support for management development. Given the everyday frustrations of consultancy there is sometimes the temptation to take measures of retribution against those whom we see as culprits. But retribution is unlikely to improve the general good.

If the cause of frustration is discriminatory behaviour and attitudes, one safe response is to ask a series of probing questions to discover the grounds for the prejudice (these 'grounds' will then evaporate). Another slightly riskier response is to give simple feedback such as 'I was very disturbed to hear you say that because it sounded discriminating to me'.

Consultancy is psychologically taxing and provides plenty to get angry about (Rowan, 1976). One needs to be careful not to overwork. Punishing oneself through overworking can bring with it the temptation to take one's frustrations out on those whom one sees as wrongdoers. Many consultants will create strong financial and 'lifestyle' pressures for themselves. It is with concern that I recommend that they regularly check that they are not punishing themselves by overworking.

In the ethics of consultancy, there needs to be more attention paid to the basic dimension of reducing misery than has been the case to date (Keeley, 1978). This need applies also to the ethics of school education. Many young people are very unhappy at school. I suggest that consultants in education inform and shape their missions by considering the needs of those who are least happy about being on the receiving end of the education system.

CONCLUSIONS: BUILDING A PERSONAL CODE OF ETHICS

I conclude with some ideas on how to build up a personal code of ethics for educational consultancy.

(1) Keep a special diary for recording the details of occasions when you feel under pressure to breach your own ethical standards of consultancy. An additional record can be kept of times when you feel wrongly treated during an assignment. At the time of writing, or later, on rereading, tease out the ethical principles involved and think about how to use these principles positively.

(2) Find a colleague whom you can trust and who can trust you not to reveal secrets. Agree to have regular conversations about ethical consultancy, drawing on your own recent experiences. Try to get to a point where you can both share and talk through current dilemmas.

(3) Suggest to participants in your consultancy interventions that they 'catch as it happens' behaviour that they regard as unethical, just as you will yourself do with them. Suggest that such challenges are best made elegantly rather than accusatorily. Try not to *defend* when challenged. Look forward to being challenged because of the possibility of learning about yourself. Be prepared to have others judge you by standards different from those you would prefer to apply to yourself. Expect to come out as rather less than perfect on the criteria that matter to you.

(4) Resist attempts to establish regulatory codes of ethics, since these tend to be impracticable (Chalk, Frankel and Chafer, 1980; Snapper, 1984). Nonetheless, read and debate codes written to stimulate self-examination and debate (Gellerman, 1986).

REFERENCES

Beeby, M., Broussine, M. and Guerrier, Y. (1986) 'Ethical dilemmas in organisation and management development'. *Management Education and Development*, **17**(1), 24–33.

Berry, A. J. and Marshall, J. (1986) (eds) 'International management and development'. Special issue: *Management Education and Development*, **17**(3).

British Psychological Society (1985) 'A code of conduct for psychologists'. *Bulletin of the British Psychological Society*, **38**, 41–3.

Bromley, E. (1981) 'Confidentiality'. *Bulletin of the British Psychological Society*, **34**, 468–9.

Chalk, R., Frankel, M. S. and Chafer, S. B. (1980) *AAAS Professional Ethics Project: Professional Ethics Activities in the Scientific and Engineering Societies*. Washington, DC: American Association for the Advancement of Science.

Crews, M. and Cunningham, I. (1986) (eds) *What Is Making a Difference in Organisations?* ATM Focus Paper. London: Association of Teachers of Management.

Gellerman, R. (1986) 'A statement of values and ethics for professionals in organisation and human system development'. New York: 372 Central Park West, Apt. 16c.

Gray, H. L. and Snell, R. S. (1986) 'Towards effective practice where management development is a recent concern'. *Leadership and Organisational Development*, **7**(2), 21–26.

Green, M. (1973) *Teacher as Stranger: Educational Philosophy for the Modern Age*. Belmont, Cal.: Wadsworth.

Hodgson, V. E. (1985) 'Distance learning and management education'. *Journal of Innovative Higher Education*, **2**(1), 19–24.

Illich, I. (1973) *Deschooling Society*. Harmondsworth: Penguin.

Illich, I. (1978) *Disabling Professions*. London: Boyars.

Johnson, T. (1984) 'Professionalism: occupation or ideology?' in Goodland, S. (ed.) *Education for the Professions: Quis Custodiet?* Guildford: SRHE–NFER–Nelson.

Keeley, M. (1978) 'A social justice approach to organisational evaluation'. *Administrative Science Quarterly*, **23**, 272–92.

Kelly, J. E. and Llewelyn, S. P. (1978) 'Abuses of psychology for political purposes: some critical remarks on the working party report'. *Bulletin of the British Psychological Society*, **31**, 259–60.

Lippitt, G. and Lippitt, R. (1978) *The Consulting Process in Action*, San Diego: University Associates.

Mackie, J. L. (1977) *Ethics: Inventing Right and Wrong*. Harmondsworth: Penguin.

Nagel, T. (1970) *The Possibility of Altruism*. Oxford: Clarendon Press.

Newby, A. C. (1982) 'Ethical issues for training practitioners'. *Journal of European Industrial Training*, **6**(3), 10–14.

Pfeiffer, J. W. and Jones, J. E. (1977) 'Ethical considerations in consulting', in Jones, J. E. and Pfeiffer, S. *Handbook for Group Facilitators*. La Jolla, Cal.: University Associates.

Phillips, K. and Fraser, T. (1982) *The Management of Interpersonal Skills Training*. Farnborough: Gower Press.

Popper, K. R. (1966) *The Open Society and Its Enemies*, 5th edition. Princeton, NJ: Princeton University Press.

Rand, A. (1964) *The Virtue of Selfishness: A New Concept of Egoism*. New York: Signet Books.

Rochester, A. (1985) 'The uses and abuses of assessment centres', paper. Bromley, Kent: Rochester-McConnell Ltd.

Ross, W. D. (1930) *The Right and the Good*. Oxford: Clarendon Press.

Rowan, J. (1976) 'Ethical issues in organisational change', in Warr, P. B. (ed.) *Personal Goals and Work Design*. London: John Wiley and Sons.

Snapper, J. W. (1984) 'Whether professional associations may enforce professional codes'. *Business and Professional Ethics Journal*, **3**(2), 43–54.

Snell, R. S. (1985) 'Non-professional local authority administrators as potential participants in educational change and development'. *Educational Change and Development*, **6**(2), 2–6.

Snell, R. S. (1986) 'Questioning the ethics of management development: a critical review'. *Management Education and Development*, **17**(1) 43–64.

Standards and Ethical Considerations for Assessment Center Operations (1975). Paper endorsed at the Third International Congress on Assessment Center Methods, Quebec, Canada. Bromley, Kent: Rochester–McConnell.

Strien, P. J. van (1976) 'Professional ethics and the quality of working life', in Warr, P. B. (ed.) *Personal Goals and Work Design*. London: John Wiley and Sons.

Walter, G. A. (1984) 'Organisational development and individual rights', *Journal of Applied Behavioural Science*, **20**(4), 423–9.

Walton, R. E. and Warwick, D. P. (1973) 'The ethics of organisational development', *Journal of Applied Behavioural Science*, **9**(3), 681–99.

Wooten, K. C. and White, L. P. (1983) 'Ethical problems in the practice of organisation development', *Training and Development Journal*, **37**(4), 16–23.

Chapter 5

Consulting as Counselling: The Theory and Practice of Structural Consulting

Stephen Murgatroyd

INTRODUCTION

A number of chapters in this text describe the similarities and dissimilarities between management consulting in education and the practice of management consulting in business. In this chapter the parallel between educational consulting and the practice of counselling is drawn, using the theory and practice of structural family therapy (Minuchin, 1974) as a basis for intervention. This chapter develops and extends ideas found in Murgatroyd and Reynolds (1984, 1985) and in Murgatroyd (1984, 1986). Throughout, the focus is upon the nature and practice of long-term consultancy aimed at improving management quality across the school as an organization. Short term, 'one-off' advising tasks are specifically excluded from consideration in this chapter, which is based on a three-year consultancy in one school and several shorter consultancies in private and comprehensive schools and local education authorities in Britain over a ten-year period.

In examining the relationship between counselling and consulting, the intention is not to suggest that some of the consulting practices commonplace within business are inappropriate to the practice of management in schools. On the contrary, schools need to be encouraged to regard themselves as responsibility centres with their own costs and liabilities and their own products which they need to market. Just as universities in Britain now compete with private and quasi-private sector institutions for their services, secondary schools compete with each other for students, staff and resources. Schools are non-profit organizations and as such they require the same level of management sophistication as many profitable businesses (Handy, 1985; Peters and Austin, 1985). Many of the tasks undertaken by consultants are intended to assist school-based managers to achieve these objectives. Counselling is seen to be relevant as a descriptor of the *process* of consulting. Indeed, the central argument of this chapter is that effective consulting is a sophisticated form of counselling.

THE FRAMEWORK FOR CONSULTING PRACTICE

Just as the family therapist works from a model of how a particular family could function, given the historiographies of family members and the quality of their interpersonal relationships, so a consultant needs to understand what a particular school or subsection of a school in which they are working could be like if it were functioning effectively. This issue needs to be addressed in a unique way each time a consultancy is embarked upon. There is no such thing as an ideal school or ideal family; however, there is such a thing as a fully functioning school, given the historiographies of the individuals who comprise that school and the quality of relationships between them. A major task for the consultant is to imagine just what is possible for this group of staff.

One way consultants sometimes express their understanding of what is possible is by offering objectives for the school. For example, at a large comprehensive school in the North-west of England a consultant recently suggested that the school's management team should have three major objectives:

(a) to increase the quality of its output as measured by public examination passes, job-placements and successful passage from school to a post-secondary educational institution;
(b) to increase the proportion of available resources within the county allocated to the school; and
(c) to reduce the level of staff turnover in the school to a level commensurate with that of the school with the lowest staff turnover in the county.

Such a clear and precise statement of management objectives represents this consultant's 'fantasy' about what this school could achieve. In setting these objectives, or revealing their 'fantasies' in other ways, consultants are using an implicit theory of the school as an organization.

In the example just given, the implicit model assumes that the staff collectively agree to setting as a priority the completion of public examinations, securing job-placements and fostering a continuing desire for learning and that they wish to pursue this for some time as a collection of staff teams working collectively and cohesively in the pursuit of these aims. It is further assumed that a good organization has a low turnover of staff. These are not trivial assumptions. They are similar to the family therapist regarding an ideal family as one in which all activities undertaken by family members are done so on a shared basis, and that the children should stay with their parents until they themselves are married and wish to start a family. The assumptions made about the nature of the school represent an implicit theory of organizations.

To be effective, a consultant needs to have a theory of organizations which they can test against the reality of the school in which they are working. The problem here is that there are a great many theories of organizations, not all of which have utility for the practice of consultancy. The theories which have utility are those which contribute directly to an understanding of a particular problem or set of problems which a particular school is experiencing at a particular moment in time. That is, the pragmatic value of a theory of organizations is more important to the practice of consultancy than the integrity of the theory *as* theory.

Given that a pragmatic theory of organizations is a prerequisite for effective consultancy, the work of Harrison (1972) and Schein (1984) can be regarded as having some utility. Schein describes two different organizations which are permeated by different sets of assumptions which in turn lead to different kinds of organizational behaviours. Organization A prizes individuals, devolves responsibility to many levels of the organization and encourages its members to be 'self-starters' and risk-takers; key decisions are fought over in groups—tension is thought to be an implicit feature of the organization as also is change; while the outsider looking at the organization may see a great deal of tension about key decisions, organizational members see this tension as both productive and safe, because of the existence of team quality in the organization. Organization B operates on very different assumptions: truth and objectivity are seen to rest on the shoulders of the older, more experienced and wiser members of the organization who are therefore given higher status; decision making is 'top-down' and the characteristic feature of a successful organizational member is their ability to follow instructions; relationships are linear and vertical, with each person in the organization having and knowing their place; and the organization takes care of its own members by shielding them from decision-making and the exercise of authority.

Organizations A and B are polarities—the consultant can use these as benchmarks against which to view the organization in which they are working. The point to note, according to Handy (1985), is that these two forms of organization are different structures which in turn give rise to different cultures. Harrison (1972) provides some particular tools with which the consultant can further explore the details of an organization's culture. To understand the organization and thus be able to begin the process of changing it, the consultant needs to understand the implicit and explicit features of its culture. A failure to do so will often lead to inappropriate interventions. The task is not to work on what the school *should be* in terms of some theory of education, but to work on what the school *is and could be* in the terms of the quality of relationships and the capacity for change evidenced within the institution.

The notion of organizational culture now also permeates the literature on family therapy (Murgatroyd and Woolfe, 1985). For example, it leads to the recognition that the behaviour of a family cannot be explained simply in terms of some summation of the behaviour of individual family members: the assumptions family members make about the culture of their family inform the interactions between family members which in turn shapes their behaviours. The culture of the family is thus all-pervasive in shaping the thoughts, feelings and behaviours of family members. Given this realization, family therapists have had to develop a theory of families *as organizations*. While there are many such theories competing with each other in the family therapy literature (Speed, 1984), what has come to be known as the structural approach to family therapy (Minuchin, 1974; Olson, Sprenkle and Russell, 1979) can be seen to have considerable utility for the practice of consulting.

Adapting the structural model of family therapy to the practice of consulting in schools suggests that the consultant should attend to six principal features of the school during the assessment period prior to any intervention. These are:

(a)   the school's structure—the arrangements that govern the transactions between organizational members,
(b)   the flexibility of the school's patterns of function, and the capacity of the school for change;
(c)   the 'resonance' of the school—the extent to which a school can be described as 'enmeshed' or 'disengaged' (these terms are explained more fully below);

(d)   the context in which the school operates, especially the level and quality of social support and the economic circumstances of the school;

(e)   the stage of development the school as an organization has reached (see Greiner, 1967); and

(f)   the ways in which the identified 'problem' (which gave rise to the consultancy) or 'symptoms' are used by the school's managers in their interactions with each other and other organizational members.

In addition, the consultant needs to understand the way in which power is organized in the school. To do this, the consultant has to observe the school in action for some time. While doing so, he or she should also attend to these features:

(a)   *boundaries*—who participates in particular transactions, who is 'in' and 'out' of transactional patterns and what rationale is given for their inclusion or exclusion;

(b)   *alignments*—what coalitions (the joining of two or more persons *against* others) or alliances (the joining of two or more members without regard to others) exist and why; and

(c)   *power*—who exercises power in different sets of circumstances and whether this power is due to their formal status or to some other feature.

All of the observations suggested here should be seen as guiding the consultant's understanding of the culture of the organization as experienced by a variety of organizational members holding different status positions within the school. It will be clear that some considerable time may be needed for observation and assessment prior to any interventions which are intended to have consequences for the management of the organization. It should also be clear that the consultant, to be able to develop such an understanding, needs to *join* the organization—become an 'acting and reacting' member of it.

JOINING THE SCHOOL AS A CONSULTANT

Joining the school as an organizational consultant is a difficult process (see, for example, Richardson, 1973). It requires the consultant to engage in a great deal of *accommodation*—adjustments made by the consultant so as to permit him or her to 'become' an organizational member. At the early stages of the consulting process the consultant does not seek to change the organization, but rather to experience it so as to discover which channels of communication are open and which are not, to understand how different members of the organization experience the organization's culture and to review the way in which power and authority are exercised through alliances and coalitions.

Some specific consulting devices may be especially useful to the consultant in this joining stage. These include:

(a)   *tracking*—the consultant systematically tracks the activities of managers or others in the school as an observer—some pupil pursuit activities (Hargreaves, 1972) or decision pursuits (tracking what happens to a decision once it has been made) can be illuminating;

(b)   *mimesis*—the consultant adopts the language and style of the organization (for example, sombre or serious, general or specific) not as a cynical mimic, but so as to reflect back to the organization a degree of empathy with both *what* is being communicated and how it is being communicated;

(c)   *multi-access*—maintaining openness to all organizational members and refusing to reveal confidences is an important element in the development of trust; and

(d)   *positive connotation*—the consultant needs to recognize that, while he or she may have doubts about the value of various transactions that take place between people in the school, their task is to enable these same individuals to become more positive about their relationships with each other so that they are more rather than less capable of change—the consultant therefore has the task of encouraging the members of the organization to see their interrelationships as having positive features.

This last point is emphasized by Palazzoli *et al.* (1978), who suggest that a failure to offer a positive connotation to the nature of interactions within a management team is likely to lead to a rejection of the consultant (and hence his or her advice).

Joining the organization as a consultant is more of an attitude than a technique. The consultant needs to display four dispositions through behaviour so as to effectively communicate this attitude. These are:

(a)   *accurate empathy*—the consultant needs to show an understanding of the school, the nature of communications and the power-relationships 'as if' he or she were a part of the school, without losing the 'as if' quality;

(b)   *positive regard*—the consultant needs to show respect for the individuals who comprise the organization, irrespective of whether the consultant likes or dislikes the strategies and tactics which the individual chooses to use as an organizational member;

(c)   *genuineness*—the consultant needs to behave in a genuine and authentic way rather than be a crass mimic or a chameleon; and

(d)   *concreteness*—the consultant makes relevant interventions which have a direct bearing on the issues with which he or she is dealing. Joining an organization involves the frequent display of all these dispositions.

Joining also requires the consultant to be a learner. He or she has to learn about the organization, about its culture and implicit structure and about the nuances of power and authority. As the Milan school of family therapists found when they sought to work in organizations (Palazzoli, 1981), consultants have to quickly abandon the illusion that they might be able to put into effect interventions to provoke rapid changes in relational patterns involving an entire organization. Rather than look for 'miraculous interventions', the consultant should instead search for patterns, test the validity of his or her findings and begin a process of intervention. These things take time. There are few 'quick fixes' for schools who have reached a point of calling in a consultant.

IDENTIFYING THE PROBLEMS

When a school seeks the help of a consultant, it usually does so in relation to some specific problem. For example, recent consulting activities have included:

(a)   assisting in the coordination of the merger of two schools;

(b)   developing management training programmes and implementing them for the heads of department in a large comprehensive school;

(c)   developing activity costing and financial management systems associated with the devolution of budget responsibility to school-based managers; and

(d)   assisting a governing body in the development of appropriate procedures for the appointment of senior managers in the schools for which they were responsible.

When a consultant is asked to work on problems such as these, they first need to understand that an organizational 'game' is in progress. One group has decided that external help is required in order that progress can be made. This group may represent the majority or may not. The group may be identifying the organizational problem accurately, or may not. The group may want the consultancy to succeed, or may not. The group may have understood the full implications of asking a consultant to become involved, or may not. The group may have a clear understanding of the outcome they desire, or may not.

From the consultant's point of view, it is essential that he or she begins by understanding the way in which two subsystems (the consultant and the organization) came together. Indeed, one way of understanding some of the structures within an organization is to look carefully at the process of commissioning the consultant. The fact that an organization turns to a consultant for help is one kind of move in the ongoing 'game' within the organization. This particular move is of great value to the consultant, since it usually represents the most recent and significant move in the ongoing strategic game being played in the school.

Given the significance of this move, it requires careful examination. Useful questions include these:

(a)   Who is the person who first had the idea of employing an external consultant?

(b)   What specific words were used in the first contact (in particular, how is the 'problem' represented and what statements are made about the support within the organization for using consultancy)?

(c)   Who is the person who comes to the consultant with the proposition?

(d)   What are the implicit communications (verbal and especially non-verbal) in this first meeting?

(e)   What time-lines are referred to and what do these references tell us about the level of understanding within the organization about their own problems and the nature of consulting as a process?

(f)   Even at this first meeting, is the consultant being offered a place in some coalition with some particular subsystem of the organization (for example, a coalition against a failing headteacher or a coalition against a group of staff)?

These questions highlight the fact that the consultant should use the first moments of contact with the organization as a key data collection activity. It is a unique opportunity to experience an organizational game in action. Typically, the consultant will experience reticence and contradiction (and sometimes deception) when seeking to explore the *how* and *why* of their employment. The very fact that this is generally the case indicates that the consultant is a part of a complex strategic game.

Another key to unravelling the nature of the organization concerns the way in which the 'problem' is first identified. For example, in one school the problem was said to be 'poor communications between management and staff, staff and management'. When unravelled, the problem was better expressed as 'poor communication between managers and a complete absence of team quality within the management team, leading to organizational uncertainty, distrust and an abundance of coalitions against others'. The starting definition and this end definition of the problem are radically different.

This phenomenon is not uncommon. In family therapy, the identified patient (the person said to have 'the problem') is often a child. When unravelled, the problem is more accurately the complexity of the family's culture—the child being a representation of that complexity. One key task of the therapist in the family is to reward the identified patient for accurately representing the problem within the family (Minuchin, 1974; Palazzoli *et al.*, 1978). The consultant has a similar task in the school: the identified problem needs to be regarded as a manifestation of the culture and organizational dynamics of the school and explored as such. While the 'problem' as expressed is often real to organizational members and concrete to them, the fact that it is a representation of some deep structural feature of the organization should not be ignored. If the consultant works solely at the surface 'problem' as presented, and does not seek to affect the deeper structure, then a new problem is likely to manifest itself somewhere else in the organization. This is a common finding of family therapists. An attempt to treat the identified patient and not affect the structure of the family usually leads to another family member developing new symptoms and becoming an identified patient (Haley, 1967). In my own early experiences of consultancy, my attempt to resolve a specific problem in one part of the organization (for example, the pastoral care subsystem) often led to new problems in other systems (for example, the academic subsystem). The consultant's focus needs to be upon the structure and culture of the organization and the way in which these features are manifested in organizational boundaries, games and coalitions. To maintain this focus often requires the consultant to reframe the problem around his or her understanding of relationships within the organization and/or the capacity of the organization to change.

The declaration of a diagnosis by a consultant is often a difficult event for organizational members to deal with. That this is the case should not be surprising. The organization itself is often poor at diagnosing its own problems since those who do so usually have something to lose. Drawing attention to the implicit features of an organization is also difficult for organizational members who would prefer implicit features to stay that way. Murgatroyd and Reynolds (1984) give the example of a diagnosis they offered to a school which almost led to an outright rejection of their services. The school concerned had identified its problem as 'underachieving pupils', whereas the consultants' diagnosis was that the problem was more accurately 'the labelling of pupils by the staff and the quality of interpersonal relationships in the classroom that resulted from this labelling'. Transferring the focus of the problem from the pupils to the staff was a cause of new and significant distress, especially amongst the management team who had invited the consultants to join the organization. From the consultants' point of view, however, a failure to offer this diagnosis would have led them to add to the problem rather than reduce its occurrence.

THE INTERVENTION FRAMEWORK

A great deal of consulting intervention can be regarded as focused upon altering the boundaries between groups within an organization. This is especially true when developing or refining management activities, when working on the development of new programmes (for example, TVEI (Technical and Vocational Education Initiative), drug education programmes) or when enabling an institution to cope with downsizing as a result of falling enrolments or budget cuts. The interests of one group (senior managers, a department, new staff versus established staff) versus another are most often seen to be the cause of the 'problem' which a consultant is asked to resolve.

Boundaries take many forms. Some are 'soft'—they relate to misunderstandings, inappropriate responses between groups and poor communication. Others are hard—reflecting deep-rooted and systematic divisions within the organization which have been compounded by personal conflicts and intrigues. The consultant wishing to affect the boundaries within an organization first needs to understand their nature. It is usually helpful to look at the four basic kinds of boundary relationship seen clearly in studies of families:

(a) *Enmeshed*—where the relationships between organizational members are so integrated that it is almost impossible to change the organization (even slightly) without having to secure the support of all organizational members. While the culture appears to be supportive of organizational members, it actually inhibits innovation, entrepreneurial activity and change. The consultant's problem with this form of relationship within the organization is that it is all-embracing. To change the relationship structure of an entire organization is almost impossible; any attempt to achieve such a change takes time and requires the consultant to take considerable risks.

(b) *Connected*—where individuals do feel connected with one another and are able to act collectively on some issue. There is a strong sense of team, but also a respect for individuals within the team. The consultant will find that this team-spirit quickly assimilates new members and that the team is adaptive and responsive when faced with change. While some individuals may find the team spirit overpowering in relation to specific issues in which they have a strong vested interest, these feelings will be unusual and the team itself is able to deal with them.

(c) *Separated*—unlike the previous form, this kind of boundary permits individuals to connect to others, but in a disinterested way. Self-interest takes precedence over the group and the group is unable to deal with these issues. The resultant effect is an organization in which power struggles are inevitable and organizational paralysis results from the insistence that every detail and nuance of every change or development be analysed in a way that seeks to meet the needs of each individual in the group. The organization experiences distress in two ways: (i) there is a strong feeling that the organization lacks direction if the senior management team can be described in this way; and (ii) because of the nature of the relationships within the group, the group itself is unable to overcome its own problems.

(d) *Disengaged*—this relationship set is an exaggerated form of the type just described. In this form, the group can best be described as a 'production-economy' of individuals who act independently of one another and have few (if any) personal or social relationships with one another. The organization is a shell in which individuals come and go without necessarily sharing any experiences, thoughts or feelings with others.

These four kinds of boundaries between subsystems within the organization (based on those described by Sprenkle and Olson, 1978) each require different kinds of intervention. The consultant needs to make an accurate assessment of the 'problem', the underlying dynamics of the organization and the boundaries around groups within the organization. In addition, he or she needs to examine the capacity the organization and its subsystems have to respond to opportunities for or requirements to change. It will be clear from the descriptions just given that different kinds of group with different kinds of relationship will respond very differently to a felt need for change or an external challenge.

In considering this last point—the capacity of the organization for change—some simple constructs from structural family therapy are again helpful. While there are many patterns of response to the opportunity or felt requirement to change, structural family therapists begin their assessment by looking at four descriptions:

(a) *Chaotic*—the group responds to challenge or change in a fruitless way, best described as disorganized. Policy decisions are made and then changed; the information used to make decisions is inaccurate; issues of policy becomes confused with personality.

(b) *Flexible*—the group looks at challenge and change as opportunities for development, and seeks to respond in a careful and rational way, adjusting their responses as events unfold. The flexibility of the response is experienced by others as a rational and considered sequence of moves, rather than a random set of events. The group regularly assesses its progress, both in dealing with some change and in learning from the process of trying to do so.

(c) *Standard*—the group has a routine set of responses to new and challenging situations which it uses as appropriate and is reluctant to try new strategies or to take risks. Challenges or a felt need to change always result from external pressure—the group itself never volunteers to change or seeks to evaluate change needs within the organization.

(d) *Rigid*—the group has a single response (usually 'no') to external or internal threats, challenges or requests to change. These responses may take many forms (for example, 'Not at this time . . .', 'Further research is needed . . .', 'While appropriate for others, not appropriate here . . .'), but is the product of an essentially emotional process which is irrational. If the group is the senior management team, other organizational members will either be embittered by the lack of change or enmeshed and supportive.

Once again, the realization that an organization is responding to some uncertainty or felt need for change in one or other of these ways (or in some combination of these ways, since these descriptions apply equally well to subgroups within the organization) will lead the consultant to intervene in different but appropriate ways.

The combination of these two dimensions—relationships and capacity for change— produces a complex matrix of organizational features which shape and inform the work of the consultant (Murgatroyd, 1986). While these dimensions are a useful starting point for the consultant's intervention, that is all that they are: *a starting point*. They provide a model of organizations more complex than that suggested by Schein (1984), but which has considerable utility in shaping the consultant's 'diagnosis' of the organization.

INTERVENTION TACTICS

From his or her diagnosis of the organization and its 'problem', the specific interventions the consultant uses will seek to affect both the problem and the underlying features of the organization which gave rise to this problem. A failure to do so will, as already has been suggested, give rise to other problems in the organization at some later date. The consultant should regard the purpose of *all* interventions as drawing attention to both the explicit and implicit features of the organization that give rise to the problem. They should also recognize that a part of their role is to accept a volume of negative feelings projected on to them by organizational members who are anxious not to be 'caught-out' in the new game the consultant begins and defines by the very fact of their intervention.

Murgatroyd and Reynolds (1984) suggest that there are a variety of intervention tactics a consultant can use to affect the organization, depending upon their diagnosis of the problem the organization faces. The available tactics include the following:

(a) *Promoting conflict*—encouraging constructive conflict within the organization so that conflict can be experienced as a normal, healthy and productive activity; to be successful, this intervention needs to involve a real conflict about a real issue, the outcome of which will affect the school as a whole; an artificial conflict created by the consultant solely for demonstration purposes will reduce rather than increase the effectiveness of any intervention.

(b) *Blocking transactions within the organization*—in order to increase the distress felt within the organization, the consultant interrupts the process of communication (for example, decision-making in a management team or the processes used at general staff meetings) by blocking the normal forms of communication and asking participants to behave differently; in doing so, the consultant seeks to affect the normal transactional patterns within a group.

(c) *Sharply marking out power boundaries*—so as to reveal the various coalitions within the organization, the consultant shows others where the boundaries are; the major tool the consultant has is drawing attention to the sources of information within the organization and constantly checking the way in which groups and subgroups seek to maintain the organization's culture.

(d) *Sharply marking out individual boundaries*—ensuring that the concerns and needs of individuals are being addressed within the organization by drawing attention to them; requiring that individuals be spoken *to* rather than *at*; seeking to develop strategies by which individual needs can be regularly identified.

(e) *Creating new alliances and coalitions*—encouraging the formation of new groups and coalitions through *ad hoc* task forces, temporary planning groups, competing teams working on similar organizational problems.

(f) *Emphasizing differences*—especially between group members within a particular group so that the idea of consensus management (frequently voiced by school-based administrators) is recognized to involve the rejection of the ideas of some people within the organization.

(g) *Manipulating space*—changing the physical arrangements for meetings, the position of individuals during meetings, and the frequently used spaces for cliques and subgroups within the organization are often quick ways of drawing attention to boundaries.

(h) *Enacting transactional patterns*—asking individuals to role-play their decision-making as if they were different members of the organization; asking for an 'action replay' of a conversational sequence.

(i) *Recreating communication patterns*—asking decision-makers to repeat a sequence of dialogue during a meeting, emphasis being given to different features of the message.

(j) *Coaching*—helping an individual or group to undertake a new task by direct advice giving, assisting in presentations, developing the resources of the group.

(k) *Sponsoring*—enabling an individual or a group within the organization to take a new position in the organization on either a temporary or permanent basis.

(l) *Confronting*—directly addressing issues and behaviours which others will not or dare not address.

These particular interventions are described briefly here for two reasons. First, they suggest that the role of the consultant is a significant one within the organization. Consultancy aimed at making a significant change in the management quality throughout an organization has to involve significant actions within the organization. Second, they suggest that consultancy is a difficult process. This is not intended to be an exhaustive listing of possible interventions, rather it is intended as representative of the kind of interventions that follow from the use of a structural approach to consulting practice.

Just as changing the relationships within a distressed family challenges the therapist to examine their motivation, exercise their skills and constantly evaluate their performance, so consultancy requires the consultant to do the same. To help them undertake this work, consultants need training in organizational analysis and intervention, need to be supported in their work as consultants through some form of supervision, and need to be asked to evaluate their work over a long period of time. They also need to regard consulting as involving more than a simple advisory role (though some consulting tasks involve little more than this)—it is a major undertaking that can affect a significant number of individuals.

It will be noted that a variety of the interventions listed here concern the quality of interpersonal relationships within the organization. It might be thought that such a focus, while following naturally from a counselling perspective, is inappropriate to many organizational consulting problems. This is not the case. Team-building and development are the major building bricks of organizational development. According to Woodcock (1979), effective teamwork requires the following features:

(a) clear objectives and agreed goals;
(b) openness and confrontation within the team;
(c) support and trust between team members;
(d) cooperation and conflict within the team;

(e) sound procedures within the team for conveying information and making decisions;
(f) appropriate leadership within the team for the issues being dealt with;
(g) regular review of the team's working patterns;
(h) attention to the needs of individuals within the team; and finally,
(i) sound relationships between different teams within the organization.

Almost all of these features concern the nature and quality of interpersonal behaviour within the team and the organization. Such a focus on relationships can therefore be seen as appropriate for consultancy aimed at affecting management quality throughout an organization.

CONCLUSIONS

This chapter has introduced some of the key concepts and features of the practice of structural consultancy within schools. Examples of specific cases of this work in action are given in Murgatroyd (1986) and Murgatroyd and Reynolds (1984).

Consultancy, to be effective, needs to begin and end with an understanding of the interpersonal dynamics of an organization and a concern for the well-being of individuals and the relationships between them. A school's capacity for change is a product of the relationships that exist within it (Murgatroyd, 1984). A consultant who seeks to facilitate change without attending to relationship issues is likely to create distress in the organization, though not necessarily that part of the organization with which he or she is directly concerned. Organizations, like families, have rules and structures which shape relationships. Change affects these rules and structures. If the focus of the consultant's work is upon the products of the consulting process without due attention to the process itself, then it is likely that the net effects of consultancy will be shortlived. Substantive change in organizations follows from an attempt to change the basis of the rules and structures which govern relationships within that organization. Given these observations, counselling provides many valuable insights and procedures which consultants in schools would be well advised to use.

REFERENCES

Greiner, L. E. (1967) 'Patterns of organizational change'. *Harvard Business Review*, **45**, 119–30.
Haley, J. (1967) 'Toward a theory of pathological systems', in G. H. Zuk and I. Boszorneyi-Nag (eds), *Family Therapy and Disturbed Families*. Palo Alto, Cal.: Science and Behaviour Press.
Handy, C. (1985) *Understanding Organizations*, 3rd edition. Harmondsworth: Penguin.
Hargreaves, D. (1972) *Interpersonal Relations in Education*. London: Routledge and Kegan Paul.
Harrison, R. (1972) 'How to describe your organization'. *Harvard Business Review*, **50**, 21–45.
Minuchin, S. (1974) *Families and Family Therapy*. London: Tavistock.
Murgatroyd, S. (1984) 'Relationships, change and the school'. *School Organization*, **4**(2), 171–8.
Murgatroyd, S. (1986) 'Management teams and the promotion of staff well-being'. *School Organization*, **6**(1), 115–21.
Murgatroyd, S. and Reynolds, D. R. (1984) 'The creative consultant—the potential use of consultancy as a method of teacher education'. *School Organization*, **4**(4), 321–35.

Murgatroyd, S. and Reynolds, D. R. (1985) *Do Schools Make a Difference?* Milton Keynes: Open University Press.

Murgatroyd, S. and Woolfe, R. (1985) *Helping Families in Distress—An Introduction to Family Focused Helping.* London: Harper and Row.

Olson, D., Sprenkle, D. H. and Russell, C. (1979) 'Circumplex model of marital and family systems'. *Family Process*, **18**, 2–28.

Palazzoli, M. S. (1981) *Sul Fronte dell'Organizzazione.* Milan: Giangiacomo Feltrinelli.

Palazzoli, M. S., Boscolo, L., Cecchin, G. and Prata, G. (1978) *Paradox and Counter-Paradox.* New York: Jason Aronson.

Peters, T. and Austin, N. (1985) *A Passion for Excellence—The Leadership Difference.* London: Collins.

Richardson, E. (1973) *The Teacher, the School and the Task of Management.* London: Heinemann.

Schein, E. H. (1984) 'Coming to a new awareness of organizational culture'. *Sloan Management Review*, **6**, 44–52.

Speed, B. (1984) 'Family therapy—an update'. *Newsletter of the Association of Child Psychology and Psychiatry*, **6**(1), 2–14.

Sprenkle, D. and Olson, D. (1978) 'Circumplex model of family systems—empirical studies of clinic and non-clinic couples', *Journal of Marriage and Family Counselling*, **4**, 59–74.

Woodcock, M. (1979) *Team Development Manual.* London: Gower.

Part II

The Industrial Perspective

The contributors in this part of the book all come from industry and have had long experience working as consultants in all kinds of business settings. But their insights are useful because they have also had considerable experience of working with schools in a consultant and training capacity, as well as both commercial and non-commercial (such as public service) organizations.

Bertie Everard (Chapter 6) has a well-established commitment to helping schools to change for the better and sees management skills as the key to success. He has spent much time in recent years working with teachers and exploring with them the applicability of management theories and practice to school situations. He explains how management's use of consultants has developed over the years and how industrial approaches have an increasing relevant applicability to schools. He is realistic about what has been achieved in industry and sanguine about the prospects for education. Few industrialists have greater insight into schools or more sympathy.

Geoffrey Morris (Chapter 7) began his career as a teacher and there is a certain clarity in his understanding of what schools need and how they may be helped. He explains clearly what consultants do and how they do it, illustrates the usefulness they can have for schools and the procedures that must be adopted for a successful relationship. He describes a variety of approaches and styles and overall provides a good summary of considerations to be borne in mind before engaging a consultant.

The chapter by Geoffrey Sworder (Chapter 8) is included because it explains how consultants are developed and trained in industry. It is unlikely that education can do things in quite the same way but the chapter makes clear that training consultants is a demanding task and cannot be undertaken lightly. Consultants themselves must be trained and given experience if they are to be really useful. In industry consultants are taken seriously and there is a danger that schools will use consultants under the GRIST funding simply because they are the flavour of the month and not because it is well understood how to make use of them.

Chapter 6

Training and Consultancy: Lessons from Industry

Bertie Everard

The practice of consultancy within the education service in Britain is ill-developed by comparison with industry, where it is more common for consultants to be engaged to help management deal with a variety of organizational or technological problems. Knowledge of the way in which consultancy has developed in industrial firms comparable in size and complexity to local education authorities may therefore help administrators to develop the use of a potentially powerful tool for school improvement. This chapter provides an overview of consultancy in industry and how the process is being and could be applied in schools.

The rationale for using consultants is that no organization or subdivision thereof can hope to have internal access to all the management and technological expertise that it needs to be effective; it would be wasteful to train every manager in all the skills and insights required to deal with all organizational problems. To use a medical metaphor, organizations have 'pathologies', and when the patient is not fit it pays to get help. Equally, a well patient needs coaching and training in order to reach a peak of physical condition. While this is an acceptable state of affairs in matters of individual health, it is only partially accepted as desirable in matters of organizational health, even when it is clear to observers that problems abound. Some managers, for example, are reluctant to admit that their departments, schools etc. have problems at all, lest this be construed as a mark of weakness or incompetence on their part.

It is perhaps the constant drive for improved performance in industry that makes its managers more willing to seek help from outside; as Peters and Waterman showed (1982), the pursuit of excellence is a deeply embedded value within successful companies. By contrast, the duty to improve a school is not among the list of duties of an English or Welsh headteacher, as enshrined in the 1986 Coventry Agreement. It is true that those heads noted for their leadership qualities are habitually on the lookout for innovatory approaches to school management, but the majority are not naturally inclined to ask anyone for help with their managerial tasks.

In large companies with a payroll comparable with that of a local education authority, there are often several groups of different kinds of internal consultant—management services, systems analysts, productivity, personnel, training and organization development (OD). Despite having these internal specialists, based either at headquarters or strategically dispersed throughout the organization, it is also the practice to engage from time to time external consultants to augment the advice and help available to line managers and to develop the expertise of the company's own internal consultants.

The nearest equivalent in the education service to the internal consultants that industry employs is the inspectorate and the advisers, though the overwhelming majority of these see their role as offering technical advice on particular subject areas in the curriculum, rather than helping heads to manage their schools more effectively.

WORK STUDY CONSULTANTS

The earliest significant use in British industry of consultants to deal with organizational as distinct from technical matters was in the 1940s and 1950s, when work study officers were brought into manufacturing plants and into offices to observe and measure the way in which repetitive work was done. In the case of work done by hourly paid employees, one of the early outcomes was the development of new payment systems designed to create an incentive for workers to give a fair day's work for a fair day's pay. At least as important, however, was the effect of work study on ensuring that workers were provided with the best-designed tools for the job. In other words, it was a means by which work, work methods and the working environment could be sensibly designed to save unnecessary effort and to enable more work to be done in a given time: not making people work *harder*, but helping them to work more *effectively*. ICI pioneered the use of work study in the United Kingdom and Russell Currie, the 'father' of work study, did much to extend the use of these techniques throughout British industry as a means of raising productivity and economic performance, not only on production plants but also in offices. A corps of trained work study officers grew up and provided consultancy services on a large scale.

Unfortunately, work study acquired a bad name, partly because of its politically sensitive links with incentive bonus schemes, and partly because of the insensitive way in which many of these experts offered their advice. However, long after other payment schemes have replaced those based on time and motion studies, the use of work study consultants still survives in companies like ICI, though much of the expertise has been assimilated into the line management system through the use of training.

I have not encountered the use of this approach in schools, yet my visits have revealed many opportunities for applying such expertise (not, of course, to the development of incentive schemes!). There are numerous examples of teachers' effort being inefficiently applied and needlessly dissipated, where it would appear that no-one has stood back to review the way in which work (especially of an administrative nature) is done, whether it is, in fact, worth doing at all, how smoothly information flows round the school, how forms are designed, how people contact one another in order to communicate, how equipment is made available in working condition at the right place at the right time, and so on. It has come to be accepted by some teachers, apparently without question, that inefficiency in work systems is a natural and immutable characteristic of school organizations and other academic institutions, about which therefore little or nothing can be done. It does not occur to the staff of a school that a work study consultant might be valuable in diagnosing the sources of inefficiency and suggesting well-tried ways of removing them. Moreover, the connection between organizational efficiency and morale is sometimes forgotten; the Local Government Training Board has recently adduced examples of this connection, when reviews of the systems for getting work done have led not only to improvements in procedures but also to the increased motivation and commitment by staff (Local Government Training Board, 1985).

One of the offshoots of work study, which stemmed from the study of how managerial work is done, was the development of a range of management techniques such as systematic problem-solving, critical path scheduling, project planning and so on. Along with the earlier work study techniques such as activity sampling, these were incorporated as topics in management training courses and instruction was given in their use. Many managers, however, encountered considerable difficulty in applying these techniques in their back-home work situations; others found them somewhat simplistic and could not see their relevance: 'It may be all right in theory, but . . .'. What in effect was happening was that the consultants who were trying to 'sell' these techniques were using mechanistic models of organization processes and were failing to recognize the importance of the human element in introducing new procedures.

OD CONSULTANTS

In the 1960s and 1970s, a somewhat different approach to consultancy began to be adopted in ICI, Shell, Rolls-Royce, Procter and Gamble, Tube Investments and other large firms. This was organization development (OD) or 'process' consultancy. It had some profound effects on the practice and outcomes of consultancy, and of training. Indeed, it was mostly in training or personnel departments that OD consultancy took root. Whereas management services departments tended to attract authoritarian, hard-nosed consultants, often with an engineering background and a high respect for rationality and quantitative approaches, the culture of training departments at that time was more influenced by the behavioural sciences. The concept of training was broadened from that of instructing individuals in apprentice schools, staff colleges, etc. in the knowledge and skills required to do their jobs, towards developing natural work groups, changing attitudes and influencing the whole culture of the organization. At the same time, more attention was paid to following up courses by providing practical support to the participants after their return to their normal jobs—a form of consultancy. Although the now familiar phrase 'management of change' was not in common currency at the time, the new breed of trainer-consultants were in fact facilitating the changes the need for which they helped managers to diagnose. Consultancy became less a matter of *prescribing* what changes were needed and leaving the managers to get on with it, and more a matter of helping managers to carry through the change *processes* that would lead to greater effectiveness. The word 'facilitator' began to be used to describe this style of consultancy.

This was a much more organic, and less mechanistic, approach to consultancy; not only did it take better account of the human aspects of organizations (for example, feelings of apprehension when people are faced with the need to change), but it achieved a better balance between the development needs of individuals and those of the organization. In the old prescriptive style of consultancy, the feelings and aspirations of people were often submerged by the imperatives of organizational efficiency.

Important though it is in any organization to take account of the needs of the individual, in educational institutions it is essential to do so, by their very nature and culture. On the other hand, as the decline in the world economy moves organizations from a relatively rich to an impoverished environment, with the management of growth giving way to the management of contraction, so the need to make organizations more efficient (that is, achieving more with less) is also vital. A good OD consultant will help an organization to manage the tension that exists between fulfilling individual needs and those of the organization. He (or she) will be interested in changing (and many will be specifically employed to change) the organization's culture, as well as helping individuals to adapt to it.

CONSULTANCY AND MANAGEMENT TRAINING

Some of the best examples of the application of consultancy and of training in ICI are those in which the analytical–rational insights of those brought up in the 'work study' tradition were blended with the humanistic insights of those involved with personnel management and exposed to the behavioural sciences. Collaboration between the two types was not always smooth, because the cultural gradients between 'hard' and 'soft' were often very pronounced; neither stereotype respected the other, and their psychological distance could only be closed by working together, for example in jointly designing and running a management training course.

My first experience of this was in the development of a one-week residential 'Group Achievement Course' in ICI during the early 1970s. The course was based on the notion of setting groups of participants some 20 interlinked tasks, with plenty of opportunity for them to reflect on how they set about doing them. This brought out some general principles of how group work can be organized more systematically, as well as how individuals interact with one another. The lessons learned from performing each task were then applied to improving the process by which the next task was tackled (Figure 6.1), and this gradually induced changes in group and personal behaviour. At first the trainers would act as consultants to the groups, coaching them in the management of the process, but soon one or two group members would be detached to act as observers, and would learn to diagnose the causes of both effectiveness and ineffectiveness. They would then conduct a process review with the group and learn how to put across their

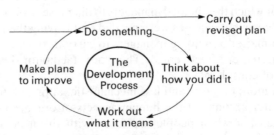

Figure 6.1 Experiential learning cycle. Reproduced with the permission of the Development Training Advisory Group.

insights about how to improve effectiveness, in an acceptable way (that is, taking into account the feelings of group members). After following this experiential learning process assiduously for a week, they became much more aware of interpersonal and intergroup processes and were able to tackle new problems more systematically than before.

I have used this course design in training head teachers on 'OTTO' (one-term training opportunity) courses designed to help them train less experienced heads in managing their schools. By introducing them to the practical value of 'process consultancy', this kind of training is paving the way for more school-based consultancy and INSET, in which real problems are tackled in a learning situation with the help of a process consultant. The adoption of a common systematic approach to solving problems is the main building block in the management of change.

CONSULTANCY CLINICS

An intermediate stage between observation/consultancy on tasks set by the course designer and in-school consultancy on real problems is the use of a training workshop as a 'consultancy clinic'. The origin of this idea was as follows. When it became apparent in the 1970s that ICI would have to face major strategic change, with fundamental reshaping of the organization structure and culture, the training function mounted a series of three-day workshops for senior managers, up to and including members of the main board, on the management of complex change. The design of these was inspired by Professor Dick Beckhard of MIT (Beckhard and Harris, 1977), who has since developed the approach into a commercially available learning package (Beckhard, 1986). The internal OD consultants and trainers who ran these workshops shifted their emphasis (which at first was inclined to be overdidactic) from training towards consultancy, and their own roles changed accordingly. Pairs of people who either jointly owned a problem (for example, two works managers who faced the need to close one of the two works and amalgamate all production in the other), or one of whom played a helping role towards the other (for example, a business manager and an internal consultant) came on the workshop in order to work systematically on the strategic problems that they owned. The ratio of participants to trainer/consultants was about 6:1. The trainers provided (mainly in written form—handouts) a general framework for the systematic management of complex change (which I have adapted for school situations in part 3 of *Effective School Management* (Everard and Morris, 1985)), and the workshop participants tackled their change problems in pairs or small groups, using this framework. The trainers acted as consultants to the managers during this process and helped each pair to think through its problem and develop plans for solving it.

As can be expected, most of the participants left this 'clinic' with loose ends untied, so the process of consultancy was continued after the workshop, either through visits by the trainers running the event or by handing over the responsibility for providing support, to other internal consultants or trainers who had been trained in the same approach and who therefore could readily tune into the process. This sort of training approach sometimes creates a demand for consultancy where none existed before.

Two examples can be given of how this approach has been applied in school management. First, the Schools Council Industry Project (SCIP) tapped into ICI's experience;

using trainer/consultants who had been responsible for running the workshops just described, they mounted a number of 'consultancy skills' workshops for SCIP coordinators and for heads involved with SCIP (Everard, 1984). As a subsequent spinoff, one of the heads who had attended a workshop changed places for a week with a colleague head from a neighbouring school; then they gave each other what amounted to an 'organization diagnosis' (Everard, 1986, p. 62).

Second, I have run at the University of London Institute of Education (as part of OTTO and 20-day basic courses) and at the University of Warwick (as part of the Advanced Diploma course in Industry and Education) a modified version of the ICI management of change workshop, in which trios of heads or senior teachers use the framework to work on their own school management problems. This is organized partly as a co-consulting process, and partly as an exercise in bringing in an external consultant (such as myself or one of a number of former OTTO 'graduates' who have been trained in the systematic approach to problem-solving) to help with particularly difficult aspects.

Unfortunately it has proved difficult to set up arrangements whereby participants can obtain continuing consultancy help after their return to school. Resources are not generally available for this kind of follow-up. Occasionally a primary adviser who has been exposed to the approach has been able to offer help, but mostly one has to rely on heads developing their own support networks or 'action learning sets', in which co-consultancy can continue.

INSET provision for management development consists mainly of external courses, and although these are useful in providing general understanding of and practice in the processes of problem-solving, consultancy, etc., there is always difficulty in transferring skills back to the job, so that real and observable improvements in school effectiveness ensue (Bolam, 1978). If more of the total INSET resources were applied to school-based INSET, with a strong orientation towards process consultancy based on real problems, expenditure on INSET would be likely to produce more tangible benefits to schools. The relative underprovision and widespread lack of acceptance of the consultancy approach to securing change and development in the education service is in marked contrast to the experience of ICI which (as I have argued elsewhere: Everard, 1986) faced problems of change remarkably similar to those that confront education today.

CONDITIONS NECESSARY FOR SUCCESSFUL CONSULTANCY

Professor Andrew Pettigrew conducted a major longitudinal study of the use of training and OD consultancy in bringing about complex change in ICI, which he regards as the leading UK company in this field. His book, *The Awakening Giant* (Pettigrew, 1985), is a mine of information about successful and unsuccessful consultancy interventions, as well as providing a valuable commentary on the theories of organizational change. He draws a number of conclusions which seem to be of relevance to education.

Although several external OD consultants were regularly working in the company during the 1960s, a major effort was made in 1970 to train a network of 50 internal consultants to work with some 40 000 middle managers. Examining the impact that these consultants had, Pettigrew noted that it is a great help if those chosen to be trained as consultants are perceived not as people who can readily be spared, but as high-energy, relatively successful managers who are capable of learning consultancy skills.

Even those who were well selected and well trained sometimes found themselves contending with a fairly hostile environment, where they were seen as an illegitimate, marginal and relatively powerless group. Pettigrew concludes that one of the consultant's first tasks must therefore be to build up credibility by giving real help on practical issues, rather than by peddling techniques. They have to fashion a social context in which it is legitimate for them to work, and not leave this to chance in a culture unaccustomed to making use of consultants. Where it is well-established, a training department can provide an acceptable base, with its course follow-up activities providing a *raison d'être* for consultancy. It is not helpful if consultants are perceived as too closely connected with the power system, otherwise they constitute a threat rather than a resource. On the other hand, if they are perceived as having no political standing or top-level support at all, they are all too readily ignored. So they need to cultivate allies and friends at court.

The most difficult environments in which consultants have to work are those in which there is little appreciation of the need for change at the top of the organization; although they may be able to create change, it is arduous and frustrating work. Organizations that are strongly segmented (as many schools and universities are) also constitute difficult environments, for change is usually seen as a threat. Consultants have to try to change the world while living in it—in other words, to retain a vision of how things ought to be, while still being seen as practical, down-to-earth and in touch with the realities of organizational life.

The environment for consultancy work becomes more benign when a serious external crisis confronts the organization; this can lend point to their activities, as they turn problems into opportunities. The education system is currently at such a point of crisis; the government's attempts to bring about simultaneous cuts and improvements in the service, exacerbated by the 'hurt' of the teachers' dispute, have sensitized heads and other senior managers to the need for obtaining help.

The response to this need in the education service has been somewhat different from that in ICI. While the DES 3/83 initiative was based on the concept of training experienced heads in management in order that they could in turn train their less experienced colleagues, the whole thrust of the resulting OTTO courses has been towards improving *management* skills rather than training or consultancy skills. Since for many heads who took part this was the first time that they had experienced formal management training, it is perhaps to be expected that there would be such an emphasis. In the case of ICI, however, there was already a thriving management training function, so the development of a management consultancy resource was more directly targeted towards turning trained managers and experienced management trainers into internal OD consultants. They formed an informal professional association or 'OD network' which provided moral and sometimes practical support for this form of consultancy. Although their initial training took place on a month-long workshop, of which two were run, other training events were regularly held so that they could build up their expertise and commitment, and also enlarge the total group of OD practitioners (some of whom were also practising managers for part of the time) to 100–200. These people exposed many more potential clients and supporters to behavioural science ideas, group relations training methods and the use to be made of third party OD consultants. Some 500–600 senior and influential managers were invited to week-long residential workshops to diagnose the reasons for resistance to change and to lay plans to overcome it. These events were generally regarded as helpful and successful, and they led to an at times embarrassing number of requests for consultancy help, especially for team-building and intergroup work. As well as using the internal consultants, the company brought in an increasing number of (mainly American) external consultants to support the strategy for enabling and energizing managers to cope with change more proactively.

RELATIONSHIP BETWEEN INTERNAL AND EXTERNAL CONSULTANTS

It is worth examining ICI's experience of using internal consultants (that is, managers and management trainers retrained as consultants) and externals, because the choice between the two is also an issue that the education service needs to confront.

McLean *et al*. (1982) have listed the advantages of externals over internals: they can act as an independent conceptual stimulant, a provider of alternative views, and by not being part of the career or political system of the organization, they are more free to act as sounding boards and counsellors. ICI also found that they helped to overcome parochialism and stretch horizons; even if a novel approach suffers from the 'not-invented-here' syndrome, a good consultant will help to adapt it to a new setting.

Independent consultants are well placed, by working in different organizations, sometimes in other countries, to survey, identify and disseminate current best practice; and by concentrating on particular aspects of organizational effectiveness, they can build up a veritable storehouse of practical knowhow which often goes well beyond that available in centres of learning such as universities and business schools. While the latter may (but do not always) develop a sounder theoretical framework for their work, the private consultancy firm is often more adept at applying and adapting theory to practical situations, as well as presenting it in an acceptable way. They also become highly skilled at interviewing people, which is necessary to draw out salient information that might not otherwise be revealed, and in some cases certainly not to other employees in the organization.

However, as Fullan remarks (1982), so far as education is concerned, 'It is an undeveloped art to know how best to select and use external consultants'. ICI's experience, summarized by Pettigrew, is that one of the most important factors in their choice is the 'personal chemistry' between the consultant and the principal client. However skilled and knowledgeable the consultant, if he comes across as arrogant, academic, insensitive to the client's needs, odd or unempathetic, then he is unlikely to be acceptable. ICI faulted some otherwise extremely able consultants on these counts, and this is likely to happen with schools. To take an example: I have just used the male pronoun; an external consultant with an industrial background who visits a school unaware of the strength of feeling within education about sexism is likely to alienate his or her client from the word go. 'Get where the client is' is one of the first lessons a consultant has to learn.

The fit required between the consultant and the organization is illustrated by the following triangle:

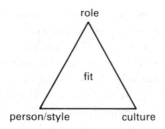

Is the role that the consultant is expected to play one that the person can fill? Is his or her style in tune with the culture of the organization? Will the culture regard the role as legitimate?

One lesson drawn by Pettigrew from ICI's experience is that external consultants should always be used to enhance, rather than compete with, the credibility of any internal development resources that are working in the same problem area. They require management, not just in the narrow contractual sense, but in directing them to people and problems where their expertise is most likely to be used. They may need shielding and protecting from short-term critics and if the use of their particular approach is countercultural, they may need legitimizing in some way.

Thus it is often helpful if someone (such as an internal consultant) is made responsible for managing the interface between the external consultant and the principal client(s), so that the visitor can be briefed about the culture and micropolitics of the situation. The external can sometimes be guided to 'do good by stealth' rather than by raising his head above the parapet.

In a consultancy assignment I have had with a school, to carry out a diagnosis of the organization and management, it was one of the deputy heads who performed this function. Although the head was the senior person to whom I related, the deputy engaged me, set up my programme with me, briefed me and generally helped to provide a 'fair wind' for my intervention into the organization.

Not only does it oil the wheels if there is a designated internal person to liaise with the external consultant, but the impact of the latter's work is likely to be enhanced. Indeed, Fullan (1982) in reviewing the research concludes that most of it shows that external consultants are effective only when there is an internal consultant or a team which supports their activities. All the major research showed that effective organizational change occurs when there is combined involvement of internal and external members. External consultants who are interested in facilitating real educational change should therefore establish some ongoing relationship with a teacher or teachers who will act collectively to follow through on the change. Certainly ICI experience supports this strategy; it was the normal practice to develop close working relationships between the external consultant and the internal team.

It is often a valuable learning experience for whoever is managing the external consultant's entry into the organization, if the two of them articulate and review the process. The internal contact (whether a consultant or a manager) should try actively to acquire the skills that the consultant deploys. The best way to do this is to review after an encounter with the organization what lessons are to be learned, why the consultant acted as he did and how else he might have acted instead. The kinds of skill a good consultant uses are applicable to other management processes such as coaching, counselling and developing staff. In the personal assignment already mentioned, it was built into my contract that I would try to pass on the skills and techniques I used, so that learning could occur not just at the content level (the feedback of the results of my diagnosis) but also at the process level, so that the school staff would become better equipped to carry out their own school reviews in future. This proved to be a useful piece of training, not only for the school's own staff but for the staff of neighbouring schools who were invited to the seminar.

USE OF INDUSTRIAL CONSULTANTS BY SCHOOLS

Another link to training arises when a consultant is in dialogue with those in the organization whom he interviews. Not only is it common for the questions he poses to set up a hitherto unconsidered line of thinking in the minds of the interviewees, who therefore experience the interview as stimulating, but from their responses he can often identify training needs at either the individual or the collective level. For example, if most interviewees are floored by the same simple question such as 'What is the purpose of your work?', or if they simply reply in terms of what they do rather than what they hope to achieve, it can signify the need for training in objective-setting. Sometimes it does not occur to an individual or his or her manager to ask the sort of questions that would reveal important training needs, because of limitations in their constructs and frameworks of thought and in their knowledge of what is possible and perhaps even common practice elsewhere. This is particularly true in schools when the consultant has an industrial background.

The encouragement implicit in a number of circulars from the Department of Education and Science (see, for example, 3/83) that the education service should try to build bridges with industry in developing management, has stimulated some schools to obtain consultancy help from that quarter. LEAs have also looked to industry for help. I have described elsewhere some of the results of using consultants from industry (Everard, 1984, 1986). For example, Duffet, a senior internal consultant in BP International Ltd, was commissioned by Cambridgeshire LEA to comment impartially on aspects of the education service from an industrial manager's point of view. The Authority and the schools that were involved found his comments very acceptable and because the teachers reacted positively to the presence of this consultant over a six-week period, they began to seek outside consultancy support from other industrial firms.

In another school two industrial training officers were invited to evaluate the management work of the head and three deputies. Their visits were spread over six months, taking 86 hours in all. The results proved rewarding in terms not only of the findings, but also of the processes they used for their review.

In Chapter 18 of Everard and Morris (1985) I give a case study of a major change programme in 'Westfield School', in which a leading part was played by an industrial training manager who was brought in as a consultant by the head. I commented on the case, and in particular his role, as follows:

> Though coming from a different culture, with all the suspicions that this is apt to arouse, he worked hard to establish credibility by introducing the staff to techniques that had short-run advantages to them, in a problem area that 'hurt'—how to make better use of their all-too-scarce time. It is from this kind of bridgehead that trust can be gradually extended.

The consultant's experience of strategic planning of change in a large organisation was very valuable to the head and new deputy in dealing with such practical issues at teacher level, and the three were able to hold fruitful strategic and tactical discussions in a high-level language of change. So effective was the partnership that the trio are in demand for providing inputs to school management training courses sponsored by a consortium of nearby local authorities.

These examples show how the expertise that training officers have in the role of consultant can survive the sometimes rough crossing of the cultural divide between industry and education and facilitate processes of change and innovation in schools.

Schools may experience difficulty in identifying the type of industrial training officer who is most likely to prove a useful consultant. Pettigrew, Jones and Reason (1982) have categorized the different roles that are generically described as 'training officer', and the one that is most likely to be useful is that which they call the 'change agent' or who operates in this capacity for part of his time. A flavour of the role is someone who is:

(a) outside the line organization;
(b) politically neutral (though not unaware);
(c) facilitating and educating about the *process* of organizational problem-solving (they see their task as helping to manage a process);
(d) client-orientated;
(e) problem-orientated (rather than activity-orientated);
(f) in the workplace but not of it (that is, intentionally marginal).

In other words, a prospective consultant from industry should be asked how he sees his role and what he tries to achieve in his organization. If the answer is about helping managers to change (culture, attitudes, practices, etc.) then he is likely to be more helpful than if he simply provides training courses.

In conclusion, I cite as an example of cultural change led by a trainer/consultant team, the objects of which should particularly commend themselves to educationists, the experience of the Sun Alliance Group, which employs some 12 000 people. The way in which the organization's culture was transformed over a period of eight years has been described in a series of articles by Bruce Nixon, the company's former training and development manager (Nixon, 1984, 1985; Allen and Nixon, 1986). They increased the level of trust in the organization and stimulated the development of networks providing mutual support. Greater attention to personal development, caring relationships and the pursuit of excellence are among the outcomes of their work. They changed the value system so that success was celebrated more than failure criticized. They worked not under the direction of top management, but with its support. The lessons they learned are ones that are worth pondering by all consultants and trainers who wish to bring about fundamental change; here are some:

(a) Develop a clear vision.
(b) Build friends and allies.
(c) Show your trust and optimism (and even love).
(d) Collaborate across the politics.
(e) Keep in touch with the politics.
(f) Get good people around you and support and nourish them.
(g) Do not take over training: enable and empower managers to do it.

(h)   Build training and development into the business.
(i)   Build a network and a community.
(j)   Spread the word to the grass roots.

In this way, they say, things can and do change for the better.

TVEI AND TRIST

For all the adverse publicity it received at first, the somewhat misleadingly named Technical and Vocational Education Initiative (TVEI) and its associated TVEI-Related In-service Training programme (TRIST) have the potential to bring about an equally fundamental change in schools, with TVEI coordinators being the change agents that facilitate the process. They may not be called 'consultants', but if they develop the skills and approach of OD consultants they could, over the sort of time-scale that was needed in Sun Alliance and ICI, really change things for the better in schools.

REFERENCES

Allen, R. and Nixon, B. (1986) 'Effective in-house management development: challenging tradition'. *Industrial and Commercial Training*. **July/August**.

Beckhard, R. (1986) *Managing Change in Organisations*. Reading, Mass.: Addison-Wesley.

Beckhard, R. and Harris, R. T. (1977) *Organisational Transitions. Managing Complex Change*. Reading, Mass.: Addison-Wesley.

Bolam, R. (1978) 'School focussed INSET and consultancy'. *Educational Change and Development*, **1**, 25.

Everard, K. B. (1984) *Management in Comprehensive Schools—What Can Be Learned from Industry?* (2nd edition). York: Centre for the Study of Comprehensive Schools.

Everard, K. B. (1986) *Developing Management in Schools*, p. 62. Oxford: Blackwell.

Everard, K. B. and Morris, G. (1985) *Effective School Management*. London: Harper and Row.

Fullan, M. (1982) *The Meaning of Educational Change*. New York: Teachers College Press.

Local Government Training Board (1985) *Good Management in Local Government*. Luton: Local Government Training Board.

McLean, A., Sims, D., Mangham, I. and Tuffield, D. (1982) *Organisation Development in Transition: Evidence of an Evolving Profession*. Chichester: Wiley.

Nixon, B. (1984) 'In search of excellent management development'. *Industrial and Commercial Training*. **July/August**.

Nixon, B. (1985) 'Some effective ways of working with managers'. *Industrial and Commercial Training*. **July/August**.

Peters, T. J. and Waterman, R. H. (1982) *In Search of Excellence*. New York: Harper and Row.

Pettigrew, A. M. (1985) *The Awakening Giant: Continuity and Change in ICI*. Oxford: Blackwell.

Pettigrew, A. M., Jones, G. R. and Reason, P. W. (1982) *Training and Development Roles in Their Organisational Setting*. Sheffield: Manpower Services Commission.

Chapter 7

Applying Business Consultancy Approaches to Schools

Geoffrey Morris

THE NATURE OF ORGANIZATIONS

Every type of organization, and indeed each individual organization, is perceived by its members as 'fundamentally different' from other organizations. Paradoxically this belief is yet another of the similarities which exist amongst organizations of various kinds. It is important to recognize differences in purpose, priorities, terminology, products, services, environmental pressures, structure and culture. However, it is equally important to recognize that organizations of all kinds, whether large businesses, small businesses, government departments, hospitals, professional practices or schools have a common *raison d'être* which is to unite the efforts of individuals in the pursuit of the organizational goals. Furthermore they have a common need to optimize the use of limited physical, financial and human resources. In consequence, we find within all organizations common requirements which include:

(a) definition of responsibilities;
(b) constant adaptation;
(c) taking and implementing decisions;
(d) development of people;
(e) motivation of people;
(f) delegation and control;
(g) financial control;
(h) purchase, maintenance and control of physical resources.

We also find common potential or actual problems, notably those of inadequacy, inefficiency and destructive conflict.

THE CONSULTANT ROLE

Controlling these activities and handling the problems is the ongoing task of 'management'. The role of the 'consultant', whether internal or external, is to supplement the activities of management in one or more of these ways:

(a) by giving an independent view;
(b) by providing a process through which longstanding problems can be tackled and hopefully solved;
(c) 'cross-fertilizing'—that is, transferring into an organization the benefit of experience gained in similar situations—this may involve formal training;
(d) by acting as a temporary, additional resource in order, for example, to 'put in a new system'.

In the competitive world of business, organizational problems are more immediately apparent than in education: financial performance deteriorates. It is not therefore surprising that the business world was the first to recognize the need to develop effective techniques of management and consultancy. Without the spectre of insolvency, or any universally accepted measure of success or failure, other types of organization have not always had their minds so sharply focused on the need for efficiency and high performance, though the need could hardly be greater than in an area, such as education, on which the capabilities, attitudes and values of the rising generation depend.

Moving 20 years ago from a senior school post into industry I was impressed by the fact that in my first month in industry I received more training than I had in ten years of teaching and I was equally struck by the relevance of the training to my former teaching career. This is equally true of management consultancy, and fortunately I have had some opportunity to continue working with schools and school managers while directing the activities of EMAS (European Management Advisory Services) for the last 15 years.

CONSULTANCY STYLES

Consultants, like managers (Everard and Morris, 1985, p. 18) have two main concerns:

(a) to achieve results;
(b) for people and relationships.

The possible approaches that a consultant may adopt when faced by an assignment are illustrated in Figure 7.1. While intermediate approaches are the most probable, the extreme styles may be described as:

(a) directive;
(b) behavioural;
(c) catalytic.

In a *directive* approach, the consultant will focus on the criteria by which the success of the client organization is measured and on the reasons for shortcomings. He will then analyse the structure and workings of the client organization and recommend changes that should be made in personnel, structure and methods. He may then be commissioned to implement his suggestions.

In a *behavioural* approach, the consultant is primarily concerned to develop the ability of the people within the client organization to handle their relationships and to solve any conflicts which may exist. In this approach there will normally be a high training content with a focus on group dynamics.

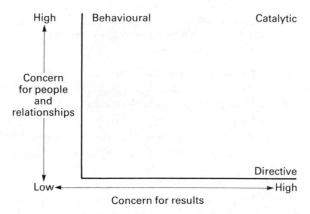

Figure 7.1 Consultancy approaches.

In a *catalytic* or participative approach, the consultant will help the members of the client organization to focus on the purpose of the organization and to find and implement ways of improving performance. This approach is likely to involve training of members of the client organization in techniques ranging from budgetary control to conflict management. It is likely to include 'workshops' in which teams of members of the client organization work on problems faced by the organization and emerge with action plans which should include mechanisms to ensure that the plans are actually implemented.

THE USE AND ABUSE OF A DIRECTIVE APPROACH

Which approach is used ought to depend on the nature of the problem and of the people involved. In practice it will depend also on the character and experience of the consultant who may use a particular approach whether or not it is the one most appropriate to the situation.

The popular image of a consultant is of someone who adopts a *directive* approach, and many of the early 'management science' consultants indeed used only this approach. It is in the nature of the approach that an 'outsider' moves into the organization in order to 'tell' the members of the organization how to do things better. The outsider will tend to rely on observation and analysis of the 'hard' data of physical systems, processes and results. People will be questioned so that they may explain what is happening rather than to seek their constructive input to solutions. Not surprisingly those subjected to the scrutiny of such a consultant may resent the interference of this stopwatch- and notepad-bearing knowall and will not be predisposed to accept his recommendations. However, the directive approach is sometimes the only one possible in cases where:

(a) the organization's results are such that there will be disastrous consequences unless there is urgent action;
(b) there are grave doubts about the ability of the organization's current management to handle the problems;

(c)   the resistance of the organization to changes seen as necessary—or indeed to any change—is perceived to be so strong that no amount of persuasion or discussion is likely to have any effect within a reasonable time.

In cases (a) and (b) above, especially where both occur together, it is likely there will be drastic changes to the existing staff, and an approach which expected their participation could therefore be adding insult to injury. In the third case an appropriate strategy may be to impose the parameters of change—for example, that two schools will be merged, that a new curriculum will be used, that the public examination system will change, that the school leaving age will be raised—and then use a catalytic or participative approach to help the school to find the best way of meeting the new requirements.

This combination of the directive and the participative has been the chosen method of government and local educational authorities over recent years with inspectors and advisers acting as the 'consultants'. The need for some degree of uniformity across schools means that it is often the only means of achieving consistency in change. However, most teachers have personally felt the resentment caused by imposed change, and the risk is that imposition is going into increasing detail—to impose 'what' is to be achieved is one thing, to impose 'how' is another. The lessons of industry are that 'directive' approaches create frustration, resentment and industrial relations problems. If methods and rules are tightly prescribed people 'work to rule' and do not apply creativity to their jobs, nor do they put in effort beyond what is required.

Two major industrial concerns were both advised that the use of microcomputers could be cost-effective in a number of areas. In the first company, microcomputers were purchased for each of the areas, staff trained in their use, some standard applications were imposed, others suggested and staff were told that they should develop further applications of their own. While a limited number of 'buffs' took enthusiastically to the computers, the majority of staff resented them—especially as the imposed applications produced information of use to a central department rather than to the department of origin. Six months later most of the computers were barely used.

In the second company, staff were trained in the use of the computers. During the training they were invited to consider what application would most help them in their work and were helped to program these applications. Those who had been trained were then told that computers would only be supplied to those departments which could produce a good, written cost justification clearly setting out to what use they would put the computer. Central information requirements were discussed, and departments were involved in developing the manual or computer systems that could be commonly used to meet the information needs. In this second company, most departments applied for and used the computers.

In the spring of 1986 my company carried out a limited research project in which we asked local education authorities (LEAs) and schools for their plans and views about the use of computers for administrative purposes. We also examined the benefits that could accrue from the use of computers in school offices. Two interesting positions emerged:

(a)   In the case of schools in particular, office microcomputers using standard packages could pay off dramatically in the following ways:

   (i)   word processing could save hours of work by both teaching and clerical staff in producing:

(1) examination papers and other teaching materials;
(2) letters;
(3) school documentation of various kinds;
(ii) a simple database could hold both pupil and staff records and instantly produce all lists of various kinds which are frequently required;
(iii) spreadsheets could facilitate the control of books, materials and finance.

(b) Most local authorities have in hand plans and pilot projects to put computers into school offices complete with programs to enable schools to provide the authorities with information that the authorities require, possibly via a network. In some cases the computers will not be capable of using standard 'user friendly' packages with which the schools could do some of their own work. In one case we were told that the computers would have the capability, but that the authority did not intend to advertise the fact. In other cases the schools would be provided with specially written programs over time to meet what the authorities believed to be the schools' needs. These programs would be much more costly than off-the-shelf standard software which could be adapted to school use, but, when we put this to the authorities, most of them said that they hoped to recoup their costs by selling the software to other authorities. Unfortunately, whilst we found many would-be 'vendor' authorities, we did not meet any would-be 'purchaser' authorities.

While the research was not in sufficient depth for us to draw definitive conclusions it would appear:

(a) that the 'directive' approach of the LEA data-processing consultants is likely to produce a negative reaction in the schools as well as taking an unnecessarily large share of scarce educational resources;
(b) that a more participative approach could produce very cost-effective results. Such has been the case in several independent schools where consultants have first trained staff and then helped them to produce solutions which have saved time, effort and money far beyond the cost of the hardware and software.

This type of problem is all too familiar to industrial consultants, and it does seem a pity that, as far as we know, education is not drawing on their advice to shape the thinking of the LEAs.

APPLYING A BEHAVIOURAL APPROACH

The behavioural approach is appropriate in those cases where relationships between individuals and behaviour in interactive situations such as meetings are clearly problems in their own right. The approach is limited in focus. This is a strength in that consultant and staff time and effort may be concentrated on a specified set of relationships within the organization and/or a specified relationship problem such as communication, decision-taking, meeting management, conflict, motivation, delegation, appraisal. The limitation of the approach is that we may be so obsessed by the particular tree that we are tending that we do not see it in the context of the wood. The result of 'team-building', 'group dynamics' or, in particular, 'T-group' or 'sensitivity training' within a part of an organization has sometimes been that:

(a)   the group has set itself apart from the rest of the organization;
(b)   people within the group have become so obsessed by contemplating the group 'navel' that they have lost sight of the group role and purpose.

However, an experienced consultant will have learned from the many mistakes in industry some 10 to 20 years ago, and will neither use the more extreme behavioural consultancy/training techniques nor allow his or her clients to forget the organizational context within which the intervention is taking place. In fact, the consultant will often find that he cannot stay within the confines of, say, decision-taking or appraisal but that the issue for which he or she is called in is merely the tip of an iceberg.

In a large comprehensive school the apparent problem was one of managing meetings which were being called with increasing frequency to try to sort out the problems of integrating a former grammar and secondary modern school. Meetings were being called by the head, the deputy head, heads of department, heads of year, the head of pastoral care and heads of house. Inevitably people were often asked to attend two different meetings at the same time with the result that decisions would have either to be postponed to a further meeting or taken in the absence of individuals whose commitment was critical to successful implementation. There was a general feeling that many of the meetings were badly structured, took far too long and went round in circles. Decisions taken by one group were often inconsistent—or in direct conflict—with those taken by another group.

Using a 'directive' approach a consultant would doubtless have prescribed decision-making roles for each meeting, set out either regular schedules or a procedure for 'booking' meeting times and venues, and suggested that those who ran meetings should be trained in meeting management (see Everard and Morris, 1985, Chapter 5).

However, in discussing the issues with the head, the deputy and one or two members of staff, it quickly became clear that there were underlying problems of relationships with deeply entrenched conflicts and patterns of negative behaviour. Instead of taking responsibility for solving problems, staff were blaming the new structure, the head, the deputy or each other, and declaring their inability to act. Meetings glossed over controversial issues between parties present at the meeting and usually focused blame on someone who was not present. If there was any result at all from a meeting it was a declaration of intent rather than a firm action plan setting out responsibilities and time-scales. Warring cliques abounded. People expressed themselves to be disappointed, frustrated, demotivated and generally behaved as 'victims' rather than as active, dynamic participants in shaping the school's destiny.

For a consultant to suggest new structures and procedures in such a case would be merely to tackle the symptoms rather than the root causes. Undisciplined stagnation and frustration would simply be replaced by disciplined stagnation and frustration. The objective therefore was to try to influence behavioural patterns and relationships so that staff would in future be better able to put the real problems and issues on the table and manage their way through them. The consultant's task was therefore:

(a)   to help those involved to obtain a common, more objective perception of what was taking place in their group;
(b)   to help them to understand the dynamics of groups and or organizations;
(c)   to develop in individuals positive attitudes and skill in managing problems of relationships;
(d)   to apply these skills to the real problems of the organization.

The phases of consultant activities are:

(a) analysis of the situation through discussions with:

    (i) key persons involved (that is, the head and the deputy head)
    (ii) a cross-section of other members of staff.

(b) feedback to the principal 'client' (in this case, the head) of the consultant's perceptions, together with recommendations for a further course of action; agreement on this course of action, possibly involving feedback to other key persons;

(c) preparation (discussion, training, counselling) of all parties for a 'new approach' to the problems;

(d) a problem-solving session, or sessions, to try to consider the issues objectively and agree a reasonable number of actions to improve the situation;

(e) follow-up meetings to review progress and to agree further actions.

The aim throughout in such cases is to persuade the parties to view the situation in a new way, to stand back and take a broader, more objective view and thereby to escape from established patterns of negative behaviour.

The time and effort devoted to each phase will vary from organization to organization. Our experience is that large industrial organizations are more likely to recognize the importance of solving problems whose impact affects their financial performance than are schools. They invest more time and effort and therefore get a correspondingly better payoff. Nevertheless, while a half-hearted attempt is worse than useless, a well-planned but short intervention can be very effective, provided always that it is followed up by regular review meetings.

In a typical school case, *phase A* (the analysis phase) involved one or two days of consultant time interviewing the head, the deputy (one hour each) and about ten other people (half an hour each). The interviews were based on the structure in Table 7.1, but this was used as a prompt rather than as a straitjacket, and issues that appeared to be relevant were followed up as and when the interviewee alluded to them. Emphasis was on asking for suggestions.

Phase B (feedback) should be based on a written report in order to ensure consistency of communication. The aim is to set the personal snippets of information and opinion in a broader and more objective context, using them as evidence of general statements. A typical report might state:

> Meetings, though frequent, are often badly organized and do not arrive at decisions. One interviewee said that she had during the past month attended five meetings of the same group to discuss the typing of examination papers and that only one decision had been reached during that time. Even that decision was rejected by the deputy head on the grounds that it was impractical.

The very process of analysis in which a third party listens attentively, and by questioning and reformulating probes the answers given, often takes much of the emotional heat out of situations. A further cooling usually takes place when people are asked for suggestions as to what should be done. In the report it is often also possible to help people to realize that what to each of two people appears as unreasonable behaviour by the other is a consequence of a vicious spiral that has developed. Thus a head of department complained that members of his department were constantly being asked

Table 7.1 *Structure for analysis meetings*

(a)	Explain that the purpose of the interview is: (i) to obtain a more complete picture of the school and its workings; (ii) to seek the views of the interviewee on ways in which the operation of the school could be improved; (iii) to discuss the particular problems and opportunities in the interviewee's own area.
(b)	Explain that information received will be fed back without reference to source.
(c)	Explore the role of the interviewee: (i) organizational relationships (departmental, pastoral, head of year). (ii) problems caused by the relationships (action taken, action planned, action needed); (iii) how personal success is measured by the interviewee and by others; (iv) use of time; (v) changes anticipated; (vi) changes needed; (vii) aims and ambitions; (viii) frustrations and what could be done.
(d)	Explore views on the school in total: (i) what are the major opportunities, problems, changes? (ii) what key events illustrate these? (iii) what actions have been taken, are planned, are still needed?
(e)	Ask for any remaining issues or suggestions that the interviewee would like to bring to your notice.
(f)	Check whether there are any matters which have been discussed about which the feedback should be handled sensitively.
(g)	Explain what will, to the best of your knowledge, be the next steps in the process and seek views.

directly by the deputy head, and without the head of department's knowledge, to undertake certain jobs which often interfered with their departmental activities. The deputy head, on the other hand, said that the members of Mr X's department were often frustrated because Mr X tried to run his department as a capsule with each person's attention focused solely on departmental activities. She was now making an effort to remedy this. Clearly the point had been reached where the more the deputy did to involve members of Mr X's department in non-departmental tasks, the more Mr X would close the doors, and vice versa.

My experience is that most reports are well received as being an accurate picture of what is taking place. Obvious references to the foibles of individuals or groups become acceptable to those concerned because they are set in a context of everyone else's problems and weaknesses, and the clear purpose is not to attack but to solve.

After discussion of the report with the head, I would normally advise that it should be circulated to all members of staff, or at least to all who were interviewed, with an invitation to comment on any inaccuracies, omissions or wrong emphasis. They can also be invited to contribute any suggestions that they wish to make at this point. In practice there has generally been only positive comment in response.

Whereas phases A and B are standard, many variants are possible from now on. In an industrial context it is common practice to organize a series of seminars to cover all concerned staff (a classic *phase C*). Often these will last for one week and participants will work in groups which are as mixed as possible in hierarchical levels and functions. There will then be some theory but, above all, practical exercises to enable the development of skills in managing:

(a) communications;

(b) relationships;
(c) meetings;
(d) delegation;
(e) conflict.

There may also be some work on identification of problems across the organization (that is, interdepartmental) with suggestions for solutions.

Following training there may then be a series of reviews by members of work teams possibly using a structure such as the one discussed below.

My experience of schools is that they do not yet appreciate the value of giving a common in-depth training to all members of staff in order to reap the considerable payoff that can result from deliberate application to school problems. Within schools, therefore, a consultant probably has to rely on:

(a) a thorough briefing of the leading person in a review meeting, that is, the head at school level—this briefing will cover how the meeting is to be conducted and above all the need to avoid falling into the trap of attack/defence;
(b) some briefing of all other participants:
    (i) a clear meeting structure;
    (ii) the consultant's presence to prompt the participants if they move into negative attitudes or if the structure and discipline of the meeting are being lost.

At *phase D* the crucial element is a meeting structure which ensures that all the controversial issues are put on the table in as objective a way as possible and dealt with systematically. In *Effective School Management*, Everard and Morris (1985, p. 256) set out a structure which has been found very effective within schools. It asks the individual staff members before attending a review meeting to compare how things are with how they would like them to be, under the headings of:

(a) decision-taking;
(b) communication;
(c) new ideas;
(d) relationship with other groups;
(e) review;
(f) objectives;
(g) planning;
(h) commitment;
(i) responsibility;
(j) use of resources.

It also asks the individuals to write down their three priority areas for improvement.

The headings in this particular structure are generalized, but they can be varied to suit the specific case addressed by the consultant. The value is that a review meeting can begin by having an agenda of individual views which means that issues cannot be avoided. Frequently, meetings will in fact say that they do not need to discuss the very issues which prove to be the most vital.

As meaningful discussion is impossible in large meetings, it will be necessary either to have a hierarchy of reviews or to have the staff work simultaneously in groups which may take various forms according to the needs of the organization. In one example, proposals for improvement were initially developed in cross-departmental groups and, after presentation, were then considered in departmental groups. At a subsequent meeting they were finalized by the head, the deputy and the top team. While various options are again possible, the most effective method for such reviews has proved in my experience to be that the head runs the discussions and the consultant runs the 'process'.

The effect of most review meetings is euphoric since staff feel that they have at last been able to tackle longstanding behavioural problems in a new, more open and objective way and that issues have been resolved with less acrimony than was feared. However, it is now vitally important to turn good intentions into firm action plans and to follow them up.

Phase E (follow-up) is critical. Without it, all else appears in vain. Clients often feel that they can now manage unaided—as should, indeed, be the case—but almost invariably the consultant needs to play the role of Jiminy Cricket and prod the client's conscience periodically.

During the review phase the three most difficult tasks of the consultant are:

(a)   to make sure that a detailed action plan is written down (preferably on a flipchart for all to see), saying who must do what by when;

(b)   to make sure that a clear date, or series of dates, are set to review progress;

(c)   to make sure that the action plan and dates are minuted to all concerned and that the review dates are faithfully observed.

Unfortunately, I cannot claim that schools have been sufficiently disciplined to follow through all that has been planned. In common with most organizations they suffer from the syndrome of being so preoccupied with pressures, crises and detail that they do not take the time to sort themselves out and prioritize so as to reduce the day-to-day pressures.

However, the effects of getting even as far as a review meeting are dramatic and relationships are fundamentally changed for the better. In one case at least, a head who was on the verge of a breakdown and resignation was re-established and became highly effective once more.

USING A CATALYTIC/PARTICIPATIVE APPROACH TO IMPROVING ORGANIZATIONAL PERFORMANCE

In the 'behavioural' approach discussed above, the consultant can be said to be a 'catalyst' and to 'participate' in solving behavioural problems within the school. However, there is a distinct consultancy approach which, in drawing on many of the techniques of both behavioural and directive consultancy, focuses primarily on helping the client to improve performance against organizational objectives.

Variation in size and complexity of projects is infinite. Clients may or may not have a clear idea of what they wish to achieve from the consultancy. They may wish in the school context to find a formula to ensure the continuing viability of an independent school; they may wish to review administrative procedures; they may be concerned at a loss of staff morale; they may wish to review curriculum. Some of these problems could suggest a directive approach, others a behavioural approach. In fact, all of them could be tackled by either of the approaches, so that, for example, an entrenched behavioural consultant might tackle even a review of administrative procedures by asking staff members how they 'felt' about them without necessarily focusing on the purpose of the procedures. He would probably find a mass of relationship problems behind apparent procedural defects and would achieve an improvement in the eyes of the staff by solving them.

The phases in a catalytic approach are basically the same as in the other approaches. However, there are many more possible variants.

At *phase A* (analysis) the client may, as we have said, already have a clear view of the change desired. Discussion with other involved staff may be more or less detailed, but what is clear is that the consultant will be concerned with what the school, the department and the individual are trying to achieve, how that achievement can be measured or judged and how improvement could be made against the criteria. They will discuss the resources available (financial, material, skills) and the experience, knowledge and skill of the interviewee.

Catalytic consultancy works on the well-proven principle that people who do not understand a subject or a proposal do not admit their ignorance; they just say 'no'. The consultant is therefore keen to discover training needs rather than to make proposals.

The *phase B* feedback may well contain proposals for customized training simulating activities which are tailored as precisely as possible to the in-school situation. School-teachers often have a very weak understanding of finance and are therefore badly placed to judge or make the case for investment. In independent schools therefore the head and the bursar can be lone voices (sometimes only the bursar) who speak a language incomprehensible to the rest of the staff who are consequently frustrated. In discussing the use of computers for school administration, discussion on efficiency can be further complicated by a 'buff' who knows only BBC micros and who insists on designing his own administrative programs in BASIC.

What is critically important therefore is to ensure that recommendations are kept strictly within the limits of what the decision-taker understands. If he needs a greater depth of understanding in order to make a meaningful decision and to be in control, the recommendation should be to train him.

In *phase C* (preparation) it is implicit from the above that this phase can be expected to concentrate on the build-up of confidence in techniques which could be relevant, so that the school staff—not the consultant—will be able to choose and 'drive' the use of these techniques. Some behavioural skills may also need to be taught.

For *phase D* (problem-solving), in the same 'workshops' or at a separate event or events staff members should be given as many hard facts as possible—possibly also some perceptions—about the current situation and asked to contribute suggestions. On the basis of these, the decision-taker can set out a new policy and action plan.

Phase E (follow-up) is likely to be less difficult to achieve than in a purely behavioural approach as far as the technical aspects are concerned, though there may well also be some 'behavioural' elements which may slip even further because of the excuse that 'at least we have set up and are operating system X'.

SPECIAL PROBLEMS AND OPPORTUNITIES RELATING TO SCHOOLS

To a consultant, most of the differences between working with industry and schools lie not in the nature of the organizations and the relationships, but in experience and attitudes in relation to consultancy, training and finance.

Industry has a long history of using consultants and most managers have experience of working with consultants. Over the period 1971–81 the industrial training boards ensured that organizations—ironically to the exclusion of the educational sector— systematically examined their training needs and developed the necessary skills to improve performance. Those working in companies have always understood that survival depends on performing well.

The culture of schools is very different and attitudes of many teachers are positively opposed to anything that smacks of industry. Among the phenomena I have met are:

(a)   a resentment of the notion that teachers and schools ought to try to perform better. This has been exacerbated by the appalling way in which appraisal was presented to teachers as a process designed to weed out the inefficient;

(b)   a resistance to the concept of 'skills' which teachers strongly associate with manual activity or robot-like performance of industrially 'useful' tasks. The distinction between education and training, knowledge and skill is seen as one between higher-level and lower-level activity rather than as the distinction between theory and practical ability whether mental or manual.

However, on the positive side is the ready response of teachers once the consultant has succeeded in showing that he understands their problems and needs and can relate his techniques to the school situation.

REFERENCE

Everard, K. B. and Morris, G. (1985) *Effective School Management*. London: Harper and Row.

Chapter 8

Developing Consultants in Industry

Geoffrey Sworder

A few years ago, when I was working as a change agent in ICI (from which I retired in 1985), I was contacted by the company's Schools Liaison Officer, Bob Finch, who asked whether I thought ICI had any help which could be given to those schoolteachers who were being moved into advisory positions as part of the Schools Council Industry Project (SCIP). These people were being given the job of influencing the curricula of individual schools within a specific local authority area, in order to increase the amount of learning about industry in schools, and to improve the quality and relevance of this learning. It was expected, and early experience had already shown, that this task would not be easy, even with the incumbent being recruited from within the teaching profession. The request to ICI was therefore whether there was some skill training which we possessed which could be used in these circumstances. My reaction was to put forward the possibility of using what ICI calls 'influencing skills' training—a programme which had been developed around 1970 by ICI and a firm of consultants, Sheppard Moscow and Associates (SMA).

This programme consists of a series of experiential events, interspersed with theory inputs, which follow the sequence of a systematic influence process from making the initial contact through to achieving successful and lasting change. It culminates in a full day simulation of an organization on which all programme participants have to carry out a diagnosis and then attempt to influence towards improvement.

In discussion with Sue Holmes (then Director of SCIP) and Ian Jamieson (then Research Director), it was agreed that this programme, in a form modified to suit the SCIP situation, would be used, and that Sue and Ian, together with about 12 SCIP coordinators, would be participants. The programme was run jointly by myself and Bryan Calvert (then also working for ICI, but now retired) and was judged successful by the participants, particularly in the light of their subsequent experience (a report on this event was subsequently written by Ian Jamieson).

I have written at some length about this project, because:

(a) it was my first and main contact with the world of schools;
(b) it was successful, and led to further development work with teachers by Bryan Calvert.

(c)   it showed that at least some of the change skills developed in industry are relevant to schools.

It is, however, essential to place the 'influencing skills' material in context with other skills developed and used in ICI and elsewhere in industry, in order to understand the activities of organizational consultants. To do this, it is necessary to describe the history of organization consultancy in ICI and the training which has been developed to enable such consultants to operate effectively.

ICI began experimenting in the 1960s with some of the behavioural science research results and theories, which were in the main being produced in the United States by people such as Herzberg, McGregor, Maslow and Argyris—most of whom were brought over to the United Kingdom by ICI at one time or another as consultants. Partly as a result of this exposure, and of visits by a number of senior ICI staff to the United States to see what was being done there, an ambitious series of programmes was initiated to change the culture, structure, and working systems of ICI in ways that were expected to lead to improvement in productivity at all levels and thereby make ICI more competitive worldwide than it was currently.

The first of these programmes, launched in 1965, was called 'Manpower Utilization and Payment Structure' (MUPS for short), subsequently becoming the 'Weekly Staff Agreement' or WSA. Weekly paid staff in ICI could at that time loosely be called 'blue-collar' or 'shop-floor' staff, as distinct from monthly-paid staff who were mostly 'white-collar'. This programme was an ultimately successful attempt to draw out the contributions of staff at the lower levels of the organization, reduce the number of restrictive work practices between members of different unions, and reduce the number of levels of supervisors and junior managers. The attraction of the programme to those affected was mainly in the improved wage rates offered in return for these changes, but also, less tangibly, in the more interesting and less supervised work which staff at these levels would do.

A second programme, which was launched in 1969 and called the 'Staff Development Programme' (SDP for short), was aimed at 'white-collar' staff at levels up to, but not including, senior management (defined as the top 200 or so managers in the United Kingdom). This programme had similar principles to MUPS/WSA in that it set out to increase productivity by releasing the latent contributions of junior and middle level staff and managers, partly by means of a similar financial inducement of increased salary rates, but mainly by the use of organization development techniques.

The development techniques used involved a substantial amount of group discussion to elicit ideas for improvement, not just in productivity, but also in quality, organization structure, and to suggest better ways of working. Specific training packages widely used at this time were Managerial Grid (to improve management style), Coverdale (to improve group problem-solving), and a variety of self-awareness training methods ranging from T-groups to less searching programmes.

It was during this period of the late 1960s and early 1970s that it became evident that using external consultants (who were still largely from the United States) had no chance of meeting the expanding needs of ICI. The requirement was for a substantial cadre of people who could act as facilitators of group discussions, training staff on internal programmes such as those described above, and advisers to middle and senior managers on how to develop the effectiveness of their sections or departments. In addition to the fact that there were insufficient external consultants to carry out these tasks (and their cost would have been very high even if they had been available), there were significant benefits to be obtained from developing internal consultants. The main benefit, in addition to availability and lower cost, was their knowledge of the organization, its culture and systems, and therefore their potential ability to become more useful more quickly than a stranger from outside the organization. Against this had to be set the problem of escaping from a previous role in order to be seen as an unbiased third party.

The first few 'agents of change' of this kind were developed partly by working with the early external consultants, and partly by going on external consultant development programmes, of which the most significant was the Program for Specialists in Organization Development Technology (PSODT) at the National Training Laboratories (NTL) in Bethel, Maine, USA. It soon became obvious, however, that a larger number of change agents needed to be trained, and that an internal ICI programme was required. In addition, this training should be done in a British context, rather than American, as even at that time it was becoming clear that organization development in a British culture was somewhat different from in an American one.

Two such programmes were organized in 1970, led by Dick Beckhard from the United States, with staff teams including such well-known names as Harvey Hornstein, Warner Burke, Roger Harrison, Herb Shepard (all from the United States), Gurth Higgin, Colin Sheppard and many others. To make it economic, participants were drawn from a variety of companies as well as ICI, particularly Shell, but including Tube Investments, Procter and Gamble, Rolls-Royce and others. These two programmes each lasted for four weeks, with 40 participants (about two-thirds from ICI) and included:

(a) extensive self-awareness training by T-group method;
(b) training in organization diagnosis;
(c) experience in group facilitation;
(d) exploration of theories, principles and strategies of organizational behaviour, planned change, and organization development.

The first of these programmes was extensively researched by Alan Dale and Olga Khaleelee, then of London Business School (LBS), and written up by them in an LBS report (Khaleelee and Dale, 1970).

The effects of these two programmes were to produce within ICI a substantial cadre (around 50) of internal consultants who had been exposed to a similar experience and therefore were likely to operate in similar ways; to increase the confidence of participants in operating as change agents; to provide them with a substantial repertoire of technology in organization development; and finally to give them some legitimacy among line managers in operating as a change consultant. As a participant in the first of these programmes, I certainly found it an enormous help in getting going as an internal consultant, and although some participants had different experiences, or never had the opportunity to practise because they went back into line management roles, the overall value of the programme was undoubtedly high.

Over subsequent years of the 1970s, the cadre was supplemented by others who either developed organically, or were trained on external programmes in the United States (particularly at Columbia), or in Shell (who had subsequently developed their own internal programme), and the role of internal consultant developed in a variety of ways according to the capabilities, orientations, and opportunities of individuals.

By the late 1970s, organization development had become part of the management process in many of the product divisions of ICI in the United Kingdom (organizations ranging in size from 1000 to more than 10 000 staff), and was beginning to spread to some of the overseas subsidiaries. At the same time, the original cadre of internal change agents was shrinking by natural processes of retirement and moving to other jobs, both within and outside the company. The director on the ICI Main Board responsible for organization and change at that time was John Harvey-Jones (subsequently Chairman), and he was sufficiently concerned about the disparity between shrinking resources and growing demand to initiate a study of the situation. This led to setting up a new series of training programmes to produce more change agents, the first of which was run in 1981, organized by Arthur Johnston, who was then the most senior and experienced internal resource.

By this time, however, views had changed somewhat about what kind of internal resources were needed. The earlier and simpler concept of a substantial cadre of highly trained full-time internal consultants had now developed into a wider concept, requiring the development of:

(a)   a small number (perhaps a maximum of one in each product division) of highly trained and experienced resources of the original kind, capable of acting as centres of excellence and experience, and able to work at the most senior levels in their operating units, at least providing a service to individual division directors, if not to a divisional board as a group;

(b)   a much larger number of people, being those in staff roles particularly (but not exclusively) personnel, training, and management services, provided with a significant understanding of organizational change and substantial skills in facilitating such change. Nowadays these roles are much more, if not wholly, about change rather than about maintaining the status quo;

(c)   a capability in most, if not all, line managers to be their own managers of change, as the rate of change was now such that few, if any, managers were likely to be in static situations for long.

The first three programmes, run in 1981 and 1982, and lasting two weeks each, were aimed at categories (b) and (c) above, in approximately equal proportions overall, and a few places were also made available to external organizations, usually through contacts who were ex-ICI people now in senior positions (this brought in participants from British Nuclear Fuels and Remploy) or through existing relationships with, for example, the National Health Service. At the same time, a series of trainees began to arrive from ICI subsidiary companies overseas, in particular Malaysia and India.

The design of these programmes was broadly in three parts:

(a)   a period during which participants look at themselves, their existing skills, and the developing requirements of their jobs;

(b)   a period spent learning about organizations and change, and acquiring skills in facilitating change;

(c)   a period spent carrying out a real change project in an existing organization, with guidance.

There is no doubt these programmes were very successful in raising the capability and confidence of participants in handling or helping with change situations, as judged by their subsequent experience. During the same period, however, a parallel initiative had been taken to provide change management capability to the much larger number of line managers who were not able to find places on this two week programme, or did not feel they could afford as large an investment of time. This initiative was (and still is) the running of short 'management of change workshops' for line managers facing current change situations, based on material developed by Dick Beckhard, much of it during his work (still continuing) within ICI. Most of his material is described in Beckhard and Harris (1977), but it has been extensively developed within ICI in a variety of ways. (There is also a video package marketed by Addison-Wesley, starring Dick Beckhard.) The key elements of these short programmes for managers are:

(a) managers come with real, current, change situations, on which they work during the programme;
(b) the problems must be sufficiently under their control so that they can have a significant impact on them;
(c) they normally come as a pair of managers (or more) who share the problem;
(d) they work through their problem using:

   (i)   a problem-solving model of change;
   (ii) pieces of change technology given to them bit by bit as the problem-solving process proceeds;
   (iii) help from the programme staff, who are all experienced change consultants.

(e) the programmes do not intend to achieve complete or tidy problem solutions, as there is often insufficient time for this, nor would it necessarily be desirable (as other people are likely to need to be involved in the solution process); they are however intended to achieve a substantial step forward;
(f) managers do learn change concepts and techniques which they can and do use again on subsequent problems;
(g) the programme can be (and is) used at any level from Main Board directors to first line supervisors.

A large number of these events has been run over the years, both in the United Kingdom and overseas, again with positive results as judged by participants and by demand for repeats, and have therefore contributed substantially to the need for raising the capability of line managers to handle change.

After the completion of the first three of the new series of two week 'change resource development programmes' (as they came to be known), Arthur Johnston retired from ICI and the opportunity was taken to review the need for these events, and their design. As a result of this review, it was decided that:

(a) It was necessary to continue providing such events, as there was an unsatisfied demand for them, particularly from overseas subsidiary companies;
(b) it was necessary, reluctantly, to concentrate on training people in staff roles, rather than line managers, as in this way it was possible to make a significant impact on the skills of this segment of the target population which only numbered several hundred, whereas it was not possible with the thousands of line managers

(who were in any case being addressed by the 'management of change workshops' described earlier);

(c)   the limited number of highly trained and experienced resources left in ICI who could staff these events required ICI to call on external resources to help with the design and management of the programme—this was expected to be a beneficial move in any case, by widening the range of professional contribution;

(d)   it would be useful to draw some participants from non-ICI companies in order to reduce the possibility of a narrow approach to change being developed.

The result of these decisions was that the next three programmes, in 1985 and 1986, were designed and managed jointly by myself and a representative of Sheppard Moscow and Associates (SMA), the organization development consultants mentioned earlier in connection with influencing skills training. A majority of participants were still from ICI, but a variety of non-ICI people were drawn from clients of SMA, the main criterion for selection being that the participant's organization was judged as being able and ready to make good use of a trained resource.

At this point it is worth giving some details of the design of the programme, so that the qualities developed in the participants can be judged. The objectives of the event are that by the end of the programme participants will have:

(a)   learned concepts which aid understanding how organizations work and how their capability can be diagnosed;

(b)   learned about the dynamics of change in organizations;

(c)   learned about the ways in which power is used in organizations;

(d)   practised some skills as a facilitator of change;

(e)   gained increased self-awareness;

(f)   developed personal application plans relevant to their own situation.

The pattern of training used to achieve these objectives is as follows.

The first two days are spent on what we call 'self-awareness development'. We have found over the years that this is an essential beginning to any resource development programme, and that two days is the minimum amount of time needed to get participants to a point where they have examined realistically:

(a)   the positions they hold in their organizations and the opportunities they have for initiating and facilitating change;

(b)   their own skills, attitudes, and values, and how far these are helpful or not to the tasks with which they are now faced.

During this period they are exposed to, and thereby learn how to use, a number of concepts and techniques for developing individuals and groups. At the end, they often have a different perception of themselves and their future tasks than the one they came with.

The next five days are spent on a variety of topics concerning organizations and how they work, with a particular emphasis on acquiring skills in facilitating beneficial change. These topics include:

(1)   A whole day on the nature of organizations, and how to diagnose their effectiveness in meeting their objectives. This day is structured mostly around the work of Nadler (Nadler and Tushman, 1980), and involves using a fairly complex case study

which allows participants to practise using Nadler's framework. This encourages them to look at more aspects of an organization than they would have done in the past—in particular, the formal and informal organizational arrangements used to transform inputs into outputs. Some time is also spent on examining dimensions of organization culture and how to diagnose them, using the work of Roger Harrison (unpublished), Schein (1984), and Hofstede (1984).

(2)   A day on the nature of change in organizations and how to manage it. This is based on the Beckhard/ICI work referred to earlier in this chapter, and takes the participants through this technology and how to use it with line managers. At the end of this day, participants should be able to help staff a 'management of change workshop' as well as use pieces of the technology when needed. The vehicle for this day, as always with this material, is a live change problem which each participant wants help with back at work.

(3)   A day on the dynamics of intergroup situations. This is done by setting up a simulation in which two groups have a common task which has to be achieved by communication between the groups using messengers. This creates most of the effects of intergroup cooperation and conflict, and enables people to experience and analyse these at first hand. They are also provided with some techniques for resolving inter-group or interdepartmental conflict which have been successfully used in a variety of situations.

(4)   A day on the dynamics of team-working, and how to achieve improvement, either as a team member or, more particularly, as a team facilitator. Two of the most useful concepts and techniques used at this time are those of Belbin's team roles (Belbin, 1981) and Coverdale's systematic approach.

(5)   A day learning the skills of being an effective influencer, particularly in one-to-one situations. This day is taken from the 'influencing skills programme' referred to at the beginning of this chapter in connection with the work done for SCIP. The process used is to work on real influence problems in trios of client/consultant/observer, where the consultant is trying to exert influence over the client concerning the client's own problems about influencing someone else. This day is deliberately set at the end of this section, so that it immediately precedes the project section, described below, during which skills of influence are particularly needed.

The next two days are spent working, usually in pairs, on real influence projects at organizations within convenient reach of the centre where the programme is running. These projects are identified in advance as appropriate for the kind of learning the participants have had during the programme, and the majority of them are not in ICI nor even in the chemical industry. Frequent providers of projects have been schools, local authorities, hospitals, police forces, and charitable bodies, who have welcomed the opportunity to have a short study of their organization's problem by an outside team. The value of these projects to the organizations is shown by the number of requests we get for further projects from the same organization or from people in the same occupation and district. The main purpose of these projects is to provide a live learning opportunity for the pair of change agents in training, with guidance from experienced tutors. The design of the two-day project period is:

(a)   the trainees are given a brief written project description;
(b)   they then meet one or more members of the client organization for about an hour,

when they hear more details of the problem, and what has been arranged for them at the organization's site (this first meeting is held at the programme venue);

(c)   they spend a whole day at the organization collecting data by interviewing members of staff;

(d)   they have half a day to prepare their conclusions and a short presentation to the organization's managers;

(e)   the last half day is spent reviewing the project experience.

Each pair of trainees is assigned a tutor, who is always an experienced consultant. The pairs are obliged to keep their consultant informed about their plans and any difficulties they are having. They are also required to go through their review process using a laid-down format of questions, and to discuss their review with their consultant.

The project period is undoubtedly the high spot of the programme, as it generates an enormous amount of energy and enthusiasm. It also increases the confidence of the trainees in their ability to influence change, and gives them feedback from their partner and tutor on their methods and style which is difficult if not impossible to obtain subsequently.

The penultimate day of the programme is known as 'cafeteria day', as it consists of a series of two-hour sessions running concurrently as well as consecutively, provided by eight or more experienced consultants who describe and discuss specific projects and/or pieces of technology with which they have been involved. Participants choose beforehand which of these sessions they wish to attend, and the small groups thereby achieved allow them to go into some depth with the visitors about their experience and methods. This day is intended to widen the trainees' knowledge of activities and technology in the field, and also to tap them into a network of experienced change agents which they well need to exploit in the future.

The last day of the programme is designed to get the participants thinking about and planning for their re-entry into their back-home situation. A framework is provided for them to examine their work situation in the light of the learning from the two weeks, to plan what they need to do on return, and what help they may need to achieve it. This process is always an essential one at the end of programmes of this kind, in order to ensure that there is a clear link between the programme learning and the real life to which participants are returning.

The programme as a whole is designed and managed by experienced change consultants, rather than trainers, as are the individual parts. This is done deliberately in order to ensure that inputs and activities are directed by people who can speak from their own direct experience as agents of change, even if this means that sometimes the training methods are not quite as elegant as they might be if trainers rather than consultants were used. The learning methods used in the programme are substantially experiential, as would be expected from a skill training programme, although there is a significant amount of interspersed input on organizational and behavioural theory and concepts.

By the nature of the programme's length and high staff/participant ratio, it is expensive to run. Because many of the staff are internal ICI resources, their cost is not fully charged; if they were, the cost of the programme would be higher, whereas at the moment it compares favourably with external programmes at reputable training establishments. The need for such training, however, clearly exists both within ICI and comparable commercial organizations which are undergoing significant change (as nearly all are), and also within other kinds of organization such as the National Health Service which are non-profit-making (the NHS has its own internal programme for this purpose). I would be very surprised if educational institutions, whether primary, secondary, or tertiary, did not have similar needs for managing change and therefore for trained resources to help with this process. I hope ICI's experience will provide some pointers towards how this can be achieved.

REFERENCES

Beckhard, R. and Harris, R. T. (1977) *Organisational Transitions—Managing Complex Change*. Reading, Mass.: Addison-Wesley.

Belbin, R. M. (1981) *Management Teams: Why They Succeed or Fail*. London: Heinemann.

Hofstede, G. (1984) *Culture's Consequences*. Beverly Hills, CA: Sage.

Khaleelee, O. and Dale, A. J. (1970) Research Report to London Graduate School of Business Studies.

Nadler, D. A. and Tushman, M. L. (1980) 'A model for diagnosing organisational behaviour'. *Organisational Dynamics*, **Autumn**, 35–51.

Schein, E. H. (1984) 'Coming to a new awareness of organisational culture'. *Sloan Management Review*, **Summer**, 3–15.

Part III

Within the School

The acid test of ideas about management consultancy is whether they can be applied or not and it is natural to look for examples or case studies. Most management consultancy in schools involves a great deal of related training and personal development. For the most part schools do not present the consultant with a problem and then sit back until they receive an answer (though as Bertie Everard reminds us in his chapter in Part One many schools would benefit from some straightforward practical advice in this way). Generally they wish to become actively involved in the change process and work alongside the consultant.

Probably quite a lot of schools have used consultants for brief periods or involved some local expert in a project but few schools have a sustained commitment to working with an outside professional for a considerable period. Yet it can be done and will become increasingly done as schools gain confidence in their own management processes and see outside skills and resources not as a threat but as complementary to the skills and resources within the school.

Harold Heller (Chapter 9) has had considerable experience of long-term working with management consultants from industry with a group of schools. The approach involved working with seconded management development trainers from ICI who conducted training workshops for heads in order to develop strategies for school development. As leader of a team of LEA advisers, he understands very well the opportunities for advisers as well as the pitfalls associated with their position as local authority employees. Certainly, the role of LEA advisers is undergoing a sea change and they will have to learn new skills and new philosophies as schools continue to develop towards being self-directed institutions. The chapter points up the ways in which local advisers can help schools but in so doing underlines just how many opportunities are missed because the advisory service is organized as it is in so many LEAs.

Stanley Putnam (Chapter 10) graduated from being a key client in a quite major management development process in the school of which he was head to being a trainer of other heads in management and organization development (OD) skills. He writes about the ways in which a school can continue to maintain the momentum to change after the engagement period of a consultant has been concluded. He shows how necessary it is for ownership of continuing renewal to fall to the members of the school and how the training programme may be continued. The self-directed, self-renewing, fully functioning, self-actualizing school—to introduce some of the jargon terms of humanistic psychology, applied to institutions rather than individuals—can only come into existence by an effort of will and determination to continue the development process within the school. Presumably this is what most teachers would want.

Don Musella (Chapter 11) provides a Canadian perspective of how consultants can actively help principals to develop fresh approaches to school organization and management. In this North American account one can detect a different climate for consultants in schools from the United Kingdom. There is clearly a more accepting and sophisticated climate for employing consultants that arises partly (perhaps even largely) from the fact that principals in North America as a whole see themselves as administrators over and above being teachers. Hence they see their role as a true management role free of the duality many British heads experience of being teacher and head. Musella writes from wide experience as a consultant and trainer from a management standpoint and offers no apology for not being a teacher as one so often feels UK writers do. In Canada, the executive function of the head is taken a good deal more seriously than is often the case in the United Kingdom.

Ian Jamieson (Chapter 12) writes about consultancy with a curriculum focus. The importance of this chapter is that it shows that management skills are essential everywhere in the system. Curriculum change has to be managed, and management skills are the skills of helping people and organizations to change. There is a danger—and in the United Kingdom the TVEI (Technical and Vocational Education Initiative) illustrates this—that every new fashion will be given its measure of 'management' training as if there were no central management needs and as if 'management' was just peculiar to each venture. Management is always about something; you cannot manage nothing, and in schools management involves people (teachers, students, parents, etc.), the curriculum and the 'technology' that permits the curriculum to be implemented. Many teachers misunderstand the nature of 'management' and assume it has nothing to do with teaching whereas the reverse is the case—management has everything to do with teaching. Jamieson shows this relationship very clearly through his explanation of strategies for managing change and introducing innovation.

The last chapter in this part (13) deals with organization development (OD) approaches to management consultancy in helping schools to change by drawing on the personal resources that they already have. Mike Lavelle and David Keith describe how the OD unit was set up by the Sheffield Education Department, what its principles are and how it works with heads and schools. The term OD—in its English context at least—refers to a coordinated and systematic process of helping an organization to become self-renewing by working with the people within it to help them to find greater fulfilment in their membership and to increase personal reward by improving the effectiveness of the organization. The point about OD is that it tries to bring the relationship between people and organization into harmony. It differs from most other approaches to management development in that it does not concentrate on a single aspect such as subjects, 'curriculum', finance, profitability, technological innovation, marketing or whatever. Although surprisingly neglected in education, OD is probably the most potent mode for bringing about sympathetic change than any other process—certainly more than the authoritarian processes that are most commonly used within institutions.

Chapter 9

The Advisory Service and Consultancy

Harold Heller

INTRODUCTION

This chapter argues that the advisory and inspectorate role in English and Welsh LEAs had reached, by the mid 1980s, a point of critical change after almost a century of sporadic and largely unplanned growth (the accounts given by Pearce (1986) and Winkley (1985) although largely anecdotal, accurately depict the idiosyncratic flavour of this development). The accretion of diverse and sometimes contradictory functions, as the Education Service became more complex over the last 20 years, has led to a profound and sometimes debilitating conflict of roles for advisers. This has, somewhat simplistically, been characterized as a clash between the supportive/developmental role and the monitoring/line-management function. It does, however, seem evident that the traditional *laissez-faire* model of support is increasingly impotent to resist central pressures for accountability in the service and that more responsive, flexible yet politically astute styles will need to be developed. It will be argued that the range of skills, perceptions, understandings and strategies usually associated with 'the consultant' may prove one of the most useful core components of any emerging style and that the shift to this model will entail considerable self-review and reorientation by advisers. The training and development implications of these role-shifts will also be analysed.

THE CURRENT POSITION

As has been implied above, the study of LEA advisory services has received no more than discursive attention until the last 15 years, with a particular burst of interest in the very recent past. The Bristol University study of 1972–76 by Bolam *et al.* (1976) was the first research to take a perspective on advisers in the context of LEA wide and national developments; the first to treat advisers as 'agents for change' with an interventionist role within the system and the first to recognize that a set of functions might be emerging which were 'system-wide' and transcended the particularities of the allegedly decentralized LEAs. The 1974 Local Government reorganization [Maud Report, 1969] had led many (including the Department of Education and Science) to advocate coherence and team-design as a principle for the structure of advisory services and a relevant example of this thinking is the paper jointly owned by the Society of Education Officers and the Advisers' professional association[1] which sought to underline the collegial, evaluatory and coordinating qualities of teams, as distinct from the individualistic or maverick specialist roles common before reorganization. Such papers tend to be over-rational and idealized, bearing little resemblance to the messy and fluid patchwork of most advisory contexts. The latest crop of research and discussion does, however, engage more realistically with the stress and lack of fit experienced by advisers in the face of growing complexity of organization, uncertainty of resources and policies, and an imperative for accountability at both ends of the political continuum.

The impetus for these more recent explorations of the adviser's function seems to have both intrinsic and extrinsic origins. This is neatly borne out by the authorship of the more influential pieces. The two works quoted at the beginning of this chapter (Winkley, 1985, and Pearce, 1986) are respectively by a head teacher and an LEA senior inspector: the important DES papers on LEA advisory and inspectorate services[2] was put together by a joint group from the DES and the local authority associations: the major NFER study of advisers to be published in 1988, which will offer the first comprehensive research into advisory roles and functions, is NFER funded and LEA monitored.

In fact, it might be claimed that this ferment of interest in advisers in the mid-1980s arose to a large extent from the policies of a Conservative government, which was set on limiting the power of LEAs and scrutinizing quality in more stringent ways. The internal government 'Rayner report' on HMI (Her Majesty's Inspectorate) had shown the important interface between that force and local advisers; the annual expenditure and quality surveys by HMI began to use the range and numbers of advisers as a benchmark for assessing LEA competence; the cost and quality conscious Secretary of State and other ministers began to recognize publicly[3] the potential of advisers as change-agents and guarantors of standards. In some metropolitan LEAs newer left-oriented administrations, coming to power with radical manifestos, either saw advisers as factors for conservatism and sought to marginalize them, or attempted to transform their role (often through new posts and appointments) with much more dynamic job-specifications.

The contrasts of these multiple perspectives of the same scene may be briefly illustrated.

A 1981 research survey (Williams, quoted by Pearce, 1986, p. 125) of six LEAs' advisory forces observed 'a cadre of inspectors in a stressful situation and experiencing increasing frustration over a self-perceived inability to maintain an appropriate balance between office and field-work'.

Winkley (1985, p. 220) identifies 'the lack of any close and convincing analysis of advisory functions, their ever-increasing shift to generality and diversity of function where specificity and specialism seem actually most effective and most needed'.

These actuality-based observations may be contrasted with bland statements from corporate, central sources: 'Expenditure on advisers is an investment, and an adviser's influence for good can be out of proportion to what he or she costs'.[4]

The purpose of an educational advisory service is to promote high standards of attainment, not only in basic studies such as literacy and numeracy, but also in education in its widest sense for pupils and students in maintained educational establishments.[5]

The striking contrasts of these positions now lead us into an examination of whether a coherent professional definition is possible.

THE SEARCH FOR A PROFESSIONAL DEFINITION

These quotations will have indicated the gulf between the idealized picture given by employers and professional associations and the 'insider' perspective with a more gritty and cynical experience of the adviser's work. What seems to be emerging from the field-work of the NFER study is a surprising variation in the range and priority of advisers' work tasks:

> These differences mean that the concept of the 'average adviser' and that of the 'list of tasks' undertaken by the average adviser are both very difficult to sustain.
>
> (Stillman and Grant, 1987)

These variations are borne out by the writer's own experience both as Chief Adviser in a fairly large LEA and in the adviser training role where liaison with a wide range of LEAs reveals significant and often arbitrary deviations from any hypothetical list of functions. These differences are not merely cosmetic; they may be structural, in a deep sense, and critically condition the effectiveness of the advisory team and its impact on the service.

A complicating factor has been the status of adviser as 'transitional agent', a role which is fraught in any complex organization with profound ambiguities. In the case of the education service this is intensified by the 'loose coupling' of the system, with its many quasi-autonomous elements and groups with whom the advisory team is assumed to maintain some organic, coordinating role (LEA members; school governors; head-teachers; Her Majesty's Inspectorate; parents; teachers' unions and professional bodies as well as office-based administrators).

At the heart of this lie issues of power and authority, which I will explore more closely in the next section. Yet, two other concepts may be introduced which I have found helpful in addressing the sometimes confused world of the contemporary adviser. The first is the notion of functional elasticity: a phrase which seems to me to describe the chronic and protean overload experienced by most advisers and well captured by Pearce (1986, p. 126):

> In the management of time they often prefer a muddle which leaves them some control to any more orderly priorities controlled by others or by the group. In consequence most of their clients and superiors regard advisory time as indefinitely extensible.

The 'corporate management' philosophy of the 1974 reorganization together with ever more stringent resource control and quality intervention from central government has served to place the LEA officer and administrator in a permanent siege-like state, buffeted into a depressed loss of spirit and morale.[6] At the same time, many new special initiatives have arrived at the LEA's door, which often carry the prospect of extra resources for the hard-pressed and squeezed authorities (examples are the introduction TVEI and the GCSE, the increasingly ragbag collection of government prized initiatives in the Education Support Grants Scheme, pilot projects on low-attainers and profiling, the complex new in-service arrangements and a whole raft of measures relating to ethnic and gender initiatives in the curriculum).

In many authorities not only the personnel and counselling support, but sometimes the planning and implementation of wholesale redeployment of teaching staff has also fallen on advisers, in addition to the traditional functions of staff and curriculum development, in-service training, school-observation and inspection and the general 'dogsbody' fetching and carrying likely to fall on field officers.

In short, many of these new and critical functions for the LEA have, with the growing bureaucratization of education officers, fallen through the LEA system to the point of least resistance—the advisory service, which, in addition to the consequent stress and overload, has the opportunity of much greater influence in key policy developments as education officers become more distant from the field of schools and teachers. The very absence of agreed job-descriptions or coherent and planned objectives, has brought advisers both great pressure and significant challenge.

The second explanatory concept which may illuminate the current confusion of professional role-set and definition is that of client-ambiguity. If a group of advisers is asked to clarify whom they are obligated to 'advise' within their professional self-image, the answers are likely to be multiple and diverse, reflecting the diversity of groups already referred to in the discussion of adviser as 'transitional agent'. This complexity is, in part, semantic, since the verb 'to advise' carries some of the elasticity of function described above; it is also—more dangerously—politically labile, with very different degrees of resonance and impact whether applied, say, to the struggling probationer or to the interventionist chairman of a major education committee. Thus, the verb has a 'weak' and a 'strong' usage, and the degree to which advisers accept either view may well, implicitly, colour the potential for their influence.

My own view is that most advisers have been recruited under the rubric of the 'weak' sense, and define themselves professionally in terms of the traditional, curriculum-based activities with the schools as their field and focus. The newer, higher profile demands exemplified above require a new layer of skills and understandings vested in the 'strong' sense of the verb. The consequent conflict and self-doubt has proved corrosive to many teams and individuals as they struggle to accommodate this basic splitting process.

Indeed, there seems a real prospect that the conceptual split may lead to a professional reclassification, in which two tiers of advisory officer may emerge: one, carrying the traditional field load; the second a central policy and monitoring function. In some LEAs this divergence has been formally marked by redesignating the second group as 'inspectors'.[7]

At the same time, a new species of adviser seems to be developing, which, in the spirit of the age of multiple births, I have styled 'quins and quads', that is, quasi-inspectors and quasi-advisers (Heller, 1987). This development is, in part, a response to the piecemeal and rapid development of new initiatives which require instant coordination and monitoring by staff with recent and senior institutional experience. This, in itself, will rule out most advisers, while the project-focused nature of the assignment argues for short-term commitment. These trends, allied with the reduction of promotion possibilities for teachers, produce a compelling case for short-term attachments by secondment from the field as the structure likely to satisfy the 'weak' sense, with the 'strong' discharged by a smaller group of policy-orientated advisers. This emergent tendency also supports the contention made by the NFER team (Stillman and Grant, 1987) that the distinction between education adviser and officer is manifestly eroding.

VALUES AND AUTHORITY

One of the correlates of the traditional, 'weak' sense of the verb 'advise' is the conviction that advisers carry the developmental aspects of the LEA while officers look after the regulatory or normative needs. Thus advisers portray themselves as holding the values of schools and teachers and being closely tuned to these. Yet experience suggests that advisers rarely articulate their operational values either as individuals or as teams and even more rarely disclose these openly with teachers. This reluctance to examine what are felt to be driving principles of the work goes along with an aversion to work in a team or corporate mode—except in the most trivial sense of an administrative aggregate of people with cognate job-titles. The writer's experience of using a structured instrument to elicit educational values both on an individual and team basis suggests that there is a greater consensus than would be anticipated by this private reticence and apparent predilection for the 'lone-wolf' or impresario style of operation (Heller, 1986).

The modesty about personal and educational values is echoed in the issue of the adviser's authority and power base. Using a development of the work of French and Raven (1960) on power in organizations I have worked with advisers on their own and others' perceptions of their power. One significant issue at the start of much of this work is a cultural dissonance at the very term 'power': many advisers will expend much energy resisting the fit of this term (a resistance in line with attachment to the 'weak' role definition). I work with six classes of power grouped into three major categories:

(a) formal power
    (i) coercive power (rewards and punishments)
    (ii) legitimate power (ex officio power)
(b) professional power
    (iii) sapiential power (expertise)
    (iv) effective power (can 'deliver')
(c) personal power
    (v) affective power (inner authority; trust)
    (vi) charismatic power (inspires strong feeling)

When asked to self-assess on these aspects of their authority, there appears to be a marked denial among advisers of power deriving from the first group (the formal) as well as a modesty about the last group (the personal). Much greater investment is made in the professional authority deriving from subject specialist knowhow. These perceptions are, to be certain, honestly held; but they are at considerable variance with the views of client groups—in particular, the teachers with whom they deal, who see the formal powers of advisers as far more prominent—even menacing—in their day-to-day contacts.

Such data would be merely diverting were it not a powerful indicator of the lack of realism in the role-concept of many advisers, and particularly pertinent to any possible modulation to a more consultant-like role. Consultants have to be clear-eyed about their own power and the threat they may represent to client groups; if advisers, in their current roles, have often failed to distinguish these formal aspects, it suggests a considerable shift of focus and personal orientation when contemplating the consultant mode of working. The conditions for this shift will be discussed in the next section on the consultancy function and in the later discussion on training needs.

However, one further historical trend needs to be signalled in considering the adviser's sources of power and influence. It has become a commonplace (and perhaps an overstated one) that the period associated with the growth of advisory services—the late 1960s and early to mid-1970s—was a stage of major expansion in the service as a whole, with a broadly expansionist philosophy exciting much development, both in plant and curriculum process. Currently, with the exception of the narrowly earmarked special projects, advisers have few resources with which to motivate change; where, in the 1970s, entry to change in schools might be secured through resource donation, the contemporary scene offers little such leverage to the adviser seeking to encourage development. Such change has now to be won through personal influence—moving the sphere of the adviser's authority to the professional and personal springs of power listed above and away from the rewards and punishments of formal power.

THE ADVISER AS CONSULTANT

I will avoid, at this point, any prescriptive definition of 'consultancy', since I have set myself not to import any general theory of consultancy (assuming we could find one to command agreement) to the world of the adviser, but to take the empirical reality of advisory work and test how far current practice reflects aspects of the consultant role and how far conditions in the future are likely to promote or inhibit such tendencies.

It may be clear from the preceding section that I would see the current role of the adviser as carrying—certainly in the eyes of clients—a deal of reward/punishment power normally seen as incompatible with the consultant's posture. In terms of the commonly accepted criteria for sound consultancy work in schools (a sensible and reasonably thorough discussion is contained in Hausser *et al.*, 1970), the adviser, in current form, carries many disadvantages.

If the move away from the patronage of relative affluence to the democracy of corporate deprivation is a countervailing factor allowing the adviser to don a more accessible mantle, other developments run in the opposed direction. The imperatives of rate-capping and grant penalties push many LEAs into harsh reappraisal of priorities, leading to contraction, restraint and the withering of many valued facilities. The adviser is invariably identified in the schools' minds with the policies leading to such negative outcomes, no matter that the adviser may be, in practice and disposition, far removed from the locus of decision-making.

One developmental trend which may help to mediate and redirect advisers to a position somewhat closer to consultancy practice than they currently occupy lies in the concept of the 'change-agent'. The very term is elusive and chameleon like, but it has, over the past three to four years, served as a sensitive marker to some of the changes in role sketched in this chapter. It has figured in DES formulations for advisory functions—with a decidedly instrumental tinge when raised by political post-holders—but it does serve to remind the hearer that, of all LEA personnel, advisers are well placed to spread innovation in a sympathetic and adaptive way, by reason of their access and links to schools and teachers. This, then, can be a useful concept when helping advisers to understand the relevance of consultancy ideals; it pitches the focus clearly towards the 'task-directed' end of the consultancy continuum (where the counselling or person-centred pole may prove beyond the training and immediate resources of many); it offers the promise of achievable goals (a promise that may, without care, turn out to be illusory); and it gives some guarantee of system protection.

The weaknesses of this conception or strategy are equally clear; it often ignores deeper organizational needs; it sacrifices process to product, and, most crucially, it often fails to deliver. The limitations to the role of 'hero-innovator' are by now very well documented (the work of Argyris (1971) may serve as well as any to illustrate this) and the 'change-agent' formulation must reasonably carry a 'health warning'; yet it does suggest a way forward for the adviser seeking to work through consultancy approaches.

I have used the following simple, linear model with advisers when introducing them to change-agent ideas.[8]

(a)   entry skills;
(b)   relationship building;
(c)   diagnostic skills;
(d)   influencing skills;
(e)   transition skills.

Such a model can itself serve as an introduction to major training modules under each of these heads (see the next section) but, at a simpler level can act as an *aide-memoire* for signposting work with schools.

Another useful marker has been the phrase of Desmond Nuttall arising out of the almost feverish self-appraisal activity of the late 1970s;[9] that is, the notion of 'the critical friend'. This, in itself, is an approachable concept and can offer safe guidance to the adviser exploring consultancy approaches with schools. Behind both concepts, however, lies the requirement (often sadly ignored) for clarity and explicitness of function in such interventions. Since the adviser has acquired a heterogeneous mix of tasks, it is unrealistic to imagine that she will be in a position to discard all those which militate against effective rapport with a school. There will be times when the adviser is the augur of bad news, or even the instrument of disciplinary action. It seems to me, as is argued by some, to be a counsel of despair (or a precious fastidiousness) to debar the adviser who is ever seen in such manifestations from the consultant role. In fact, such mixed interventions will limit the kinds of consultancy available to the adviser, and will place on her the obligation to ask the good consultant's question of herself—'Am I the appropriate person for this situation?'; and of the school—'Why me?'. If these questions can be dealt with honestly, then issues of contract become even more critical for the adviser. This often turns into a question of having the clarity and flexibility to register to herself and the school the shift of mode and orientation between line-manager and consultant. I accept that the second will, inevitably, be compromised by the first and that this will rule her out of involvement in some of the more sensitive areas of consultancy. I also accept that, temperamentally, some—perhaps many—advisers will not show the personal qualities of non-defensiveness, trust, and empathic warmth which seem to me to be core-conditions for effective consultancy alongside the empirical skills of analysis, diagnosis, planning and evaluation. As I have found in teaching counselling skills to advisers, it is rare to find a colleague with the interests or capacity to work at a level which would satisfy most counselling agencies, even at a minimal level. Nevertheless, it is possible to provide a simple framework which allows the adviser to reflect on her own interpersonal dealings with teachers in such a way as to enhance her 'helping skills', or, at least, to be sensitized to difficult areas or practices. Similarly, in the conceptual world of consultancy, one is seeking to illuminate and redirect practice rather than force it into unacceptably demanding transformations. In doing so, an understanding of basic processes of organizational dynamics needs to be presented in clear formulations, such as Edgar Schein's (1969):

> The process model, in contrast, starts with the assumption that the organisation knows how to solve its particular problems or knows how to get help in solving them, but that it often does not know how to use its resources effectively. . . .

At this point it may be instructive to switch perspective to an outside observer of the advisory scene who writes with insight and honesty—who may, in this context, be styled 'a critical friend'. David Winkley, towards the end of his study (Winkley, 1985, p. 218) turns towards the issue of an LEA consultancy service for schools.

> Putting major initiatives such as the Cleveland Goathland courses aside, there was no general sense . . . that there was anything like an adequate consultancy service offered to teachers. Only a small proportion of teachers were involved with advisers in depth, and only a small proportion of teacher/adviser contacts were of the higher level variety.

He concludes this final section of the book with some well-founded doubts about the viability of a narrowly conceived advisory service, adopting a patronizing and controlling stance towards the schools, and advocates a collegial partnership of interests with the classroom practitioner and the academic alongside and interchanging with the adviser.

In this writer's view, consultancy work by advisers needs to emulate a climate akin to Winkley's ideal if it is to succeed.

TRAINING FOR CONSULTANCY

The writer of this chapter has had the privilege of moving to open the first national training centre for advisers (the Centre for Adviser and Inspector Development—CAID—based at Woolley Hall College, West Yorkshire) after serving as a Chief Adviser for eleven years. I am conscious of the distance by which my own efforts in leading a team of advisers fell short of the consultancy model outlined above. In designing (with a very free hand) development programmes for advisers, in a variety of settings including team consultancies as well as more formal training modes, I have explicitly attempted to highlight the skills and competencies of consultancy styles of work.

This can best be illustrated by looking at the outline framework for the six-week 'extended development programme' for experienced advisers. The time is divided equally between assignment-based work in his/her own or other LEAs and three residential weeks at the centre. The philosophical basis for the residential work is the reflective self-development group, borrowing much from the traditions of the NTL in the United States (for a concise account of this development see Cohen and Smith,

1976) and Tavistock approaches in the United Kingdom (Lawrence, 1979). The climate is both challenging and nurturing and I see the event as an opportunity to live the experience of being in an exemplary advisory team in which new behaviours can be risked without damage, while critical feedback and self-disclosure can be safely encountered and rehearsed.

As in Schein's quotation, the basic assumption is that the participants are themselves capable of resolving their own difficulties and satisfying their own needs if the surrounding climate is sufficiently supportive and stimulating.

The norm of self-review is set in advance of the event through a set of diagnostic materials in which the adviser is invited to assess her current position and competence. In this, the areas of competence are those given below—which form the spine of the taught programme. The formal diagnostic tool is a simple grid which combines the advisers' felt competence in the areas under review with an estimate of the relevance of that area to their roles. A simple overlay then highlights the relative priorities of each of the 15 'profiles', as a basis for a learning contract between tutor and participant.

The learning profiles

Residential week 1. Towards greater awareness of self:
(a)   Career planning and development;
(b)   stress management;
(c)   helping and counselling skills;
(d)   self-esteem and values;
(e)   learning style and needs.

Residential week 2. Towards greater awareness of the role:

(f)   goal-setting;
(g)   problem-solving;
(h)   time-management;
(i)   innovation;
(j)   consultancy and communication skills.

Residential week 3. Towards greater awareness of the environment:

(k)   adaptability;
(l)   leadership skills;
(m)   skills of influence;
(n)   current awareness;
(o)   evaluation and appraisal skills.

The resulting picture of learning needs is seen as a base which is itself to be reviewed over the six-week period, and beyond, since it is the habit or practice of continual self-review which is being developed. This seems close to the attractive but elusive notion of 'praxis' (reflection-through-action/action-through-reflection) which attempts to integrate theory and practice in our split-off and divided social organizations (see discussion in Lukacs, 1948), and which Winkley seems to be aspiring to with his notion of an integrated and interdependent educational development force (Winkley, 1985, p. 223).

Several of the familiar tensions and dilemmas of the adviser's role come to the surface at this point—Is it task or process centred? Is it supportive or judgemental? Is it controlling or developmental? Is it managerial or catalytic? Is it entrepreneurial (as some of the most successful and individualistic advisers have seemed) or 'intrapreneu-rial' (finding the points of energy, growth and innovation within the system boundaries and constraints)? These tensions are not merely theoretical, nor can they be resolved by the bland and eclectic response that, at different times, advisers must do and be all of these and that the job is living with tension and ambiguity. The uncertainty of such a multiheaded role breeds the considerable stress now evident in the profession.

In a training and development role, such as leading the extended development programme with its opportunities to work in some depth at these core issues of role, while enabling individuals to share their personal struggles and aspirations, it would be avoidance to wish away or fail to engage with such frustration and ambiguity. Paradox-ically, it is by confronting and accepting the impossibility of carrying all the conflicting roles and tasks that advisers become able to reassert control in order to achieve greater personal satisfactions and better performance. The energy that is often turned on ourselves in guilt or self-blame, in a sense of failure or inadequacy, or in the manic overcompensation of the 'workaholic', can be redirected to more adaptive goals.

Thus, learning to restore the internal locus of control through realistic work-planning; learning to say 'no' without guilt through assertion training; becoming more sensitive to one's strategies of flight in groups or manipulation of others—all are likely to be common features of the programme's life. Equally important will be the opportu-nities to rediscover our creativity—whether through formally structured experiences in the music room, art studies or movement hall—or (just as often) through the human interplay of the group, with its fluidity of mood and exchange. Advisers are usually appointed from among the most creative and successful cadre of teachers; for many, the constraints of the role appear to put these talents into remission; re-energizing these forgotten springs of creativity can be joyful, but may also elicit less comfortable feelings of anger.

A programme which invites participants to look deeper than the surface issues runs the risk of evoking such feelings and leaving behind a sense of impotence or of being 'disconfirmed'—the basis for one's current functional style being attacked without adequate alternatives being available. I dwell on this risk partly because I have to be conscious of the need to 'contain' in an appropriate way such feelings, but also because it is precisely the kind of risk the process consultant takes in working at any depth. The adviser is thus party to a development contract analogous to a consultancy and has the opportunity to generalize models of practice through direct experience and reflection. The modelling process is conscious and explicit. For example, I will liken the whole experience to the formation of a temporary advisory team, with myself as its leader. This allows issues of 'transference' to be acknowledged and dealt with within the programme, offering the possibility of illuminating and improving 'back-home' rela-tionships with senior or significant colleagues (for a brief discussion of this concept see Osipow *et al.*, 1980). At the more explicit and conscious level these same issues of relationship building will also be approached through more empirical—even behavioural—methods, such as boundary-management exercises and sequences.

When dealing with the teaching of consultancy skills in the advisory setting, the same cautions are in play as with the earlier discussion on counselling. The goal is a modest one, of giving some realistic insight into the meanings and justifications for working in a consultancy mode, and since this is part of the 'subtext' of the whole programme, such insights are pervasive as well as particular. The use of role-play and simulations, of clinic sessions in which difficulties in work with schools are explored and viewed through a consultancy framework, the setting of specific consultancy tasks within the group—all may be attempted in the light of the individual needs and progress. Here again, a sensitizing process seems as crucial as skills teaching. To learn to recognize when a consultancy approach may or may not be relevant may be the critical issue for advisers with their Joseph's coat of a role.

It would also be pertinent to refer to another aspect of the training experience which is, I think, relevant to the wider issue of using consultants in schools. There is a strong body of opinion warning against the facile translation of models from industrial or commercial management to the very special case of schools as systems (Charles Handy's (1984) treatment is a robust example). In looking at these aspects—some of them very new to advisers—I often work with trainers from industry whose culture has been very receptive to notions such as 'the change-agent' or consultancy. Major cultural resistance and covert sabotage are often encountered when such consultants themselves work with advisers. I judge it very important to use this experience of the alien 'feel' of the industrial model to help advisers recognize how schools may greet such new approaches.

By working with whole-team groups in-house, as well as with individuals at the Centre, I hope to strengthen the already considerable interest in consultancy approaches for advisers.

CONCLUSION

While I remain hopeful of the possibility of disseminating such strategies, it would be prudent to recall the not unsympathetically intended critique of advisers by David Winkley (1985, p. 218) which remains sceptical of the current contribution of advisers as consultants. In support of this head's view I shall also cite the judgement of a respected trainer and writer on management, Bertie Everard, who has done considerable work with Heads' training. In his recent book (Everard, 1986) he talks honestly of his impression of the advisory contribution.

> . . . on the other hand, I note the low regard in which many heads hold their advisers when it comes to giving them useful advice on management problems. They say that . . . advisers know nothing of management, never having managed themselves. The credibility of the advisory service does not stand very high, outside curriculum issues.

While this apparently comprehensive refutation of advisers' skills had been qualified in the earlier part of the paragraph, the fact that it is genuinely held by a sober and honest reporter, and echoed widely by teachers lends legitimacy to the claims that advisers are role-bound into a coercive mode which severely inhibits their potential for consultancy.

Were we living in a static educational world, I might tacitly agree to this handicapping diagnosis. It is apparent, however, that the structural transitions which will free at least some advisers to work in this fashion are already under way, as the 'weak' and 'strong' aspects of the role are more clearly identified and distinguished. If both schools and

LEAs can see value and gain in the consultancy method, then, I conjecture, new forms of agency and role may develop both within and outside the local authority structures. Furthermore, my work with newly appointed advisers (who are currently entering the profession at a rate of more than 200 a year, a turnover of more than 10 per cent), suggests an understanding and openness to such work that needs to be supported in systematic development programmes in the early years of service.

Nor do I despair of helping more experienced advisers to enter into some understanding of the world of consultancy, despite the very real difficulty of learning to work in new ways and to put aside old habits. For the majority of advisers I meet can still be fired by the eternal challenge of learning.

NOTES

(1) SEO/NAIEA joint paper 1979.
(2) DES draft paper 1985, final version 1987: The role of the LEA advisory services.
(3) See Better Schools, DES 1985 and Sir Keith Joseph's North of England Conference speech, January 1985.
(4) DES draft Statement, paragraph 27.
(5) SEO/NAIEA, section 2.
(6) See, for example, the 1987 presidential address to the Society of Education Officers by Dennis Hatfield, reprinted in *Education*, 23 January 1987.
(7) The Croydon LEA is a notable instance.
(8) As employed as an introductory model by Nick Heap in the Brunel University Workshops.
(9) In Schools Council report on self-appraisal in schools (1981).

REFERENCES

Argyris, C. (1971) *Management and Organisational Development*. London: McGraw-Hill.
Bolam *et al.* (1976) *LEA Advisers and Educational Innovation*. Bristol: Bristol University.
Cohen, A. and Smith, R. (1976) *The Critical Incident in Growth Groups*. La Jolla, Cal.: University Associates.
Everard, K. B. (1986) *Developing Management in Schools*, p. 207. Oxford: Blackwell.
French, J. and Raven, B. (1960) 'The bases of social power'. In *Group Dynamics: Research and Theory*. pp. 607–23. New York: Row, Peterson.
Handy, C. (1984) *Taken for Granted*. London: Schools Council.
Hausser, D. L. *et al.* (1970) *A Manual for Consultants*, pp. 135–59. La Jolla, Cal.: University Associates.
Heller, H. (1986) *OPUS: An Action–Research Model for Schools*. York: CSCS.
Heller, H. (1987) Paper delivered at CAID seminar, October 1986.
Lawrence, G. (ed.) (1979) *Exploring Individual and Organisational Boundaries*. Chichester: Wiley.
Lukacs, G. (1948) *Existentialisme ou Marxisme?* pp. 302 ff. Paris.
The Maud Report (1969), Vol. 3, Appendix II. London: HMSO.
Osipow, S. H. *et al.* (1980) *A Survey of Counselling Methods*. Homewood, Ill.: Dorsey.
Pearce, J. (1986) *Standards and the LEA*, pp. 16–23. Windsor: NFER/Nelson.
Schein, E. (1969) *Process Consultation*, p. 134. New York: Addison-Wesley.
Stillman, A. and Grant, M. (1987) Paper delivered at CAID seminar, October 1986.
Winkley, D. (1985) *Diplomats and Detectives—LEA Advisers at Work*. London: Robert Royce.

Chapter 10

The Use of Consultancy in Schools

Stanley Putnam

INTRODUCTION

One of the difficulties which a manager often faces is that he 'knows' there is a problem within the organization but he does not know what he is really looking for and, in fact, feels unable to put his finger on it—something like trying to find the slippery bar of soap when bathing. It is not surprising that he does not normally have the process skills necessary as this has never formed a part of the head's management training. Further, it is difficult to admit that he has a problem because there is a view that managers are paid to solve problems and he can feel threatened by those who expect him to find the answer or, worse, expect him to prevent the problem in the first place.

So a consultant will hopefully be able to help the *manager* to diagnose and locate the problem. I have italicized 'manager' because he is a major key to success and must 'buy in' to this method of working. If he does not do so, it is unlikely that process consultation can work successfully in the school or the institution concerned. The consultant will see clearly that the manager's and the organization's problems can only be solved by the people who work in the organization and not by the consultant. So the overall task of the consultant will be to help the members of the organization to be clear about what is happening within it, both overtly and covertly. This solution is found by the consultant seeking to give understanding to the individual(s) with whom he works, into what is happening around him, between himself, others and within himself. In other words, the consultant is primarily concerned with process, hence he is often called a process consultant (PC). So often the energies of an organization are put into trying to get the structure right, believing that the new order will solve all the problems, when in fact, the underlying issues that exist between people are largely ignored. This is not to say that structure is unimportant for that would be absurd, but I would wish to stress the importance and priority of working with the issues that arise between people in the organization. It is interesting to reflect that the answer is probably to be found in the affective area—in other words, within the emotional rather than the rational areas. For, after all, it is likely that rational arguments have already been examined without their coming up with the key to the problem.

Three stages of consultancy have been suggested by Schein (1969):

(a) establishing a helping relationship;
(b) knowing what kinds of processes to look for in the organization;
(c) intervening in such a way that organizational processes are improved.

ESTABLISHING A HELPING RELATIONSHIP

It is essential (a) that the manager (head, head of department etc.) recognizes that there is a problem and wishes help in solving it; (b) that a contract is drawn which clearly defines the way of working and that the contract is clearly understood by all of those involved in the exercise. The contract may be written but this is not essential. What is vital is that everyone knows and accepts without duress, the nature of what is about to happen and contributes to the contract. Some of the conditions might be:

(a) An agreement about time: namely that sufficient, uninterrupted time will be made available and that it will be a priority as against other claims on time;
(b) that there is a right setting for discussion both individually and collectively. It is no good trying to do it in the corner of the staff room. Comfort is important also. It is difficult to think and feel, except in one area, when sitting on a hard chair!
(c) confidentiality: the consultant and members will likely have an agreement that what is said is in confidence unless an understanding is reached between the consultant and the member or members, on what can be said to others. This is essential if the levels of trust necessary are to be achieved. So when working on a one-to-one basis, for example, only at the end will the decisions be reached as to who can be told what and what can be said to another member or members;
(d) the way in which such negotiation shall be done must be agreed: the consultant might agree to work in a Kissinger fashion, namely moving backwards and forwards between two members (say) of the department or alternatively, the two members might agree to meet with the consultant acting as a third party facilitator. Trust is built by the consultant making sure that each member knows what is happening in the process: for example the PC having talked to A and then to B, informs A of the discussions that he had with B when it concerned A.

This list is by no means exhaustive but is intended to give some idea of the contract and the way of working that has been agreed by the members. The consultant will attempt to establish trust. He will know of the group's fears and possible fantasies which will block the intervention if not recognized and dealt with.

KNOWING WHAT KINDS OF PROCESS TO LOOK FOR IN THE ORGANIZATION

The starting point will certainly be for the PC to be clear about the way in which members communicate with each other: who talks to whom; who avoids whom; who interrupts most; for how long people talk; what does their body language 'say'; who listens; who 'hears' (at the deeper level of understanding of the real message) not the words but the meaning; what appears to be blocking individuals as they try to communicate; what distortions take place as a result of preconceived ideas about each other which group members hold; how the fantasies about influence and power over others are seen.

Quite obviously, the PC must have a social-psychological background and this is discussed below.

INTERVENING IN SUCH A WAY THAT ORGANIZATIONAL PROCESSES ARE IMPROVED

I would suggest that there are four broad categories of intervention:

Getting at the agenda

This might be discovered by asking questions such as 'What do you (members) feel are issues between you?' The PC uses his skill to make certain that the underlying issues are also revealed.

Analysing the processes 'What is going on between A and B and why is C so often excluded?' the PC helps the group to look at these processes and to work with them. This will help give the members some way of conceptualizing the processes that go on in groups and that are going on between themselves.

Feedback

This is done by giving individuals and groups feedback on what the PC sees taking place. It is essential that the members 'see' for themselves what is happening (the processes) when the PC is acting as facilitator.

Counselling

As a result of feedback, questions such as, 'How can I act differently?' are bound to be asked and the consultant then moves into a counselling mode of operation. The counselling mode will be based upon the premises that:

(a)   Each member can solve his/her problems once he/she is clear as to the nature of the problem.
(b)   This is done by the PC in his reflecting back what he hears the member say; at no stage does the PC offer advice or answers.
(c)   If the member has a problem, it is fairly certain that he/she has gone through all the rational answers to the problem but without satisfaction. This suggests that the problem is not of a rational nature but rather lies within the emotions. The counselling will often, if not mostly, work with feelings. Perhaps this can best be illustrated by using the Johari window approach (Figures 10.1 and 10.2).

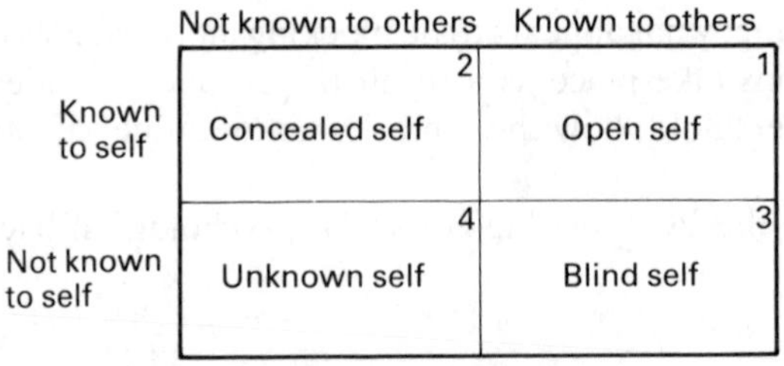

Figure 10 The Johari window

Quadrant 1: the open self, that part of ourselves of which we are aware and which we are prepared to share with others; it is sometimes called the area of free activity (public self).
Quadrant 2: the concealed self, those parts of ourselves of which we are aware but which we try to conceal from others ('bad breath' area).
Quadrant 3: blind self, where we unconsciously conceal from ourselves things which are clearly seen by others.
Quadrant 4: unknown self, which are areas of which we are not aware and which others cannot see but which operate as an emotional 'contagion'.
(After Schein, 1969).

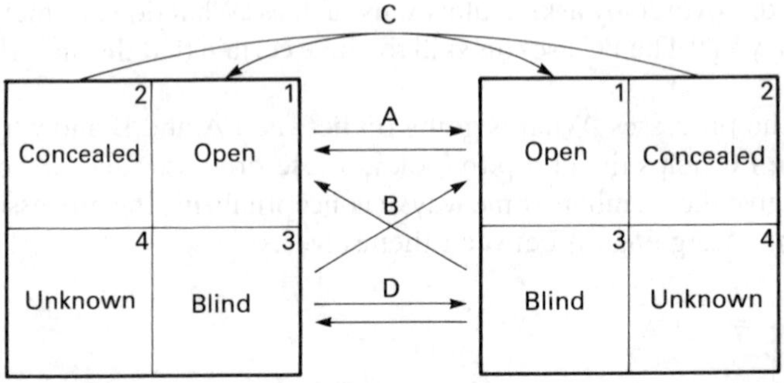

Figure 10.2

Arrow A: Open communication; most communications are of this type but they are often considered the only type of communication.
Arrow B: leakage or unwitting revelations; these messages are picked up by signals which are transmitted by the concealed self.
Arrow C: confiding or levelling; these are messages which are often of a confidential or 'levelling' kind: 'Please treat this information about me as confidential' or 'I must come clean'.
Arrow D: emotional contagion; these communications are at a deep level with both parties being unaware of them—a kind of contagion; an inner panic of one may result in an inner panic for another though both will put on a show of bravado etc.
(After Schein, 1969).

The PC will be aware of the messages as shown in these figures and will be able to make what is covert, overt.

THE WAY AHEAD

As a result of the work, the PC is now in a position to enable the organization to discover the way ahead. He will act as a facilitator in that, while the members will work with the task, he will consider the process, and because of his early efforts the members themselves will be more open and more aware of process ('What is happening to us now?') Finally, the contract is concluded and the members now take on *total responsi-*

bility. If the PC is to return, it would require a new contract to be drawn because it is essential that the members see clearly their non-dependency on the PC—in other words, he is not easily available at the end of the phone.

FROM THE IMPOSSIBLE TO THE POSSIBLE

Two immediate difficulties here are that:

(a)   there are very few people within education possessing the necessary skills;
(b)   the cost of employing PCs from outside the teaching profession would seem to be impossible. The financial implications—£200 per day plus expenses, is probably beyond the school's resources! Reference is made to this problem in Chapter 1 of this book.

So the answer has to be found either from within the institution, in this case the school, or from within the authority and that assumes that the idea of process consultation is acceptable. I wish to deal with the first of these, namely by training staff already in the school.

TRAINING OF STAFF

At Brookfield School we have instituted a two-tier training and it is hoped that all heads of department (called coordinators at this school) would be involved. The training is designed to enable staff to have the necessary skills which can be inferred from the previous paragraphs (Table 10.1).

Table 10.1   *Tier 1 and tier 2 training; the training in both tiers is done experientially*

Tier 1 training

Who am I?
Can I recognize my own frustrations?
Authoritarian, *laissez-faire* or cooperative leadership?
What 'power' would I like?
Listening
Hearing (hidden agendas)
Agenda setting
Giving and receiving praise
Confrontation
Agenda action and ending meetings

Tier 2 training

(This is 'spiral' in nature in that it attempts to 'deepen' many of the understandings from the tier 1 training)
Working with feelings
Hearing (via feelings and intuition)
Group dynamics
Third party consultation
Process consultation

Preferably, the PC should not have anything to 'gain' personally from his intervention. I use the word 'gain' advisedly because the fantasies that surround role are very powerful. If the head sets the agenda of a staff meeting, the fantasies of staff will prevent positive outcomes because of the assumptions made that lead on from fantasies ('All he wants is a rubber stamp', etc.). If a head takes the chair it is almost certain that the meeting will be, at least, partially blocked. So, it is almost impossible for a headteacher to carry out PC work in his own school, though he can do it in other schools. The head's function in his own school is probably that of training staff in process consultation. However, it is possible for a head of department to work in another department both in terms of chairing meetings and in process consultation, because he is seen by the members of that department as having nothing to 'gain' as a result. Quite obviously, this is not ideal, but it is a way of working which will free the energies of the members of staff and lead to development both individually and collectively. It is possibly the only way to carry out consultation because of financial restraints.

Process consultation has very considerable implications for the head for he must be prepared to 'give' away his leadership—that is, he himself will not work in a hierarchical way; his orientation will be that of a counselling mode—facilitative.

The difficulty in writing on this subject is to give the reader a 'feeling' for something which is learnt experientially. It is not possible to deal with all the related areas such as leadership etc. which are corollaries to the work of consultation without writing at much greater length than is possible here.

TWO EXAMPLES OF PROCESS CONSULTATION

Example 1

A head, whom we will call X, felt that somehow he and his two deputies, whom we will call A and B, were not working as well together as they should have done. The head could not understand this as the relationships between them were very warm and they seemed to speak honestly together. X discussed this with the deputies, who also felt that things were not right and it was decided to ask another head who had training in consultancy, as outlined previously, to act as a PC.

The PC decided to set one day aside for the intervention and meet the three people concerned to seek the nature of the problem. This took 20 minutes. The PC then decided to meet each separately for one hour. It was also agreed that each was free to talk about any matter relating to X, A and B. The confidentiality of each discussion was agreed and the three also agreed with the PC in seeking, at the end of each discussion, areas that were felt could be passed on or revealed to the other members of the trio, A, B and X. Finally the PC would meet with all three, acting as a facilitator in the hope that X, A and B would:

(a)   be clear about the problem;
(b)   come up with ways in which the problem could be solved.

Some thumbnail sketches might help at this point.

X had been at the school for 12 years and had recently been under pressure from the governors over external examination results, and also from the staff about the physical conditions under which they worked. The second was particularly hard as enormous effort had been put in by X to little avail. He very much enjoyed working on training courses and wondered whether the time had come for him to leave the school and concentrate on training. He felt he was suffering 'burnout' as far as the school was concerned. Early retirement was also a possibility.

A, the female deputy, was in her early 30s, and had been on the school staff for ten years prior to her appointment as deputy, which she had held for six months. She felt tremendously supported by X, though sometimes overwhelmed by his paternalism, and felt unable to say so because of her fear of hurting X. He, X, tended to shelter her from difficult areas of school life in order, as he thought, that she might 'establish' herself in the new role.

B, the male deputy, was in his 40s; X very much wanted him to obtain a headship within four years largely because the authority was not totally in favour of his appointment and felt that he did not have the potential for headship whereas X did. X therefore, gave him jobs in which he could succeed. B had had great difficulties resulting from medical problems with his eldest son and he was aware of the great support given him by X. B felt that he wanted to tackle more difficult, possibly non-successful areas, but could not say this to X for fear of hurting him.

During the separate interviews the PC had become aware of several matters that she was able to bring to the final session:

(a)   That her feelings during the individual sessions mirrored those of the three people; for example, X had seemed too closed and this mirrored his closure around his own feelings of confusion. A was very open and B less so. It became important to reflect on these as similar feelings were found to be present when the three had met prior to the intervention. However, it had been necessary to have the intervention in order to recognize and verbalize them.

(b)   The issue of X's paternalism was now clearly recognized as was the need to 'separate' warmness from the blocking caused by overprotection. A and B asked for the right to fail.

(c)   X had a need to be confronted by A and B and to be 'fought' over issues. Such stimulation brought the best out of X. A and B had been given the freedom to do their own thing but had avoided doing so because of the fear of hurting X.

(d)   As a result of the intervention, A, B and X were now clear about the issues and were then able to resolve the issues and hence solve the problem. Tremendous energy was released as a result.

(e)   Finally, it was agreed that the PC meet with them again in a month to see what progress had been made before making her final withdrawal.

Example 2

A department in a school, consisting of a head of department and eight members, was in difficulty in that the members felt a sense of dissatisfaction yet they were unable to locate its source. However, the energy behind the dissatisfaction was splaying out in many directions. The head of department had his share of the 'flak'—'He doesn't spend any time with us in our lessons', 'He controls the stationery and we never get it when we need it', 'He is always at meetings' etc. Furthermore, their feelings were confused and diffused because they knew the head of department to be very supportive of them particularly in times of personal stress. Some members complained about scale posts and the way they had been distributed and what was *not* done for the extra money, though such talking was seemingly never in terms of themselves as individuals but about other members of the department. Younger, ambitious members did not recognize how ambitious they were nor could they have coped with the idea of 'What is in it for me?'. There was a great deal of turbulence hidden under what seemed to be a calm surface.

Several members of the department had had the experience of being in an encounter group and felt that an opportunity to spend time together looking at tasks, personal reactions and relationships would be valuable. The department agreed to spend two days together at the teachers' centre—one school day and one Saturday. An organization development (OD) consultant acted as facilitator. The outcome was a freeing of relationships and an ability to confront one another which led to the energies of the staff being directed towards working together rather than being used to repress feelings which 'professional' teachers never express!

It was then agreed that the head would work with the department as a facilitator. He could only do that because the initial work had been carried out by a consultant from outside the school. An evening was set aside, working from 4 pm to 9 pm. The process was that each member stated what he or she felt good at and enjoyed, and then to state alternative activities—least enjoyable, uninteresting and not easily able to cope with. For example, one member felt that organizational matters like the distribution of paper etc. drove him 'up the wall', and his colleagues agreed that this was obvious! He went on to say that he felt that he was good at working with people but he needed to check this out in case he was deceiving himself. The members affirmed him in his belief that he was good at working with others and wished to use him in that way. Another member liked the organizational aspects, and he in turn was recognized by his colleagues as being good in that area. The results were displayed on a flip-chart. Then each member began negotiating with colleagues until a plan of working together had been devised. The good feelings that arose from confirmations and affirmations were enormous (the word 'enormous' is used advisedly).

The department continues to meet from time to time, to carry out a checking out process and a renegotiation of what members wish to contribute and what areas of their work they would like to exchange. This self-directed task releases energy from the renewal into the work of the department.

The head of the department had to be absent on frequent occasions because of his union duties and his membership of examining boards, etc. The department turned their resentment into a positive working with this because they saw:

(a) the value in what he was doing; and
(b) because by so doing, his personal needs were satisfied and therefore he was able to give more to the department; for, after all, he now had no need to work with the negative feelings that were once present.

CONCLUSIONS

In summary, the following seemed to have taken place:

(a) the needs of individual members were recognized and acted upon;
(b) the departmental head had 'given away' his authority and in turn had gained it.

This is a paradox about leadership, in that it is gained when it has been given away because it is the holding on to, the paternalism/maternalism coupled with the fears arising from what will happen if functions are released that are a cause of blocks and frustrations in organizations;

(c)   the members of the department did confront one another; frictions did arise from time to time but they could deal with them;

(d)   trust grew from them being 'real' with one another, that is, they could congratulate as well as face the frictions that occurred;

(e)   the release of energy into the department was truly remarkable.

FURTHER READING

De Board, R. (1978) *The Psychoanalysis of Organisations*. London: Tavistock.

Gray, H. L. (1985) *Change and Management in Schools*. Crewe: Deanhouse.

Gray, H. L. (ed.) (1982) *The Management of Educational Institutions*. Lewes: Falmer Press.

Lawrence, P. R. and Lorsch, J. W. (1978) *Interpersonal Peacemaking: Confrontations and Third-Party Consultation*. Reading, Mass.: Addison-Wesley.

Schein, E. H. (1969) *Process Consultation*. Reading, Mass.: Addison-Wesley.

Chapter 11

School Leadership and Consultancy

Don Musella

INTRODUCTION

The title of this chapter connects two concepts, both of which can be interpreted in quite diverse ways. School leadership often refers to the formal leaders of the school, that is, those with titles—head, principal, vice-principal. On the other hand, school leadership can refer to the process of influencing change, with only tangential reference to any one specific role. In fact, if you use this definition of leadership, many individuals in the school are exerting leadership. Their ability to influence others, however, depends on a host of factors, including those described in the theory of situational leadership espoused by Hersey and Blanchard (1977). However, there is enough research to support the notion that the key player in the process of change is the school principal (Barth and Deal, 1982; Greenfield, 1982; Leithwood and Montgomery, 1982; Persell, Cookson, and Lyon, 1982; Yuki, 1982). It is quite defensible then to merge the two definitions and think of school leadership as referring to the head of the school and the process this person (and others) can use to exert effective leadership, that is, influence others to undertake change leading to improvement in schooling.

The second concept in the title, consultancy, also needs some clarification. In some jurisdictions, consultants to schools are essentially locally employed staff who respond to requests from the school principal for assistance, or in some cases, who come to the school with a directive from central office on how to change things for the better. In some jurisdictions, consultants are government employees, that is, Ministry of Education personnel, who have a mandate to assist when asked and/or to propagate the message from the Ministry. Sometimes the consultants are external 'experts' who are asked to do a specific task leading to some form of improvement in the operation of the school. In many jurisdictions, all three forms of consultancy are available.

In this chapter the focus is on the process of consultancy as it applies to leadership as a process of influencing change. The term *consultancy* is used in this context to refer to the actual activities undertaken by the consultant to assist the client.

The topics covered include: clarifying the role of the consultant; setting the objectives of the consultancy; identifying internal change agents; analyzing potential for change;

key skills of consultants; developing and maintaining relationships; and using leadership for school renewal.

CLARIFYING THE ROLE OF THE CONSULTANT

The initial consideration in any relationship of consultant to client is the perceived and actual role of the consultant. Lippitt and Lippitt (1978) offer a descriptive model that presents the consultant's role along both a directive and nondirective continuum. Behavior varies in its degree of directiveness (Figure 11.1). This model is useful in that it covers a variety of roles along one of the *most critical* of dimensions, that of directiveness–nondirectiveness. However, the consultant's role is not a static one. It is dependent upon a number of factors: (1) formal role and agreed-upon role relationship between consultant and clients, and (2) situations arising in the process of the consultancy. For example, consultants who are employed by the school system often have a mandate that requires an advocate role. Consequently, the agreement with the school principal might be one of assisting teachers to change to the new program adopted by the school board. Other times, the consultant is asked to assist a teacher the principal thinks needs assistance. The role of the consultant in this case might initially be that of observer, and after building some confidence with the teacher, the consultant might move to be a joint problem-solver. The consultant's role must change with the needs of the situation; school leaders can assist consultants by providing valid information of the situation.

As Fullan, Anderson and Newton (1986, p. 330) say:

> The role of system consultants is shifting from being technical experts in the content of curriculum (although this will still be essential for specialists) to being experts in the process and procedures of managing change.

This is one of the conclusions made by these researchers in analyzing four case studies of implementation in four different school boards. This implies then that consultants need to combine and integrate expertise in curriculum and change. The authors refer to knowledge of how people learn, effective in-service education designs, and the ability to assess progress and to work with others at various levels in the organization—teachers, principals, other consultants, and supervisory officers.

CLARIFYING THE OBJECTIVES OF THE CONSULTANCY

The first contact between consultant and client should come from the senior administrator responsible for the unit under consideration. In the case of schools, the client is the school principal. Some would disagree with this for, in their experience, successful consultancies have resulted from contacts with a variety of personnel. However, to gain organizational support for any change, administrative commitment and support is *essential* (Fullan, 1982).

The objectives of the first contact are essentially three: (1) establishing a relationship with the client and other relevant key players; (2) clarifying the objectives of the intended consultancy; and (3) clarifying the extent of administrative and organizational

Multiple roles of the consultant

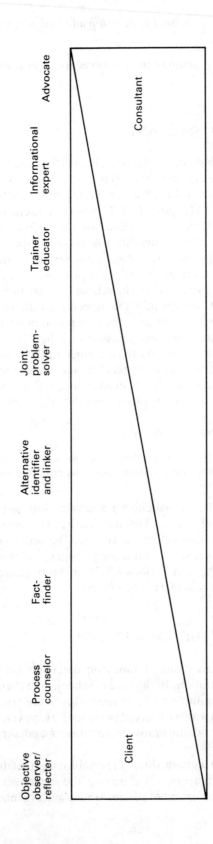

Level of consultant activity in problem solving

Non-directive							Directive
Raises questions for reflection	Observes problem-solving process and raises issues mirroring feedback	Gathers data and stimulates thinking interpretives	Identifies alternatives and resources for client and helps assess consequences	Offers alternatives and partici-pates in decisions		Trains client	Regards, links and provides policy or practice decisions	Proposes guidelines, persuades or directs in the problem-solving process

Objective observer/ reflecter | Process counselor | Fact-finder | Alternative identifier and linker | Joint problem-solver | Trainer educator | Informational expert | Advocate

Client

Consultant

Figure 11.1 Description of the consultant's role on a directive and nondirective continuum (Lippitt and Lippitt, 1978, p. 311, reproduced with permission).

support for the intended activities. Further, clear understanding of the entry role is desirable prior to the beginning of the consultancy. To achieve this understanding, both problem identification and role clarification should be the focus of the initial discussion phase with the school principal or other identified leaders of the client group. These objectives sound simple enough to achieve. However, let me provide an example of the first contact importance and how to recover from misinformation provided during the first contact.

Case 1

The school principal of a large secondary school calls. He wants to discuss the possibility of my undertaking some team building with its executive council (total of seven— principal, three vice-principals and three department heads elected by the group of department heads). Since the principal and I knew each other from previous contacts, the relationship between us had already been established; it was an open and honest one of long standing. I suggest a meeting in my office to discuss this undertaking before making a commitment. My first question to him was: How do you know you need team building? What tells you that? The principal thinks that the total group could work together much better than it does. He also indicates that the others believe this is so and are committed to trying to improve the working relationship. We arrange a day to conduct our first session on 'team building'. Shortly after I arrive to start the session, my experience (intuition) tells me that all is not right. Consequently, I start the session off with several questions to test the assumptions I have made based on the meeting with the principal (I call this process the reliability check). First question: Why do you think I am here? I get several somewhat unrelated responses. This is followed by another question: Do you think this session is necessary? After some pause, several of the respondents indicate that they think this meeting is a waste of time, that all is well, and they should get back to their heavy workload. I suggest to the principal that we do not continue; I am prepared to leave at this point. Others, including the principal, disagree. They indicate there is a problem with the workings of the council and think we should discuss the situation further. We decide on the objectives for the day. They agree that the objectives should be to analyze what has been happening and to make recommendations for change. The final outcome of the day was a decision to disband the council. It was interfering with other areas of responsibility in the organization and served no useful purpose.

COMMENTS ON THE CASE

In the example given above, the assumptions held by the principal, as well as the commitment to the task, were not shared by others. The initial discussion with the principal did not reveal the 'real' situation. It became important, therefore, to clarify the objectives and the extent of commitment by all participants; otherwise chances for success in the activities that follow would be extremely limited. The principal was sincere in what he assumed was so. The council was not acting as an effective group. Individual concern overrode group concern. However, the 'real' problem(s) were not surfacing. The council was not effective in that it had no significant role to play in the organization. 'Team building' was not the solution to the problem. The solution lay in reorganization and role clarification. This was uncovered in the first contact with the total group. It took extensive 'leadership' on the part of the consultant to facilitate the setting of those objectives that would ensure the emergence of the *real* problem. What followed then was 'teamwork' which led to a successful solution, that is, one that related directly to the problem.

Setting objectives and problem-identification usually go hand-in-hand. Obviously, when asking the question 'why', the consultant is forcing the client, in this case the formal leader, to grapple with the objectives, for *the* objective is to solve the problem. (Problem here is defined as a situation that someone wants resolved; that is, a situation that demands change.) The problems fall usually into one or more of the following categories:

(a)   participants lack relevant information;
(b)   participants lack necessary skills;
(c)   participants lack understanding of role and role relationships;
(d)   participants are in conflict; and
(e)   participants cannot decide on what to do.

Given this category of problems, the objectives of the activity then must relate directly to the problem(s) identified:

(a)   to acquire additional information;
(b)   to acquire additional skills;
(c)   to improve understanding of role and role relationships;
(d)   to resolve differences; and
(e)   to decide what to do.

The case study cited above involved categories (c), (d) and (e). However, at time of the initial contact, the assumption was made that the problem was of the third type—lack of understanding of role and role relationships. This was based on the position taken by the principal that the solution to the problem was team building. As the session progressed, it became clear that the problem was also centred on both the inadequacy of the organizational structure (the council) and the differences among the council members. Therefore, the objectives changed midway through the session.

In summary, although the first contact is critical in identifying the problem and setting the objectives, both the consultant and the formal leader must never assume that the problem and objectives are constants. One is never certain what the 'real' problems are until the interaction between consultant and participants, as well as among participants, has started. The consultant must be ready to shift objectives if the situation requires the shift. The onus for problem identification rests primarily, however, with the formal leader. The leader must do some homework before contacting the consultant. The leader must be able to answer the question: 'How do you know there is a problem?' The answer must be backed up with good information.

IDENTIFYING INTERNAL CHANGE AGENTS

The consultant does not play an official role in identifying those persons in the school or school system who have the leadership potential to influence change. The formal leader, the principal, must assume this responsibility. However, the consultant can influence the outcome, that is, by assisting the principal in identifying the change agents with the greatest potential for success.

One approach is to consider all change as solving a problem. If, for example, a new program is to be introduced, the logical question to ask is: what is the problem this new program is to solve. Is it to replace an old program? If so, what is the problem with the old program? Is it to be an additional program to fill a gap that needs filling? Of course, if the questions have no defensible answer, then one must question why the change. However, if there are defensible answers, then we need to identify those persons who see the problem as theirs. We want persons committed to trying the intended solution. Therefore, the next question then is: who, on staff, recognizes this change as a solution to their problem? Can we identify those who have something to gain by the successful implementation of the change? Can we get them to volunteer? This then is the group we need to in-service prior to and during the initial or pilot stages of the change.

However, there are other considerations that cannot be ignored in identifying change agents. If we define leadership as the act of influencing others, then we have to consider which persons have the greatest potential for influencing others. The theory of situational leadership provides one set of criteria that can be useful. Leadership ability in any situation depends on the use of potential power. The power bases are legitimization, identification, reward, punishment, information, connection, and expertise. However, in the educational environment, all power bases are not equal and all power bases do not fit all situations. The key power bases in the educational environment seem to be *identification*, *information* and *expertise*. Consider the school principal who relies on title, reward, punishment and connection to influence staff. This is not the person to bring about significant change. In the school culture of today, the greatest potential for influence rests with a person who is perceived as a credible expert with information or assistance needed and desired by the recipient, that is, the person who wishes to change. Consequently, if the principal wants to bring about significant change in the school he needs to identify persons who have the greatest potential to exhibit leadership in that situation, that is, they are perceived to have useful information, to be competent as teachers and consultants, and to have the expertise needed to assist those teachers who depend on them for success in the change.

This process is not unlike one that is used to identify or become one of the key actors in the school power structure. If one wants to have influence over others, that is, to exert leadership, then one should take steps to increase one's key power bases. For example, one can volunteer or get elected to committees. This may lead to an increase in legitimate power, as well as information, expertise, connection, and possibly reward and punishment power, depending on the function of the committee. However, lack of power in any one of the key power bases might be enough to limit the extent of influence a person has. For example, if one is perceived as an ineffective teacher or principal, then this lack of identification power might reduce one's ability to influence others in any situation.

In summary, the key to identifying change agents is to identify those with the greatest potential to influence others. This goes for the selection of consultants as well as formal leaders, such as the school principal, and should be a major consideration when delegating tasks which are intended to impact on others in the school.

ANALYSING POTENTIAL FOR CHANGE

The consultant can easily be led to assume that because the school principal or the chief education officer has called, the staff are ready and willing to change. Often this is the furthest from the truth. Often the administrator calls the consultant because he cannot get anyone on staff to accept his/her ideas of change. Consider another case.

Case 2

Upon the recommendation of the senior administrators, the Board of Education of this rather large school board (25 schools) had passed a policy which stated in effect that all classroom teachers were to implement changes that would be consistent with the government guidelines recommending language teaching in all subjects. In other words the practice of 'language across the curriculum' was to be implemented in all schools by the end of the school year. The senior administrator responsible for program development, implementation and evaluation, with the support of the chief education officer of the board, decided to hold a one-day in-service session for all principals (25) and all senior administrators (four); the in-service program was to be conducted by the two language consultants.

The purposes of the day-long session were to review the objectives of the changes, to discuss implementation strategies, and to clarify any questions or concerns that the principals responsible for implementation would have. Each principal, then, was to hold a staff meeting the next day (after school) and inform the teachers of the new policy and expectations for change. I was asked by the senior administrator responsible for programs to attend this in-service program as an observer and to present a summary of my impressions at the end of the day, that is, to provide an evaluation of the in-service event and offer any recommendations to assist the principals and other participants in the implementation process.

Given what we know of the research on implementation of program change, it is obvious what resulted. However, it was even worse than expected. As the day went on, it became clear to me that no-one (even the consultants) knew what they were doing or going to do in the schools as follow-up to the day's activities. Further, although the principals were 'polite' and willing to 'follow the leader', the frustration and concerns about the lack of preparation for the change were evident. Given the severity of the situation, I decided this was not the time to congratulate them for initiating a worthwhile program change. My presentation, therefore, was not what the senior administrators expected. I read through a list of factors that must be considered in bringing about a change of this magnitude—all of which they had ignored—and concluded that they did not know what they were doing. My recommendation, in summary, was to spend one year studying the situation, developing a long-term plan with realistic goals, acquiring sufficient resources for in-service and implementation, and providing extensive in-service for all participants. The response from the principals was enthusiastic endorsement. From the chief education officer I received a letter indicating that I had set back curriculum change in that board by three years; however, six months later I received another letter from the senior administrator of the program saying that I was right in stating what I did at the time. She indicated that they were still studying the situation and were in the midst of developing a plan.

Analysis of the case study

In examining the nature of the changes required by the teaching staff and the process used to prepare for the implementation, one finds obvious obstacles to change. The content of the changes intended by the policy included changes in curriculum content and methodology in most of the subjects, changes in the style of teaching by most of the teachers, and changes in student activities and expectations. Most of the constraints to successful implementation were present and ignored:

(a)   teachers were not involved in the planning or goal setting process;
(b)   the problems the changes were to solve were not clearly articulated, nor was there acknowledgement and acceptance of the fact that there was a problem;
(c)   the information about the nature of the change was not consistent nor clearly understood by those responsible for facilitating and implementing the changes;
(d)   the resources available to assist in the implementation process were inadequate to say the least;
(e)   it was not clear what specific changes were expected, hence no way of knowing if the changes could be implemented;
(f)   what were perceived as minor changes were, in fact, major changes in teacher role;
(g)   the time-line set for implementation was far from realistic.

It was obvious that any attempt to facilitate the implementation of the policy would lead to frustration on the part of principals, who were responsible for implementation in their schools, and anger on the part of most teachers already burdened with other curriculum changes. At best the effect would be token acknowledgement of and adherence to board policy by the principals, but no real change.

KEY SKILLS OF CONSULTANTS

It is rather difficult to develop a taxonomy of competencies and skills for consultants; the very nature of the consultative process is a personal relationship between people trying to solve a problem. As alluded to earlier, the consultant should be able to influence this relationship in four ways: by communication of helpful concepts and ideas, by behavioral competence, by degree of acceptance, and by the client's legitimization of the consultant's role. The competence and creativity of the consultant alone are not sufficient to be successful. The last two factors—acceptance and legitimized role—are essential both to the consultant's opportunity to contribute and actual contribution to problem solution.

One way of identifying what makes a good consultant is to think of the consultant(s) the principal has invited into the school to work with staff during the past year and evaluate them using the following four categories developed by Menzel (1975) as criteria: *educating*, *diagnosing*, *consulting*, and *linking*. If we consider the role of the consultant primarily as change agent, then this list of change agent skills is most appropriate.

Educating

Educating includes the skills required of a researcher, writer, teacher, designer, advocate, conference leader. Is the consultant familiar with the theoretical bases for change? Can the consultant write clearly and persuasively? Can the consultant design educational workshops and events? Is the consultant successful in helping others to learn? Is the consultant able to lead, and teach others to lead, a participative meeting or conference?

Diagnosing

Diagnosing includes the skills required of an action researcher, diagnoser, survey designer, data analyst, and evaluator. Can the consultant use research and survey data to apply to the present situation? Can the consultant identify what needs to be analyzed, what data to gather, and how to obtain and use them? Can the consultant obtain the data in the simplest way and draw correct conclusions from the data? Can the consultant use evaluation as an ongoing process?

Consulting

Consulting requires one to be a role model, relater, expert in process, confronter, intervener, and adapter. Does the consultant practice what he/she preaches and use interpersonal skills to maintain credibility with all staff? Does the consultant possess expertise in the change agent's tools of the trade—process skills? Can the consultant face issues and people head-on and execute interventions forcefully? Can the consultant apply his own experience and that of others in a creative and relevant way?

Linkage

Linkage requires the knowledge and use of the process of connecting human and nonhuman resources. Does the consultant have the skill in linking the best resources with the correctly identified need? Can the consultant identify, enlist, train and employ people as resources within the school to effect change? Can the consultant identify appropriate external resources, facilitate their entry and effective functioning?

This approach to the identification of competent consultants draws our attention to the role of the consultant as change agent. Consultants are asked to assist, to help. This implies that the present situation is not good enough. Hence the desired outcome is change for the better. The consultant, therefore, must be good at helping to bring about change. This means being a master of change agent skills.

DEVELOPING AND MAINTAINING RELATIONSHIPS

Much has been said of relationships as the key to good management and effective leadership (Miles, 1965; Schein, 1969; Snyder, 1985). Obviously, if one is to have an impact on another, the relationship must be one of mutual interdependence; in other words the situation is such that it is to the mutual advantage of both parties to work together.

The key to developing and maintaining relationships lies in the ability of the consultant to 'get inside the heads of the clients' and to behave in ways that take account of the needs of the individual and group, as well as the objectives of the consultancy.

If one is applying the problem-solving approach to the consultancy then certain beliefs tend to produce relationships that lead toward and support interdependence. Consider, for example, the list provided by Filley (1975):

(a) belief in the availability of a mutually acceptable solution;
(b) belief in the desirability of a mutually acceptable solution;
(c) belief in cooperation rather than competition;
(d) belief that everyone is of equal value;
(e) belief in the views of others as legitimate statements of their position;
(f) belief that differences of opinion are helpful;
(g) belief in trustworthiness of other members;
(h) belief that the other party can compete but chooses to cooperate.

Developing and maintaining relationships depends to considerable extent on the ability of the consultant and principal to develop trust between and among the participants. Developing trust is a difficult and long process; unfortunately, it only takes one deed or word to destroy the trust that has been built. Consequently, the appropriate behaviors are those that are perceived as consistent and predictable and as being of benefit to the person to be influenced.

USING LEADERSHIP FOR SCHOOL RENEWAL

Schools do make a difference (Rutter *et al.*, 1979). School principals make a difference (Shoemaker and Fraser, 1981). Does it follow then that consultants should make a difference? The response probably is, as with most proposed solutions, *it all depends*. Leadership must come from the principal. To be an effective principal one must be an effective leader; after all, if the principal cannot influence others, specifically his staff, then his effectiveness as a facilitator of change is limited. The same can be said for the consultant. To be an effective consultant one must be an effective leader. If the consultant cannot influence others, in all likelihood he/she will not be given many opportunities to provide leadership in bringing about change.

School renewal, defined as an attempt to improve the present state of schooling, should be an ongoing process that includes self-assessment followed by planned change in areas in need of improvement. The principal and consultant(s), together, can provide the leadership necessary to mobilize staff toward planned change. Systematic employment of planned change procedures under the leadership of the school principal (Leithwood and Montgomery, 1982), along with the effective use of change agent skills by the consultant, should contribute substantially to desired outcomes in the form of more effective schooling.

CONCLUSIONS

Several factors are worthy of consideration if one is to increase the consultant's chances for success in bringing about effective change. First, the external consultant must have the skills and be perceived as a credible source of assistance by those who are interested in desired changes. Second, the role of the external consultant and the clients, as well as the objectives of the intended interactions, must be clarified to the satisfaction of both consultant and recipients of the consultancy. Third, the objectives of the consultant/ client interactions must be worked out together; that is, the problem to be solved must be arrived at through a 'working together'. Further, the clients must see the problem and be able to describe it clearly. Fourth, internal 'consultants', that is, those with the greatest potential for influencing others, must be identified and encouraged to be on the implementation team from the very beginning. Finally, all participants must believe that the process of developing and maintaining good relationships is an essential component of all procedures directed to the desired changes, for in the final analysis all change is directed to improving (changing) the performance of others.

REFERENCES

Barth, R. R. and Deal, T. E. (1982) *The Principalship: Views from Without and Within*. Washington, DC: National Institute of Education.

Filley, A. C. (1975) *Interpersonal Conflict Resolution*. Glenview, Ill.: Scott, Foresman and Company.

Fullan, M. (1982) *The Meaning of Educational Change*. Toronto: OISE Press, The Ontario Institute for Studies in Education.

Fullan, M., Anderson, S. and Newton, E. (1986) *Support Systems for Implementing Curriculum in School Boards*. Toronto: Ministry of Education.

Greenfield, W. (1982) *A Synopsis of Research on School Principals*. Washington DC: National Institute of Education.

Hersey, P. and Blanchard, K. H. (1977) *Management of Organizational Behavior: Utilizing Human Resources*, 3rd edition. Englewood Cliffs, NJ: Prentice-Hall, Inc.

Leithwood, K. A. and Montgomery, D. J. (1982) 'The principal's role in program improvement'. *Review of Educational Research*, **52**, 309–40.

Lippitt, G. and Lippitt, R. (1978) *The Consulting Process in Action*, 2nd edition. San Diego, Cal.: University Associates, Inc.

Menzel, R. K. (1975) 'A taxonomy of change-agent skills'. *Journal of European Training*, **4**(5), 287–8.

Miles, R. E. (1965) Human relations or human resources. *Harvard Business Review*, **43**, 148–52, 154/5, 156, 158, 160, 163.

Persell, C. H., Cookson, P. W. and Lyon, H. (1982) *Effective Principals: What Do We Know from Various Educational Literatures?* Washington DC: National Institute of Education.

Rutter, M., Maughan, B., Mortimore, P. and Ouston, J. (1979) *Fifteen Thousand Hours: Secondary Schools and Their Effects on Students*. Cambridge, Mass.: Harvard University Press.

Schein, E. H. (1969) *Process Consultation: Its Role in Organizational Development*. Don Mills, Ontario: Addison-Wesley.

Shoemaker, J. and Fraser, H. W. (1981) 'What principals can do: some implications from studies of effective schooling'. *Phi Delta Kappan*, **64**(3), 178–82.

Snyder, R. (1985) 'Organizational culture', in Warren Bennis *et al*. (eds), *The Planning of Change*, 4th edition. New York: Holt.

Yuki, G. (1982) *Managerial Leadership and the Effective Principal*. Washington DC: National Institute of Education.

Chapter 12

Consultancy in the Management of Curriculum Development

Ian Jamieson

INTRODUCTION

It is only relatively recently in the United Kingdom that there has been any attempt to link up the ideas of consultancy with those of curriculum development. This is not to say, of course, that those who have been engaged in the process of curriculum change have not acted as consultants and used consultants—they have. But they have not been aware of it, just as Molière's Monsieur Jourdain discovered that for more than 40 years he had not been aware of speaking prose. This lack of awareness has been important in the sense that it has hindered curriculum developers in clearly articulating the change processes in which they were engaged, and from exploring the range of consultancy styles which were theoretically open to them.

Curriculum development, the process of changing what is transacted in schools, is of course ubiquitous. Teachers are constantly changing the content of what they teach and their pedagogy. To corrupt Heraclitus, few teachers ever teach the same lesson twice; the process of teaching and learning is too interactive to allow this to happen. This process of change is influenced by a large number of factors—colleagues, subject associations, examination boards, LEA advisers and inspectors, Her Majesty's Inspectorate (HMI) and the Department of Education and Science (DES), and agencies specifically set up to bring about curriculum development. Nearly all of these individuals and bodies can act as consultants to teachers in the process of curriculum change. Two of the other chapters of this book specifically consider the role of inservice training and LEA advisers as consultants to schools and teachers. This chapter concentrates on the role of curriculum development projects that are specifically set up to bring about curriculum change. I will offer case studies of two projects that have, in their different ways, consciously worked with the concept of consultant: the Industry Project (SCIP) and the Careers Guidance Integration Project (CGIP).

THE WORLD OF CURRICULUM DEVELOPMENT

Lawrence Stenhouse has argued in his seminal work on curriculum development that, 'modern curriculum development can be taken to be characterised by the setting up of "projects"' (Stenhouse, 1975). The first programme of projects in England and Wales was initiated by the Nuffield Foundation: 'Nuffield Science, Nuffield Maths and Nuffield Modern Languages are the classic programmes in English curriculum development' (Stenhouse, 1975). Later the Schools Council became the major locus of curriculum development projects and one of our case study projects, the Industry Project, began life as a Schools Council Project.

The first generation of curriculum development projects had certain distinctive features. In the first place they focused on specific areas of the curriculum—mathematics, science, languages, English, etc. Second, they also began with a reasonably clear formulation of the type of change they wanted—either in content (most usually) or pedagogy, or both. Third, they recruited a group of school teachers who were chosen because they were thought to be leading practitioners. The task of these practitioners, who constituted the project team, represents the fourth feature of such projects. Typically their task was to construct some new materials that were to spearhead the new approach in the schools. These new materials would include pupil materials and a handbook on the new approaches for teachers. Fifth, these new materials were to be trialled in specially selected schools and then modified. Finally, once the publication stage had been reached, or possibly before, 'it was necessary to encourage the teacher training agencies, including local education authorities, universities, colleges of education, and the Inspectorate to cooperate in providing those teachers who wanted to use the new materials with appropriate training courses' (Halsey, 1971).

There is of course a model of planned change built into such projects. In terms of Havelock's models of innovation it falls reasonably clearly into the research, development and dissemination category. Experts at the centre research develop new ideas and materials, and these are offered for adoption to a passive consumer (Havelock, 1973). The assumptions concerning change are also clear: following Bennis, Benne and Chin (1961) we can say that they tended to follow the rational–empirical model. That is, change is seen as the outcome of rational persuasion on the basis of clear and objective evidence. The project's materials are offered by leading practitioners in the field, backed by the nation's curriculum development agency, the Schools Council, and after extensive research (trialling) in schools.

These models of change, and others, are of course well known to academics, but they were not part of the everyday knowledge of the *practitioner* world of the early Schools Council and its projects. Neither was the Schools Council particularly good as a corporate body in learning the lessons of curriculum development and change strategies and passing them on to new projects. The reasons for this are complex but the major ones are clear enough. The Council was dominated by a practitioner mentality—although it had academics and educationalists on its committees these were in a minority. As a body it was suspicious of theory and of factors that were not immediately related to the realities of teaching. Second, although project evaluation was part of the Council's strategy almost from the beginning, many evaluators were recruited with little knowledge of project evaluation or change strategies. Their evaluations were one-shot affairs that shed little light on the *general* process of curriculum development. It was largely left to the Impact and Take-up Project (of Schools Council Projects), which was initiated right at the end of the Council's existence, to gather data on which strategies were successful and which were not (Steadman, Parsons and Salter, 1980). Finally, the

Schools Council began its life with a publishing section that owed its existence to the view that curriculum development was essentially about experts producing written materials for use by teachers and pupils. This section grew in power during the life of the Council and made alternative models of change difficult to pursue.

The result of this combination of factors was that the early Schools Council projects acquired an almost 'natural' model of change—the R, D and D, centre–periphery, rational–empirical model. I say natural model because my own experience with a variety of curriculum development initiatives suggests that this model is the one that comes most naturally, in the British context, to those given charge of curriculum development and, just as importantly, it is the one which is expected by most teachers. Of course this model has its strengths, and under certain sets of circumstances it can be very effective. As the Impact and Take-up study showed, some of the most successful projects 'adopted such a model'.[1] What the Council did not learn, however, until it was too late, was what set of circumstances fitted what model.

During the later years of its life the Schools Council did launch some projects which started to break away from the R, D and D model of curriculum development. Projects like the Humanities Curriculum Project, Project Technology and the Industry Project do not fit into this mould. This later generation of projects had a number of features in common which made them distinctively different from the first generation projects. In the first place they tended not to be concerned with particular curriculum *subjects*, rather they were concerned with areas or dimensions of the curriculum to which a number of subjects might contribute. This fact led to their second distinctive feature. Curriculum development projects which do not focus on clearly defined school subjects are immediately faced with the problem of who are the clients for change; that is, on which particular groups of teachers should they focus? This problem brought the question of *change strategies and models* to the forefront of curriculum development. In some ways this later generation of projects was in a better position to handle this problem because the project teams were not recruited exclusively from the teacher-practitioner world simply because there were very few teacher-practitioners in the fields in which they were working. The new projects were more likely to recruit their teams from the ranks of educationalists and academics situated in universities and colleges of education. Faced with a distinctive and obvious problem of change these projects thought much more carefully about change strategies. This meant that they quickly made the breakthrough into the literature on planned change.

This breakthrough was undoubtedly assisted by the fact that these projects were not locked into single subject disciplines. The notion that ideas can be culled from a variety of disciplines helped these curriculum developers to leap over the boundaries enclosing education, and to make use of the change literature, which in the 1960s and early 1970s was to be found predominantly in the business and management fields. The reality of the curriculum development problem facing these projects, *and* the planned change literature, both indicated the centrality of two concepts. The first is that of *ownership*. Effective change will only take place if it is essentially self-directed. Project teachers had to somehow own the same problem as the project workers. This meant that most of these curriculum development projects saw themselves squarely in the business of 'people change'. The second concept which spanned both fields was the centrality of *process* as against product. The model of change adopted by many of the projects tended to be one which emphasized helping teachers to solve their own problems in the particular field of interest of the project by helping them acquire the relevant skills. The acquisition of these process principles, rather than the simple adoption of project materials became the mark of success (although not one that was necessarily accepted by the Schools Council, which tended to label such projects as invisible, for example Project Technology). Such a model has been supported by recent changes in the 14–18 curriculum, and particularly in prevocational education, which emphasize the negotiated curriculum, and student-centred teaching based on the students' ownership of particular problems.[2]

In this second generation of curriculum development projects it is possible to discover the consultancy concept. In other words some of these projects consciously made use of the idea of the project workers acting as consultants to teachers in the curriculum development process. In such projects the process of change has itself become the central issue on the agenda. The majority of them wrestle with one key problem. These curriculum development projects have models or maps of the sort of changes that they wish to bring about, yet some of them are also wedded to models of change and consultancy styles that stress the importance of the teachers' own definitions of and solutions to these problems. The attempt to square this circle is one of the central tensions of the new wave of curriculum development initiatives.

CONSULTANCY IN CURRICULUM DEVELOPMENT

There can be few medium or large-size industrial or commercial companies in Britain which have not used the services of a consultant at one time or another. And of those companies which have not made use of such consultancy services, they would probably all know of consultants they could use, and would know something of the range of services that consultants offer the industrial world. The same could hardly be said of the education service. Few schools have made use of the services of external consultants (ignoring LEA advisers). There are in fact remarkably few people operating in the education system as consultants, although their numbers are probably growing. Finally, few teachers who would be in a position to call on the services of an external consultant would ever think of doing so. Most would have little idea about the range of services offered, or about the style and strategies of consultancy. In short the external consultant is not part of either the language or the world of schooling and curriculum development. The reasons for this state of affairs go beyond this chapter but must include the following. First, the system has its own in-built consulting service—the LEA advisory service. Second, the system also provides a limited external consultancy service in the form of the curriculum development agencies, most notably the School Curriculum Development Committee. It might be argued that Her Majesty's Inspectorate (HMI) also act as consultants. Third, the vast majority of schools in Britain are in the public sector which means that schools have little financial autonomy to pay consultants and also little finance to pay for such services. We might add two other factors to this list of impediments to the consultancy idea. The first would relate to the traditional conception of teaching—something that was transacted by individuals, operating alone. Consultants generally work at the level of structures, teams and processes. This idea of teaching as a 'secret act' operating in the 'secret garden of the curriculum' (lately a little trampled through), can be connected in the British context to the obsession that we have in our society with secrecy and personal privacy (Shils, 1956). This ethos of individualism and secrecy means that aspects of schooling constitute something of a closed society. Few conceptions of consultancy work well in this situation.

Whether one accepts the argument that consultants and consultancy have been relatively absent from British schools must depend a little on one's definition of consultancy. A number of writers have suggested that it is possible to see consultancy models working in in-service education, much of which is of course focused on curriculum development (Davies, 1977; Erault, 1977; Bolam, 1978; Lewis, 1985). Although the definitions of consultancy advanced by these authors do differ one from another certain common themes emerge.

(a) the relationship between the consultant and client must be *voluntary*;
(b) the relationship between the consultant and client must be *temporary*;
(c) the relationship between the consultant and the client must be *advisory*;
(d) the consultant is assumed to be '*expert*' in some aspect of the 'problem' under discussion.

It seems difficult to see the LEA advisers, the in-built consultants of the system, as consultants on this definition despite Erault's view (Erault, 1977). They have difficulty in qualifying on the first three criteria, and they would seem to offend against one of the accepted precepts of consultancy, that the consultant is not in a superordinate position *vis-à-vis* the client. The people who most easily qualify for consultant status are people working in university and college departments of education and those working for curriculum development projects.

There seems little doubt that more college and university-based personnel are being drawn into assisting schools with the process of change. This is the result of a number of factors coming together. We can point to the increasing number and variety of problems facing schools as education, like the rest of society, moves away from a period of relative stability to one marked by considerable turbulence. Changes in assessment (profiling, GCSE); radical curriculum change (prevocational curriculum, GCSE); organizational changes (because of falling rolls and educational reorganization); the demands for greater accountability (changes in governing bodies, publication of examination results)—all these mean that schools are more likely to need external help than ever before. The focus of help is also changing. The move is towards school-focused problem-solving and school-focused INSET, rather than the more traditional cafeteria courses offered in higher education. Such a move generally assists the consultancy model which has traditionally involved the consultant working with the client 'on-site'. Finally, changes in the way that in-service education is funded via the new GRIST (grant-related in-service training) programme are likely to reinforce the development of the school-focused approach. While these changes are slowly creating conditions that favour the development of a consultancy-based model of curriculum development, what is lacking is any systematic development, dissemination and training in what the consultancy model entails. The available literature in this area is nearly all American, although the school-based evaluation movement has produced some British examples of consultancy in action (Hopkins and Vickers, 1986). The main British development that is cited is the GRIDS projects (guidelines for review and internal development in schools) which in operation can be viewed as an example of process consultancy drawing on the organization development (OD) tradition in consultancy.

CASE STUDIES OF CONSULTANCY IN CURRICULUM DEVELOPMENTS

The two case studies that are to be examined present some interesting differences and similarities in their use of consultancy strategies. Both the Industry Project (SCIP) and the Careers Guidance Integration Project (CGIP) are recent curriculum development exercises; SCIP began in 1977 while CGIP started in 1979. Neither project had a clearcut area of the school curriculum in which to work nor therefore an easily identifiable teacher–client group. As a consequence of this both projects faced particularly difficult problems of curriculum change. The final similarity is to be found in the 'industrial' connection that both projects had. As we shall show this connection was influential in the development of consultancy strategies in both cases.

The differences between the two curriculum development projects are less significant than the similarities but they are worth recording. The first is one of size. The Industry Project eventually became one of the biggest curriculum development exercises in England and Wales involving the majority of LEAs and hundreds of secondary schools. The CGIP was conceived as a small-scale project with only one full-time worker which operated in less than a dozen schools and colleges. Finally, the Industry Project was born as a child of the Schools Council, the largest curriculum development agency in England and Wales. It inherited a tradition of what a curriculum development project entailed. By contrast the Careers Guidance Integration Project was a joint DES/ European Community Project that was based at the National Institute for Career Education and Counselling (NICEC). Such mixed parentage meant that there were few traditions of what constituted a curriculum development project.

The Industry Project

The Industry Project, or SCIP as it is more commonly known, was part of the great concern about industry and education that originated in the 1970s (for a full account of its origins and development see Jamieson and Lightfoot, 1982). The CBI (Confederation of British Industries) was concerned about the lack of knowledge of, and poor attitudes towards, industry in the schools. The TUC was similarly concerned on behalf of the trade union movement. Together they convinced the Schools Council of the need for a project about industry.

Interestingly both the TUC and CBI, as centralist organizations external to the education system, saw the project in classic R, D and D terms. A small central team would produce 'authentic materials' about industry, broadly interpreted, for the schools. There was even talk about trying to 'teacher proof' such materials. Although there was dissent from the teacher representatives on the Schools Council about the idea of 'teacher-proofing', the basic model of an expert-led, materials-producing project received general assent.

Few had any illusions about the difficulties facing the project. How would the project be staffed given that there were no 'experts' in the schools? Would it be possible to produce materials that would be acceptable to industry, the trade unions and education? Who would use such materials, there being no 'teachers of industry' in the schools?

The project team that grew with the development of the project was unusual by Schools Council standards. Its first three members were respectively an industrialist with experience of educational administration, an ex shop-steward who had been a tutor for the WEA (Workers Education Association), and an industrial sociologist from higher education. A teacher was not added to the central team until the project was well underway. Partly because of this unusual background the team managed to resist being incorporated into the traditional curriculum change models that were current at the Schools Council. The organizational model that emerged was this. The project chose to work in five LEAs. These LEAs were chosen to give a reasonable geographical spread and to provide contrasting employment and industrial environments. The project made a 'contract' with each LEA to jointly fund and manage a teacher-coordinator to bring about change in a fixed number of schools, generally about five or six.

The model of change that the project embraced also slowly emerged. The director of the project put it like this (Jamieson and Lightfoot, 1982, p. 59):

> You need to try and ensure that whatever is done within schools should be genuinely *transferable*. 'High-flying' and 'self-selected' schools should be avoided and should in any case not form more than a small proportion of the schools with which the project worked.
>
> The exercise must be realistic, both in terms of costs and in terms of the kind of people which it used to develop the processes.
>
> Some means should be found of ensuring that the change is permanent. The central project could not be expected to be around forever.
>
> As far as possible, teachers should instigate the change themselves. They can be prodded, helped and encouraged, but the initiative must always be seen to come from the classroom.
>
> Insofar as materials have a role, they should be assembled on the basis of the experience of teachers who have actually been through these processes. Materials should be derived from the experience of change rather than be used as a method of inducing it.
>
> The exercise should be *locally* based. This should allow the building up of relationships at the local level, provide a mutual reinforcement between groups of teachers working in several local schools, and maximize the potential use of local contacts in industry and trade unions.

This model was evolved in the face of very considerable opposition from the Schools Council. The project seemed to lack clearcut direction from the centre; the role of materials had been seriously downgraded; there was scepticism whether local teachers could manage to change anything or produce anything of benefit for the project. The Schools Council, the CBI and the TUC all felt that they had lost their central control of what was going on.

The worries of those at the centre were not assuaged by the publication of the project's aims which seemed extremely vague. The project said that it was attempting to foster (Jamieson and Lightfoot, 1982, p. 81):

> a deepened sense of the nature of the working world combined with insight into alternatives to existing practice;
> an awareness of the interdependence of society, and hence of the ways in which authority can become legitimized; and
> an understanding of the ways in which certain groups in society operate collectively and—by extension—a readiness to participate in the processes involved.

At the forefront of this model were the project's teacher-coordinators who were working in the five initial LEAs. They suffered considerable stress and confusion at the beginning of the project. Their LEAs tended to see them as advisory teachers or advisers, as this was the nearest equivalent role model. In most LEAs such a model entails an authority relationship between adviser and teachers, and advisers are supposed to have clearly worked-out ideas about what constitutes 'good practice' in their schools and curriculum area. All the industry project's coordinators possessed was an uncertain model of change which involved sitting down with teachers and local industrialists and trade unionists (adults other than teachers as the project called them) and trying to work out a programme of action.

It is possible to see an interesting cascade model of the change process working its way through the project. At the top the project's central team attempted to *support* the project's coordinators. This support entailed helping them to develop their own local aims and strategies. The central team acted as consultants to the local coordinators. Back in the LEA the local coordinators attempted to support local change by acting as consultants to teachers and local adults other than teachers. Finally, the project's teachers, by placing an emphasis on their students solving their own problems via active and experiential learning strategies, themselves acted as facilitators and consultants to their students.

There were two great impediments to the process. In the first place the consultancy model was not recognized for what it was. This was partly due to poor communications, but largely because such a model only slowly evolved and the idea of the Industry Project's coordinators as consultants in curriculum change was a relatively late development. The second ingredient was that so many of the participants in the project held on to the 'expert' model as one appropriate in education. This was true at all levels in the project: at the Schools Council and TUC/CBI; in the LEAs amongst teachers; and just as importantly amongst the students themselves. They expected their teachers and the adults other than teachers they come into contact with to be experts.

The gradual emergence of an identifiable consultancy approach to curriculum development in the Industry Project was catalysed by SCIP's industrial connections. As industrialists became more and more involved in the project several of them began to see parallels between their own work as managerial change agents and consultants in industry and the work of the project. They noted that most of SCIP's in-service training was focused, quite properly, on improving the quality of student learning. But they were particularly interested in the role and strategy of SCIP's major change agents, the local teacher coordinators, the number of whom had grown enormously as the project had expanded into more and more LEAs. ICI, one of Britain's largest companies, and an organization with long experience of the management of change, offered a one week's residential training course for SCIP's teacher coordinators. The course focused on their role as managers of change and explored experientially the different consultancy styles available. It allowed the participants to explore their own strengths and weaknesses as consultants, and to understand, via techniques like force field analysis, the factors influencing the change process.

This course on consultancy skills has become the key element in SCIP's curriculum development strategy. It is now run by senior staff from the management development unit of British Gas and concentrates on getting the coordinators to see themselves as consultants in the process of curriculum change. The course is built around Blake and

Mouton's (1976) book *Consultation*. The coordinators are actively introduced to the five styles of consultant interventions: acceptant, catalytic, confrontation, prescription, and theories and principles.[3] SCIP encourages the catalytic consultation model which gets a school, with its local economic community, to study its own situation and jointly decide what changes it wishes to make. The coordinators often facilitate the process by promoting an action research model (a 'suck it and see' approach) and by trying to avoid specific prescriptions. The accent is always on local teachers and industrialists defining their own problems and solving them themselves.

The consultants' course, which was built on the foundations of the model of change that SCIP was already developing, has had two very important effects. In the first place it has allowed the continual development of a consultancy model of curriculum change. The project's change agents, the teacher coordinators, are clear about their role as consultants. They are specifically trained in consultancy skills. The second interesting development is how the consultancy model has spread into the very fabric of the project. Following the previous success of the consultant's course for coordinators, SCIP ran similar courses for the headteachers of project schools focusing on the management of change. A typical course is described by Holmes (1985).

Day 1 and 2
Theories of organisations and organisational change with particular emphasis on the change process. The emphasis is on the development of personal skills in managing organisational change through experiential exercises and intensive counselling.

Day 3
Personal influencing styles. The identification of personal styles and development of personal skills through active involvement of heads who act as *consultants* for each other, with feedback from the rest of the group.

Day 4
An opportunity to try out the skills developed on the course by carrying out a one day *consultancy* exercise in local industry. Companies are asked to identify a genuine problem concerned with change in their enterprise, to which they seek a solution. Headteachers work in small groups on site. The exercises are arranged by SCIP coordinators, advised by the ICI consultant.

Day 5
Debriefing centres around a discussion of how heads can use these newly developed skills when they return to school, and how the embryonic network which the course has established can be used [my emphases].

These courses have encouraged local headteachers to form consultancy groups amongst themselves, and to use local industrialists as school consultants. The consultancy model has also filtered down into the classroom. SCIP coordinators, by acting as catalytic consultants are setting an example of the sort of personal pedagogic style that they would like Industry Project teachers to adopt. In terms of pedagogy SCIP has been one of the leading organizations proselytizing active and experiential learning with the teacher taking on the role of facilitator. In many of the simulations of work developed by SCIP the teacher is cast in the role as consultant (Jamieson, Miller and Watts, 1988).

The Careers Guidance Integration Project

Like SCIP the Careers Guidance Integration Project was begun in the wake of the Great Debate and particular concerns about young people's transition from school to work.

The project focused on a difficult area of the curriculum, careers guidance, on which there is little agreement or standard practice. Like SCIP the project did not operate with a clearcut set of aims and objectives of what it wanted to achieve. The project's proposal declared that its aim was, 'to explore ways of supporting and integrating approaches to career guidance which are not confined to specialists but make use of a wide variety of resources both inside and outside school or college' (Evans and Law, 1984).

The project was concerned to stress that unlike so many curriculum development projects, it was not in the business of offering a 'product' or a 'package' to schools. It was concerned with the *process* of achieving integrated careers work. In stressing this it was trying to reinforce a view of careers education which itself stresses the processes of decision-making.

One can immediately see certain similarities with the Industry Project. Both projects operated with an action research model and both stressed the primacy of process over product. One important point of difference was that while SCIP gradually developed its ideas about consultancy based models of curriculum development, the Careers Guidance Integration Project started life with a relatively sophisticated view about the potential role of the project as a consultant to schools. There are several reasons why this occurred. In the first place the project's host organization NICEC, undertakes a variety of curriculum development projects in schools and further and higher education. It contains people with experience outside of education, in industry and elsewhere. Unlike the Schools Council it was not dominated by an atheoretical practitioner mentality. It did not have a vested interest in publishing materials. Second, the project's full-time worker had a background in organization development (OD). She characterized her previous organization development work as, 'working, usually as an external consultant to groups and organisations, assisting people to generate information about their ways of working which will assist them to improve their means of handling tasks' (Evans and Law, 1984). She saw these organization development skills as being 'relevant to questions of (careers) integration, since it is about balancing individual interests with the goals and tasks of the current education system' (Evans and Law, 1984).

The project did not operate with one clearcut consultancy model, and certainly not with a straight organization development model, although there were elements of this in some of their work. The operational model proposed by the project is depicted below (Evans and Law, 1984):

CGIP's Sequence of Action

(a) *Preparation visit*
     To talk with those in a position to report on the state of careers guidance within the organization.
(b) *Study visit*
     To decide on the viability, need and form of intervention that might be undertaken. To describe the way careers guidance relates to organizational objectives, to make an analysis of careers guidance activities, and to evaluate potential for further development.

(c) *Colloquium*
     Included where the organization seems ready to integrate its guidance activities
     more effectively through an intergroup consultation between role-groups con-
     cerned with careers guidance, including community contacts. To close with con-
     sideration of short, medium and long-term planning objectives.
(d) *First report*
     An analysis of the project's intervention and of the training needs of staff involved
     in careers guidance work.
(e) *Training visit*
     In some organizations, on-site training in specific guidance skills.
(f) *Follow-up visit*
     To assess outcomes of interventions.
(g) *Second report*
     To describe the outcomes observed in the follow-up visits.

In the course of the project the change strategy shifted from one phase to another and
from one intervention strategy to another. This was consonant with the view that the
project was itself a learning system and that its strategy changed as it assessed the
success of its various approaches.

If we consider those aspects of the project where the consultancy model was consciously embraced then certain distinctive features are revealed. The project talked in
terms of finding 'clients' in schools, that is of finding personnel in the schools who had a
concern which was of interest and relevance to the project. Finding a client is closely
related to the issue of 'readiness' for change. This classic organization development
concept became an important one for the project, and schools were assessed in terms of
their readiness for careers integration. Another important concept to be found in the
project in its initial work with schools is that of 'contract'. After initial entry the project
attempted to negotiate a contract with each school which involved those in the decision
to proceed with work in the school. The contract typically included a 'Clear remit for
project negotiated, plus commitment of time on part of school or college. Clear
statement concerning ownership of information. Date set for review and renegotiation' (Evans and Law, 1984).

Each contract specified something about information collection and feedback to the
school. The feedback of data became an important feature of the project. The process
of feedback to the schools differed in different situations and reflected the different
models that the project workers adopted to fit those situations. They represented the
differences diagrammatically in the following way (from feedback of data, Evans and
Law, 1984).

Reflection	Selection	Interpretation	Diagnosis	Perception
Project workers as 'facilitators'			Project workers as 'experts'	

$$\longleftarrow \qquad\qquad \longrightarrow$$

The feedback continuum, which runs from project workers as 'facilitators', to project
workers as 'experts', exemplifies a dilemma in consultancy styles in curriculum development. On the one hand one has the model of consultancy based on *expertise* in the
context of a particular task to be undertaken. Here the expert is brought in to offer
solutions to a stated problem. This can be contrasted with consultancy based on *process*

skills. Here the consultant is not offering solutions to problems, but rather is seeking to assist the client to develop his or her own problem-solving capacity. The focus is not upon the content of the task, but rather on the ways in which it is tackled. The client finds his or her own solutions to the problem with the assistance of the process consultant in a non-directive role.

The Career Guidance Integrated Project found itself attracted to the latter model, as did the Industry Project, but like SCIP it found strong forces pushing it in the opposite direction. Project workers do naturally have views about 'good practice' in schools and it is always tempting to play the expert and push schools in the direction one would like them to go. Teachers themselves very often expect such a stance. The CGIP project workers often found their reports, which were intended to catalyse responses, being taken as expert assessments. As representatives of the leading national body for careers education this was hardly surprising. The project also argued, however, that process consultancy is not part of the world of teaching and education, and that this was a major reason for misapprehension. They argued that the very term consultancy is used in conventional terms for a situation where the 'client' pays for somebody who is supposed to be an expert.

SOME KEY ISSUES FOR CONSULTANCY IN CURRICULUM DEVELOPMENT

I have argued that a key vehicle for curriculum development in Britain has been the specially constructed project. Both the case studies that I have described illustrate the delicate balancing act that projects have to engage in. On the one hand, they need to spell out their curriculum programme with sufficient clarity and detail to convince sponsors that it is worth funding. On the other hand they need a sufficient amount of 'space' to negotiate with schools and teachers so that the latter group feel that they own both the problems being addressed and their solutions.

We can identify several pressures that are exerted on curriculum development projects that tend to push them in the direction of the consultant as expert models. The first of these is derived from the needs and interests of sponsors for quick results. As temporary systems most curriculum development projects are anxious to make their mark on the system before they disappear and the temptation to play the expert and give teachers the 'answer' is very strong. I have argued that many teachers expect curriculum development project workers to be experts and supply 'answers'. The difficulty is that very often the advice does not fit the particular circumstances of the teacher or school, or even worse represents a solution to a problem that the teacher does not have. The final source of pressure is the understandable desire on the part of the sponsors for their role in the curriculum change process to be acknowledged. This is rarely problematic in the consultant as expert model but faces severe problems in more process-based consultancy models. Such consultants often rework the old Chinese maxim that the best 'leaders' [curriculum developers] are those who are not even noticed, those in fact whose clients when the change has been implemented, say, 'we did it ourselves'.

The problems with centre–periphery models of curriculum development, and their associated 'prescriptive' and 'theory and principles' consultation styles, raise important questions about the role of the personnel in curriculum development projects. As we have seen, traditionally they have been leading schoolteachers in specific subject areas. They have nearly always been regarded as experts by teachers in project schools. The question we have to ask is—expert in what? The original answer was expert in their subjects and this generally embraced both subject content and pedagogy, although historically the claims were always stronger in the former area. Our two case studies of curriculum development show how the claim to expertise has been extended. In both the Industry Project and the Careers Guidance Integration Project the project workers claimed knowledge and expertise in the process of change itself. Although the idea of curriculum developers as change agents has been around for a long time, it is difficult to find many examples of curriculum development projects which have taken the idea seriously, and concentrated on giving their workers the requisite skills and knowledge.

There is some debate about the requirements of curriculum developers who see themselves as consultants in the change process. There seems general agreement that such consultants should have a knowledge of the relevant curriculum area, and be familiar with the clients' setting. There is less agreement about whether the consultant should possess a particular set of personal and interpersonal skills that are relevant to the change process, and still less agreement about whether it is possible or desirable to train likely consultants in such skills. The Industry Project represents a case of a curriculum development project which takes such training very seriously, while the Careers Guidance Integration Project is an example of a project which deliberately set out to choose somebody with such skills. Finally, there are those who insist that consultants in curriculum change should have a knowledge of 'established principles of organizational change' and of 'theories and methods of change' (Hoyle, 1971).

The final issues that confront curriculum developers operating as consultants are those posed by their clients, the teachers. The concept of client is itself problematic. Although we naturally think of consultants as having clients, it is unusual to conceptualize teachers as clients in the curriculum development process, and this itself is an indication of the underdeveloped nature of consultancy in curriculum development. There seem to be several problems that are integral to the very concept of client. The first is the idea of the client as somebody who receives/approaches the consultant *voluntarily*. The history of curriculum development projects is full of unwilling schools and teachers who have been put forward by LEAs and headteachers to be 'developed'. In such a situation only a process-based consultancy is ever going to have much of a chance of success. The second problem is related to the first. The experience of both the case study curriculum development projects was that for the consultant–client relationship to work well the clients needed confidence in the work that they were already doing in their schools. In other words the client needed sufficient stature and confidence to be full and equal partners in the relationship. This factor was usually an important *sine qua non* for the client to be sufficiently 'open' to the consultant. This is one of the central problems of LEA advisers acting as curriculum consultants. As one headteacher in the Industry Project vividly put it:

I'm reticent to talk about our weaknesses when I know that the advisers have to make recommendations about the next round of cuts. We have to be competitive in order to survive, and that means marketing our strengths rather than our weaknesses [quoted in Holmes, 1985, p. 203].

Curriculum development projects that focus on specific subject areas of the curriculum usually have few problems in identifying their clients even if they have subsequent problems in persuading them to change. I argued earlier, however, that many of the later curriculum development initiatives focused their attention on much broader areas of the curriculum, many of which crossed traditional subject boundaries. This presented them with a problem of identifying clients. Ultimately this problem of client focus has been beneficial to the development of consultant strategies in curriculum development. It has forced the projects to think much more thoroughly about the problem of change, and in particular to grasp the fact that change agents need a much wider range of knowledge and skills than simply those attached to curriculum and pedagogy. In short they have come to realize that the process of change in these areas requires an understanding of the structure and process of schooling itself.

CONCLUSIONS

In this chapter I have been concerned to show the gradual emergence of models of consultancy in the process of curriculum development. It can of course be argued that curriculum development projects have always acted as consultants to schools. In the early days they merely embraced *one* model of consultancy, the subject expert offering prescriptive solutions. I would resist this interpretation, however, because I believe that a crucial ingredient in any serious view of consultancy is the possession of a set of concepts and skills that are related to the change process itself. In other words, it does not seem to me that the concept of consultant in the curriculum development process can be extended to the early curriculum development project workers. Most of these teachers did not view themselves as change agents, neither did they consciously possess change agent skills and concepts.

We recognize that it is important not to define the concept of consultant in curriculum development too narrowly, and we are aware of a growing tendency only to consider those consultants who embrace a process consultancy approach as being worthy of the term consultant. It is interesting to note that both the curriculum development projects in our case studies strongly incline towards this model. Curriculum development consultants can and should make use of a variety of models of the change process and consultancy techniques. Eventually I would expect to see the development of a full-blown contingency model of consultation in the curriculum development process. In this model the consultant would select the strategy according to the context of the situation and the needs of the client.

The English model of curriculum development has mirrored the English model of education. We have operated a devolved model where the responsibility for the curriculum has rested squarely on the shoulders of the LEA and its schools. Such a model has great strengths, particularly in its untrammelled capacity to develop innovation. The curriculum development agencies and their projects have been an important support to such a system and the source of much innovation. But this system looks as though it has reached a watershed and it is the weaknesses of the system that are now at the top of the political agenda. The major identified weakness is the piecemeal, uncontrolled development that the system produces.

There seems general agreement that the state is about to take a much stronger role in defining the curriculum. The interesting question for us is where this leaves the role of consultants in the curriculum development process. If change is to be dictated from the centre then the curriculum development agencies and their characteristic projects look as though they will be confined to the margins, although of course a lot will depend on exactly what model of the centralized curriculum the state chooses.

If, as seems likely, the main burden of curriculum change shifts to the state, then the role of the curriculum development project seems likely to be confined to small-scale feasibility studies of specific innovations. The consultant's role in such a model will surely be close to that of a process consultant, working within an action research framework, exploring the strengths and weaknesses of curriculum initiatives. Such a model is close to those that have been elaborated in our two case studies.

NOTES

(1) It might be agreed that the indicators of success used by the study deliberately favoured materials producing projects founded on the R, D and D model.
(2) Such an approach is exemplified in the Technical and Vocational Education Initiative (TVEI), the Lower Attaining Pupils Programme (LAPP), and in developments like the Certificate of Prevocational Education (CPVE).
(3) These are defined as follows (Blake and Mouton, 1976):

Acceptant: the intention is to give the client a sense of personal security so that when working with the consultant he or she will feel free to express personal thoughts without fear of adverse judgements or rejection.
Catalytic: this assists the client in collecting data and information to reinterpret his or her perceptions as to how things are.
Confrontation: this challenges the client to examine how the present foundations of thinking may be colouring and distorting the way situations are viewed.
Prescription: the consultant tells the client what to do to change or rectify a given situation or does it for him or her.
Theories and principles: by offering theories pertinent to the client's situation, the consultant helps the client internalize systematic and empirically tested ways of understanding.

REFERENCES

Bennis, W. G., Benne, K. D. and Chin, R. (1961), *The Planning of Change*. New York: Holt, Rinehart and Winston.
Blake, R. R. and Mouton, J. (1976) *Consultation*. London: Addison-Wesley.
Bolam, R. (1978) 'School focussed INSET and consultancy'. *Educational Change and Development*, **1**, 1.
Davies, B. (1977) 'Consultancy—some of the issues'. *British Journal of In-Service Education*, **3**, 2.
Erault, M. (1977) 'Some perspectives on consultancy in in-service education'. *British Journal of In-Service Education*, **4**, 1.
Evans, K. and Law, B. (1984) *Career Guidance Integration Project: Final Report*, vols 1–3. Hertford: NICEC.
Halsey, P. (1971) 'Role of research and development projects in curriculum development: an address', in Maclure, J. S. (1973), *Curriculum Development: An International Training Seminar, Norwich UK*. Paris: OECD.
Havelock, R. G. (1973) *Planning for Innovation Through Dissemination and Utilization of Knowledge*. Ann Arbor, Mich.: Centre for Research on Utilization of Scientific Knowledge.

Holmes, S. (1985) 'Using industrial managers as a resource for the in-service training of teachers', in Jamieson, I. M. (ed.), *Industry in Education*. Harlow: Longman.

Hopkins, D. and Vickers, C. (1986) 'Process consultation in school self evaluation'. *Cambridge Journal of Education*, **16**, 2.

Hoyle, E. (1971) 'The role of the change agent in educational innovation', in Walton, J. (ed.), *Curriculum Organisation and Design*. London: Ward Lock Educational.

Jamieson, I. M. and Lightfoot, M. (1982) *Schools and Industry*. London: Methuen.

Jamieson, I. M., Miller, A. and Watts, A. G. (1988) *Mirrors of Work*. London: Falmer Press.

Lewis, H. D. (1985) 'Consultancy, the tutor, and INSET'. *British Journal of In-Service Education*, **12**, 1.

Shils, E. A. (1956) *The Torment of Secrecy*. Glencoe: Free Press.

Steadman, S. D., Parsons, C. and Salter, B. G. (1980) *Impact and Take-up Project*. London: Schools Council.

Stenhouse, L. (1975) *An Introduction to Curriculum Development*. London: Heinemann.

Chapter 13

Internal Organization Development Consultancy in a Local Education Authority

Mike Lavelle and *David Keith*

THE CHALLENGE OF THE TURBULENT ENVIRONMENT

Ours is a society in which massive changes are occurring at a rapidly accelerating rate, and increasing numbers of us seem to be feeling that life is somehow out of control—we feel bewildered and confused and rather powerless. Yet if we can retain, or regain, a sense of control over our lives and our futures, while not being able to predetermine them, perhaps the shaking free from some of our old certainties can be a liberating and enhancing experience.

If we are to transform the fear of the dangers of uncertainty into a celebration of the possibilities of openness, however, we need to understand the nature of change and actively engage with it, so learning to manage change rather than being overwhelmed by it. We shall not, through such active engagement, find readymade solutions, but we shall discover and refine processes by which we can *create* solutions and shape our futures.

Such is the speed and complexity of change that we can neither return to the past nor accurately predict the future. Of course, the present is interwoven with the past and the future, but we have to learn to value the past without being fixed in it, and to look to the future without feeling swept along into it.

The responsibility for creating our own futures is not easy to accept. We tend to fear freedom (Fromm, 1960); we are afraid of the responsibility of taking control of our own destiny. Yet we need to create for ourselves and our children a new security and confidence in *processes of seeking* our way forward, processes in which we all share. We need to learn how to feel secure in the unknown because we have the process-understandings which will help us explore meaningfully. Our old certainties, concepts and paradigms are proving inadequate. We need to develop a whole technology of change, based on seeking together, by which we can conceptualize new experience and map out where we are going in the process of journeying together. What we can define is the nature and quality of the journeying, not the precise destination. Quality of process, not clarity of ends, is the key to this 'seeker' mode of change (see Bruner, 1962, on knowers and seekers).

Rather than fearing, and being immobilized by, the absence of absolute certainty, then, we may learn to welcome it, to experience a sense of adventure rather than of insecurity in journeying into the unknown with as much sensitivity and integrity as we can muster. Of course, our journey will be never-ending, for each step we take into the future, each problem we solve, creates a new situation which in turn creates new challenges and new problems. The process is, however, evolutionary not circular, because each new step forward, each emergent solution, advances our understanding one step more.

In the light of this, processes of review and reassessment have a clear psychological as well as strategic value, for 'the ability to re-evaluate decisions and policies from time to time seems fundamental to coping with complex, changing environments' (Hamburg, Coelho and Adams, 1974, p. 435).

If, then, in our turbulent environment, we are to transform the paralysis of uncertainty into the opportunity of openness, to respond proactively to flux and change, we need to perceive our world in new ways, especially to see things whole and to understand reality not as fixed and static but as dynamic and shifting. We need to take stock of where we are and of the complex factors affecting our situation. We need to understand the nature of the change processes, to develop holistic, configurational 'maps' of where we are and what we are caught up in, to identify and mobilize the resources we have available to engage with change and create our futures. There are no absolute certainties, no tablets of stone—yet this need not deter us, rather it may free us to take responsibility into ourselves. Fixed in the false certainties and securities of old precepts and paradigms, we can never resolve the human dilemmas in our world.

We do need faith—faith in our values, faith in the potential of human beings to develop deeper and broader perspectives which will empower us to transform our world. For some of us this will be a spiritual faith, for others a humanistic faith—but it will be *faith not certainty*. It will be commitment to the best that we can know, while recognizing that, in Bronowski's (1973) words, 'there is no absolute knowledge. And those who claim it, whether they are scientists or dogmatists, open the door to tragedy.'

We must commit ourselves to action, but that action must be continually reflected upon, reviewed and modified in the light of new understandings. It is in this seeker mode, this seeking for patterns and connections, this spirit of review and re-evaluation and this understanding of process-realities that organization development (OD) operates—indeed it is out of this emergent paradigm of growth and change that organization development has itself emerged; (see, for example, Beckhard, 1969; Bennis, 1969; French and Bell, 1978; Margulies and Raia, 1978) and from which the Organization Development Unit within Sheffield Education Department has developed.

SCHOOLS AND CHANGE

For over 30 years there has been a growing interest in planned change in schools. The Schools Council's curriculum development activities tended to set the style of educational innovation in the 1960s and early 1970s. What was adopted was a centre–

periphery pattern of change, with the Council funding a team of experts to *research* a curriculum area, *design* and develop a curriculum programme (usually materials-based), test and evaluate the programme, and modify and *disseminate* the finished product (the R, D and D model).

Although such an approach was soundly research-based and the materials developed were generally well-produced, the involvement of teachers in the development process was very limited, a high level of conformity of need in schools was assumed, and the approach was applicable largely to materials rather than, for example, to pupil-grouping, teaching methods, etc.

Critically reviewing this approach to curriculum development, Hopkins (1982) delivers the devastating verdict that 'top-down or linear approaches to change which ignore the user do not work', and Elliott-Kemp (1982) cites evidence from several countries of a growing dissatisfaction with the centre–periphery model—a dissatisfaction which is encouraging a shift of emphasis 'from mass-production of curriculum materials to the school setting: the unique context within which the fate of an innovation is ultimately determined'. Work by Fullan and Pomfret (1977) on curriculum implementation supports the view that the locus of control of curriculum development needs to shift from the external developer to the school itself.

There have been in more recent years, in consequence of this criticism and dissatisfaction, moves towards a problem-solving model which places the individual school at the centre of the development process. In this approach, innovations are not specified in advance or from the outside, but arise from the perceived needs of the school in its own context. Thus the diagnosis of need, the development process and the implementation of innovations are all internally administered and controlled, any 'external' support being in facilitating the development process. A school using this approach needs to develop an open problem-solving orientation, be adaptable to change and growth, and be able and willing to invest a considerable amount of staff time to the development process. (At the recent International School Improvement Project dissemination conference at Nene College, Northampton,[1] a great deal of emphasis was placed on the notion of a school's 'readiness' for change.) While schools generally make use of both externally and internally generated curriculum development programmes and processes, the implementation of new approaches is ultimately in the hands of teachers, and much of the recent emphasis on the study of educational innovation has been upon institutionalization—that is, the operationalizing of new curriculum proposals and the development of strategies to handle the problems created by this process.

CONDITIONS FOR EFFECTIVE CHANGE

Hilda Taba (1962) has noted that curriculum change cannot take place without a change in both people and institutions, and, as Hopkins points out, 'the more complex the change, the more the need to co-ordinate the actions of more people and the more need to change the assumptions and norms that they hold'. The dialectical relationship between individual and systemic change is noted by Emrick and Peterson (1978) who found in their synthesis of five major studies of educational change that

> there are two separate but parallel dimensions to this change process: a personal dimension which involves the change process occurring within individuals (cognitive, behavioural,

affective) as they acquire and make use of new knowledge, and a systemic dimension, which involves the concomitant changes occurring in the user environment (organizational, social, political). . . . These separate but parallel processes appear to unfold as interdependent stages, both within and across dimensions.

As well as the interplay of personal and systemic dimensions of change, there is the dynamic interplay of the innovation itself and the context in which it is being introduced—that is, an innovation changes to meet the unique set of circumstances in a specific school, as the school is changing in response to the innovation. Berman and McLaughlin (1977) call this process 'mutual adaptation'. Without careful attention being paid to such dynamics, the structural and organizational changes so necessary to a full assimilation of an innovation may lead to new patterns as rigid and inflexible as the old, making it difficult to modify the new patterns and even to overcome any unintended outcomes of the change process (see MacDonald (1973), quoted in Stenhouse (1975), on unanticipated consequences of change).

A school able to undertake effective change needs to be in a state of readiness—to be what Bolam (1982) calls a 'problem-solving' school. It needs, for example, effective communication and support processes, for 'without adequate structures for communication and support, innovation is unlikely to survive' (Rudduck, 1973). It needs, above all, what Stenhouse (1975) refers to as 'reflexiveness', by which he means 'a capacity to review critically and reflectively its own processes and practices'.

Such a school is able to exist creatively within its environment, responding to that environment without being enslaved by it. For Nisbet (1972) the creativity of a school has three elements: confronting problems, responding to problems and evaluating the response to problems. Programmes and processes of school improvement should, therefore, enable schools to become more proactive—to internalize more the locus of control over their destinies. This implies 'a school which takes more responsibility for: the development of its own curriculum; the professional development of its staff; innovation and change; its own development . . . and the wider society which it reflects and the community which it serves' (Hopkins, 1982).

Jane David (1982) describes four assumptions upon which proactive school-based educational change needs to be based: first, that the particular characteristics of a school and its context are taken into account; second, that for staff to be committed to a change effort they need to be involved in decisions about it; third, that the school should have a school-wide focus—'a set of shared goals and a unified approach to instruction as opposed to separate, uncoordinated projects and approaches'; and fourth, that change processes encouraging self-awareness and reflection on the part of school staff will greatly increase the chances that behaviours will change.

The findings on the conditions and strategies for effective change in schools are neatly summarized by Hopkins (1982):

. . . the school is widely regarded as the prime unit of change, its autonomy (and that of its constituent members) has become a major goal, and internal and external support systems have been created to achieve this end. Change strategies are increasingly being based on a multidimensional concept of implementation tied to the organizational features of the school, and individual school improvement efforts . . . are typically conceived of in a wider context.

THE EMERGENCE OF AN ORGANIZATION DEVELOPMENT UNIT IN THE SHEFFIELD LOCAL EDUCATION AUTHORITY

The primary assumption lying behind a shift from a centre–periphery to a problem-solving model of planned change in education is that an innovation is more likely to be successful when a need for it has been recognized by the school than when outsiders decide that it would be of benefit to the school. Innovation occurs *inside* the school and 'change which is not internalized is likely to be distorted and temporary' (Day, 1985, p. 1), so the focus of the problem-solving orientation is 'the user himself: *his* needs and what he does about satisfying his needs are paramount' (Havelock, 1975, p. 316).

However, a problem-solving orientation involves a total-organization perspective if all the factors which may impinge upon any innovation are to be taken into account. Indeed, as we have seen, planned change in schools is seen increasingly as involving not simply discrete developments within specific sections of the school system: rather, coordinated change efforts in the context of an overall process of school improvement are required (Bolam, 1982; Hopkins and Wideen, 1982; Dalin, 1983). This may pose a problem for schools whose management and teaching staffs are unlikely to have received much training as organization analysts and diagnosticians. It is not surprising that some schools are, therefore, beginning to seek the assistance of an outside person, not as an expert who provides predetermined, packaged solutions, 'which will be applied to the situation without rigorous analysis' (Gray and Heller, 1982), but as a process helper, a consultant, who acts as

> a facilitator, helper or objective observer; as a specialist in diagnosing needs and in identifying the means of meeting these needs. The consultant concentrates on the how of problem-solving in contrast to the conveyor who tells what the solution should be. The consultant's underlying rationale is that only the client . . . can really determine what is useful for him and thus the consultant's role is to act as a collaborator and encourager (Bolam, 1976, p. 58).

In the light of the developing need for, and understanding of, consultancy processes in education, an Organization Development Unit was set up within the Sheffield LEA, in September 1983, with ourselves as the two part-time consultants.

Our shared involvement, in the 1970s, with curriculum development in social education had led to a close partnership being developed between us, based on shared perceptions of the need for a whole-school perspective on social education. Our concern had been for the congruence between what was taught as social education in the classroom and what was learned by pupils about social education through the ethos, relationships, authority patterns and organizational structures of the school. It was this concern which led to our being asked by the Second Deputy Chief Education Officer (DCEO) to offer ourselves as consultants to headteachers who wished to explore processes of school improvement and organization development.

As consultants, we soon became involved in detailed processes of school development through an intensive, voluntarily contracted programme defined by our clients (the individual schools). While, therefore, the consultancy service was offered through the Education Department as supplier of that service, and our overall contract of employment was with the LEA, our primary responsibility within a specific consultancy contract was with the individual school as client. Any material generated through that primary consultancy contract was seen by us to be confidential to the school involved, except by agreement with the headteacher, and similar levels of confidentiality needed to be agreed within secondary contracts with individual teachers or pupils.

The nature of our consultancy roles, our relationship to the Advisory Service, our answerability to LEA and headteachers, and the organizational subsystem to which we would belong, all had to be explored, negotiated and defined before the Organization Development Unit was established. Discussions within the Education Department resulted in what Her Majesty's Inspectorate (HMI) have called a 'formal working agreement' being established as a basis for our work. The main points of this working agreement are that the Organization Development team:

(a)   is available to 'schools, agencies and departments within the Education Service in Sheffield . . .' offering 'insights, drawn from careful diagnosis and consultation, into the relationships between the organizational, cultural and personal aspects of a unit's life and work in a particular setting. These insights then provide the data by which problems might be resolved and developments implemented';

(b)   relates to clients 'by their invitation, on the basis of short-term contracts with specific foci, any authority to act in a given situation being subject to negotiation with the clients, not vested in the consultancy role per se';

(c)   reports to a small management group within the LEA;

(d)   should, for the purposes of liaison, inform the Chief Adviser of any consultancy contract being considered by the OD team;

(e)   may act in a referral capacity, 'recommending to clients approved services and people both within and outside the LEA structure';

(f)   should contribute to, and sometimes initiate, conferences, courses and seminars;

(g)   may be available to attend regional and national conferences and seminars;

(h)   may allocate time to 'reading, exchanging ideas, liaison and consultation with others in similar fields, and continuing to develop and refine their methodology . . .'

A diagrammatic 'map' of our consultancy relationships with clients and the Advisory Service is shown in Figure 13.1.

The Organization Development Unit offered consultancy help from the first day of the autumn term, 1983, and initially we wondered whether we would be used. We had sought a role in which we had no right of entry into schools or educational units except by invitation, and now we felt very vulnerable. However, we were introduced by the Second Deputy Chief Education Officer to the secondary headteachers at one of their meetings and were quite well-received, though no one approached us at that stage. Then we were invited to participate in a meeting of the headteachers' discussion group, which met periodically with the Second Deputy Chief Education Officer to discuss matters of interest and concern to headteachers. The focus of the meeting on this occasion was headteacher–staff development and we, among others, were able to outline what contribution we might make to this process. After the meeting, three headteachers (one secondary, one primary, one special school) approached us and we soon had our first three clients. This meeting established the basis of two major strands of our subsequent organization development work—first, work on a headteacher development strategy, and second, school-based consultancy work.

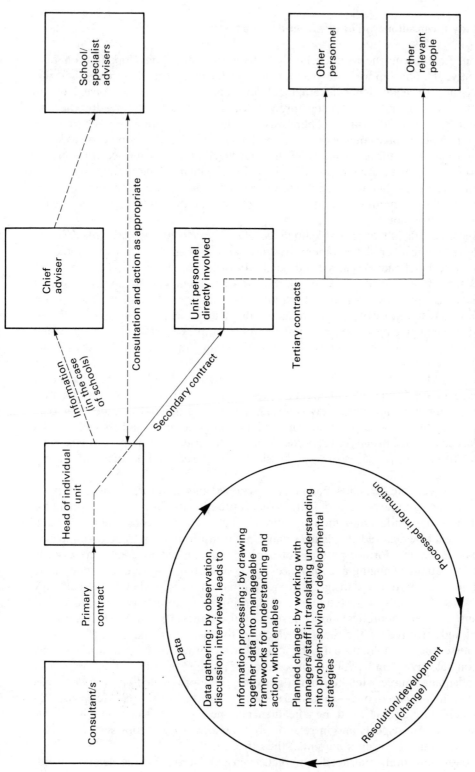

Figure 13.1 Consultancy relationships with clients.

Case study 1: consultancy in headteacher development

From our first visit to the headteachers' discussion group we developed an ongoing consultative relationship with the group, through which we were able to highlight two crucial issues for headteacher development. First, as the discussions proceeded, the locus of control of the development process was perceived by the headteachers as shifting from them to 'the office'. There was no deliberate intention on the part of the Education Office to take control; it was more that headteacher development was being perceived mainly in terms of matching headteachers' needs to the existing INSET provision, rather than matching provision (which might be much more than courses) to the expressed needs. Second, the actual process of planning a coherent strategy for headteacher development was complex, having to take account of many factors, needs and types of provision.

We recommended that the group should *develop a strategy for managing the development of* a headteacher development strategy, and that such a strategy should be responsive to headteachers' perceived needs. In order to gather initial data for this process we offered to interview all the headteacher members of the group (three secondary, five primary, two special schools) about their development needs. A remarkably consistent priority need emerged—the need to deal with high stress levels resulting from managing schools at a time of rapid, complex and turbulent change, and to feel that change was being *managed*, in a developmental mode, rather than being *reacted to*, in a survival mode.

It became clear, in these and other conversations with headteachers, that many headteachers are facing a fundamental role-dilemma in finding a healthy balance between maintaining and creatively adapting the life and functions of their schools.

In the past there was a premium on stability and continuity, and the role of the headteacher was, in a broad sense, predetermined. A pattern of role-performance was inherited from one's predecessors and decisions were based on precedent and experience.

Now, however, the demands made on our schools, and therefore on headteachers, seem ever more complex and turbulent. In such a situation it is increasingly difficult for any one person to understand and keep abreast of all the aspects of a school's life and work, in each of which radical changes and rapid transitions seem to be taking place. Past experience and former patterns of decision-making are no longer necessarily relevant to rapidly changing circumstances, and old certainties are questioned in the light of new information and insights. In such a situation, headteachers cannot act only on the basis of a tried-and-tested model of headship, nor can they turn uncritically to some untested new theoretical model devised by academics. Rather, the headship role relevant and effective for the times in which we live has to be discovered.

Of course, there is a great deal to be learned from former practice, but it has to be drawn on selectively and critically, as a resource, rather than depended upon as a totally adequate source. Headteachers today are, therefore, called upon to *develop* a role rather than to *inherit* one—that is, to undertake a sort of action-research process of carefully redefining what it is to be a headteacher and testing this new definition over time, in its various aspects and in relation to others involved: senior staff team, the whole staff group, governors, parents, 'the office', etc.

Two basic developmental needs emerged from our interviews: the need for headteachers first to find space and time to reflect on the nature and meaning of the turbulent changes in which they are caught up, and second to decide whether to respond to these changes by adopting a traditional, 'top-down' headship paradigm (with its inherent assumption that the headteacher is capable of making all the major decisions in all aspects of school life), or the emergent exploratory paradigm (in which the head-teacher involves all his/her staff in seeking the resolution of the issues/concerns/dilemmas facing the school).

In September 1985, the new Deputy Education Officer (Schools) set up a head-teachers' staff development group and we presented a paper to this group entitled 'Management Development—A Choice of Paradigms'. In this paper we argued that as the 'top-down' and 'exploratory' paradigms of headship would demand very different forms of headship development programme, the LEA should consider carefully whether its proposed headteacher development strategy would be based on one or other of the two paradigms or would attempt to meet the needs of both. As a result of this paper, and the group's deliberations on the issues raised by it, we were asked to consider the implications of basing a headteacher development strategy on the 'explora-tory' paradigm of headship. This we did in a further paper, 'Planning For Headteacher Development—An Overview', in which we suggested that there were three sets of needs being expressed by headteachers—understanding needs, development needs and support/resources needs.

If effective headteacher development is likely to be more a process of exploration than of moulding, then the first stage is for headteachers to be given the opportunity to step back from the pressures and stresses in order to reflect on some key questions. The first question is, 'What does it mean to be a headteacher in our turbulent age—how are my role, my identity, my values, my directions affected?' This argues for a development process which creates opportunities for *understanding*. The second question is, 'Where am I going and how do I retain responsibility for getting there?', which argues for a development process which supports levels of headteacher control of that process—that is, *proactive development*. The third question for headteachers is, 'Having understood where I am and having retained some control over where I am going, how do I get there?' This raises the question of commitment, both from headteachers and from the Education Department. For the headteacher it demands that thought be given to individual and corporate commitment to headteacher development (for example, should involvement be voluntary, required or a balance of both?). For the Education Department it demands a commitment to providing personnel and resources in order to respond effectively to headteacher development needs. This argues for a development process which offers, supports and ensures take-up of *opportunities*.

Our paper went on to point out the clear implications that the identification of understanding, proactive development and opportunities as key development compo-nents has for an LEA strategy:

(a) The need for *understanding* suggests the provision of supportive and reflective learning processes (through, for example, advisory, consultative and colleague support; counselling, study groups and support groups, etc.).
(b) The need for *proactive development* suggests a process by which each headteacher can build a self-selected pattern, or profile, of development for him/herself based on the understanding arising from (a) above. This profile, while being flexible and

renegotiable, will be a carefully sequenced pattern of developmental experiences (reading, support, consultation, group membership, courses, job exchanges, secondments, etc.), which might also include certain required elements.

(c)   The need for *opportunities* suggests as flexible and comprehensive a range of provision as can be offered by the LEA.

These strategic considerations have within them, we pointed out, implications for the terms of reference of the headteachers' staff development group. A group commissioned to implement such a wide-ranging, interdepartmental strategy will itself need to be interdepartmental, with strong headteacher representation. Within the parameters of its answerability to the Education Department, the group will require the necessary authority to:

(a)   *make provision* for the implementation of the strategy;
(b)   *coordinate* the contribution of a number of departments and agencies within and beyond the LEA;
(c)   *directly resource* provision where necessary, within budgetary constraints;
(d)   *take action* on reviewing existing provision, providing or negotiating for the provision of new programmes and processes, etc.

Of course, the notion of the 'effective headteacher' cannot exist in isolation; it is critically interrelated with the notion of the 'effective school'. In the final section of our paper, therefore, we suggested that a headteacher whose staff development needs are being met through the processes discussed will more effectively be able to meet the needs of the school.

(a)   Headteachers whose developing *understanding* of their role is facilitated and supported by the LEA, will more effectively enable their staffs to understand the nature of change, the pressures of change, the changing processes of learning and teaching and the nature of the effective school. For headteachers and their staffs, a participative process of exploring, learning, and growing together will engender a school *ethos*, and an educational and social climate which values and reflects these processes in the curricular, pastoral and social life of the school.

(b)   Headteachers who are *proactively engaged* in their own professional development will in turn engender a proactive approach among staff towards staff and curriculum development. A self-developing and self-reviewing headteacher will better facilitate the emergence of a self-developing and self-renewing school, in terms of both *curriculum and organization*.

(c)   Headteachers who are themselves contributors to and beneficiaries of a participative process of resource deployment, to provide *opportunities* in response to their own developmental needs, will be better able to manage such a participative process in deploying school *resources* in relation to the developmental needs of their schools.

By drawing together the relationships we had traced between an 'exploratory' paradigm of headship, a strategy for headteacher development, the terms of reference for the headteacher staff development group, and the core roles and responsibilities of headteachers in relation to the ethos, curriculum/organization development and resources management of their schools, we outlined what we hoped was a coherent model upon which to proceed (Figure 13.2).

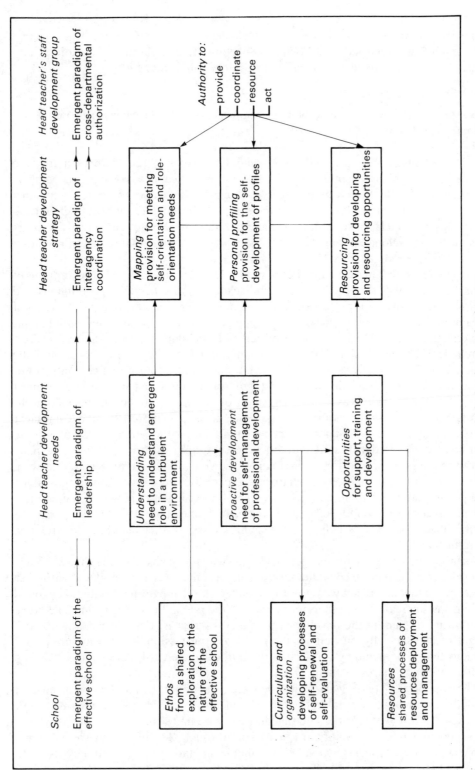

Figure 13.2 A model for headteacher development.

The paper was well-received by the headteachers' staff development group, and subsequently was received by the Schools Subcommittee of Sheffield Education Committee as a basis of its headteacher staff development strategy.

Case study 2: an organization development approach to school review in a large primary school

The head of this nursery, first and middle school was a man in his 50s, very experienced in headship and highly respected by his professional colleagues. He approached us on the basis that, while there were no great 'problems' in his school, in his few remaining years before retirement he would like the school to become as happy and effective a place as possible. He also admitted that he wished to see how effective a process organization development might be so that he might recommend us to his colleagues if he found our approach a useful one.

We worked with him over a number of weeks, learning more about his perceptions of his role, his staff and the structure of the school—and especially the religious and philosophical roots of his professional commitment and self-image. In the later stages of the school improvement process we would regularly check out and review with him his personal thoughts and feelings as he explored his leadership role. For example, he drew a great deal in his leadership style on theological models of 'the good shepherd' and 'the loving father', not in any superficial sense but imbuing his role with a commitment of caring for his staff and seeking to protect them from undue stress and pressure. Almost inevitably, however, he was transferring many of the stresses and pressures to himself, so adding to the stress he was already experiencing. As we explored this, it became clear that he was at times overlaying the 'father' role with that of the 'servant'. Part of the data that we later gathered from staff about their perceptions of his role was that while many of the teachers felt cared for by him some also felt rather overprotected and were reticent about taking their own intitiatives—especially where this involved risk-taking and possible stress for them, because any sign of stress in them, however, deliberately risked in order to grow, induced stress in the head. Some of the staff actually declared a desire to care for *him* and help him reduce his stresses, rather than have him take on more of theirs.

As this feedback began to emerge, we worked with the head on it and he felt at his age and stage in his career he could not easily relinquish the basic role-model of 'father' to his staff, but that he did not want this to engender a kind of paternalism that they found stifling and uncreative. We therefore explored the possibility of his caring role being clearly that of guiding the development of adults—that is, that his care for his staff would focus especially on helping them to grow professionally into mature, autonomous teachers, including supporting them in calculated risk-taking and in dealing with any resultant stresses themselves.

The data on the head's leadership role were a small part of the data on a range of school issues that we were able to gather by means of informal interviews with staff members. Before we embarked on this, however, we had several stages of 'entry' into the school and 'negotiation' of our role to work through. The first stage was becoming known to the deputy heads, whom we first met by invitation of the head. He wished to begin including them in our discussions, but it was important that they should meet us, explore with us some of the possibilities of a school improvement process and decide for themselves whether they would be happy both to be part of our discussions with the head and for us to work with the school. One deputy head was aspiring to a headship and the other deputy head was exploring possible career alternatives to headship, so each had a professional interest in exploring processes of school improvement in addition to that of being committed to a creative deputy headship role in the school. Both were very interested in becoming part of a developing school improvement process, subject to some further exploration of the implications.

After spending some time with this management triad, we all felt ready to approach the rest of the staff. We met them first at a staff meeting, outlining how we might talk individually with them about various aspects of school life and structure, then feed back, in a collated and anonymous form, what we had heard. We left it with them to decide whether or not they would like to participate in such a process, both individually and as a whole school. The head rang us later to say that the staff would like to participate, so we arranged to meet with them again to fix interviews. We made it clear that any individuals wishing not to be involved in the interview stage could opt out. If they wanted this to remain confidential, they could come to the interview and tell us then that they did not wish to contribute.

Only one person took up this option, and he chose to reinvolve himself in the later stages of the process.

With the exception of this one person, all the members of the staff—teachers, child care assistants, nursery nurses, school secretary and YTS trainee—participated in the data-gathering process. The interviews were semistructured, that is, we asked for responses around certain themes (previously identified with the management triad and the staff), then allowed time for any other comments people wished to make about any aspect of school. It is not possible, because of the confidential nature of the exercise, to deal in detail with the content of the feedback we received, but the main headings that emerged were:

(a)   Resources
(b)   One school or three?
(c)   Inset, staff development and support
(d)   Staff meetings and information systems
(e)   Learning style and focus
(f)   Parents and community
(g)   Roles and staffing
(h)   Curriculum objectives and evaluation
(i)   Leadership and management style
(j)   Team teaching

The first feedback session, after we had collated all the gathered data, was a rather 'stiff' and formal affair in the school library, because clearly there were some feelings of anxiety and ambivalence around. However, it soon became clear that while some frank criticisms had been expressed, there was much in the feedback that was positive and affirming. We felt it important to set the feedback in the context of our changing times and the effects of the 'turbulent environment', so we ran a follow-up session with the staff to explore some aspects of the nature and meaning of change both socioculturally and educationally. A third meeting was held and the atmosphere by now was much more relaxed. Tea and biscuits were served and we all sat in a circle in easy chairs, as we posed the questions, 'Do you want to use the feedback as a basis for a school develop ment process?', and if so, 'Do you want us to help with it?'. So that the staff would not feel embarrassed if they did not wish us to work with them any further, we withdrew from the meeting while the second question was being considered.

A large majority of the staff expressed an interest in exploring further the issues raised by the feedback, and we were invited to facilitate the process of reflection, decision-making and developmental action. Over the next few weeks, small groups were formed to reflect on specific themes, the groups meeting together later to share their thoughts and plan any necessary action. Out of this a number of suggestions were made for improving internal communication processes in the school, and in reflecting on curriculum issues the groups found themselves driven back to some basic questions, such as 'What is education for?' and 'What do we really believe about the nature of people?'. The head had offered members of staff the opportunity not to participate in these group sessions, emphasizing that voluntary participation was the essence of the exercise, but out of some 30 or so staff, only three or four withdrew.

Sadly, the development process in the school was, at this point, seriously disrupted by the teachers' national industrial action. It was only when the action had ended and the post-action problems were becoming resolved, that we were able to think of proceeding further with a full-scale school improvement programme. The attenuation of the development process had, however, made things difficult; since we had begun work with the school one deputy head had moved to take up a headship, the other had begun a year's secondment, other staff changeovers had taken place, and of course the period of industrial action had quite radically affected teachers' attitudes and morale.

At our last meeting at the school, the senior staff decided that the time was not ripe for us to attempt to pick up the development process—we would have needed almost to start the process again from the beginning—but we were invited to attend a review meeting later in the year.

THE ORGANIZATION DEVELOPMENT UNIT—GROWTH AND FUTURE PROSPECTS

The decision of our Education Department's School Subcommittee, in June, 1986, to consider the establishment of a permanent Organization Development unit with a core team of two full-time consultants gives us hope that we shall be able to respond to the rapidly increasing number and variety of opportunities opening up to us. It may well be some considerable time, however, before the principle becomes reality, in the current economic climate—although the local branches of the two major headteachers' associa tions (NAHT and SHA) and a number of individual headteachers have offered their full support to the unit.

In the meantime, we have several consultancy contracts established in Sheffield schools and are involved around the country in workshops and seminars on consultancy with schools. We are also in the second term of a two-year rolling programme of experience exchange and shared development between twelve Sheffield and twelve Cleveland LEA headteachers, based at the Centre for the Study of Comprehensive Schools at York University. This was a shared development between the Organization

Development Unit, Cleveland's Chief Adviser, the Director of CSCS and headteacher-consultants from the two LEAs.

Sheffield's former second Deputy Chief Education Officer, Dr Bill Kneen, who encouraged and supported the work of the Unit in Sheffield, is now Director of Education in Oldham. As a consequence, there is a growing interest in organization development consultancy in the Oldham LEA, with which David Keith has developed a wide-ranging freelance consultancy brief. He is currently working, for example, on the management of a schools' merger, the review of a secondary school's maths department (in partnership with the LEA's maths adviser), a development programme for staff development tutors in the secondary sector, a whole-school review and a senior management team development process.

The Unit has working links with, and opportunities to contribute to the work of, the Regional Headship Unit at Woolley Hall, Wakefield and the North West Education Management Centre at Padgate, Warrington, and during the past year we have also received our first student placement from Sheffield City Polytechnic's MSc course in organization development.

Along with networking visits to others in the field of educational development and consultancy, and attendance as participants at courses and conferences, we have been and look set in the future to be, very busily engaged in a still-emergent professional field and discipline which offers exciting and creative prospects for the future, but which clearly cannot be sustained for much longer on a part-time basis.

NOTE

(1) 'Improving the Quality of Schooling', International School Improvement Project Conference, Nene College, Northampton, 8–9 April 1986.

REFERENCES

Beckhard, R. (1969) *Organization Development: Strategies and Models*. Reading, Mass.: Addison-Wesley.

Bennis, W. G. (1969) *Organization Development: Its Nature, Origins and Prospects*. Reading, Mass.: Addison-Wesley.

Berman, P. and McLaughlin, M. W. (1977) *Federal Programs Supporting Educational Change*, vol. VII. Santa Monica, Cal.: Rand Corporation.

Bolam, R. (1976) 'Innovation at the local level', in *Supporting Curriculum Development*, Units 24–26, OU Course E203. Milton Keynes: Open University Press.

Bolam, R. (1982) *Strategies for School Improvement*. Paris: OECD.

Bronowski, J. (1973) *The Ascent of Man*. London: BBC Publications.

Bruner, J. S. (1962) *On Knowing: Essays for the Left Hand*. Cambridge, Mass.: Harvard University Press.

Dalin, P. (1983) *Can Schools Learn?* Windsor: NFER-Nelson.

David, J. L. (1982) *School Based Strategies: Implications for Government Policy*, Bay Area Research Group (mimeo), quoted in Hopkins and Wideen (1982) p. 17.

Day, C. (1985) 'The role of the external consultant in professional development', unpublished paper presented to·a CSCS/BIS seminar on consultancy in schools, May 1985.

Elliott-Kemp, J. (1982) *Managing Organizational Change*. Sheffield City Polytechnic: PAVIC Publications.

Emrick, J. A. and Peterson, S. M. (1978) *A Synthesis of Findings across Five Recent Studies in Educational Dissemination and Change (revised)*. San Francisco: Far West Laboratory.

French, W. L. and Bell, C. H., Jr (1978) *Organization Development*, 2nd edition, Englewood Cliffs, NJ: Prentice-Hall.

Fromm, E. (1960) *The Fear of Freedom*. London: Routledge and Kegan Paul.

Fullan, M. and Pomfret, A. (1977) 'Research on curriculum and instruction implementation', *Review of Educational Research*, **47**(1), 335–97.

Gray, H. L. and Heller, H. (1982) 'Helping schools change', *School Organization*, **2/4**.

Hamburg, B. A., Coelho, G. C. and Adams, J. (1974) 'Coping and adaptation: steps towards a synthesis of biological and social perspectives', in G. C. Coelho, B. A. Hamburg and J. E. Adams (eds), *Coping and Adaptation*. New York: Basic Books.

Havelock, R. G. (1975) 'The utilization of educational research and development', in A. Harris, L. Lawn and W. Prescott (eds), *Curriculum Innovation*. London: Croom Helm/Open University Press.

Hopkins, D. (1982) 'What is school improvement?', in D. Hopkins and M. Wideen (eds), *Alternative Perspectives on School Improvement*. Lewes: Falmer Press.

Hopkins, D. and Wideen, M. (eds) (1982) *Alternative Perspectives on School Improvement*. Lewes: Falmer Press.

Margulies, N. and Raia, A. P. (1978) *Conceptual Foundations of Organizational Development*. New York: McGraw-Hill.

Nisbet, J. (ed.) (1972) *The Creativity of the School*. Paris: OECD.

Rudduck, J. (1973) 'Dissemination in practice', *Cambridge Journal of Education*, **3**.

Stenhouse, L. (1975) *An Introduction to Curriculum Research and Development*. London: Heinemann.

Taba, H. (1962) *Curriculum Development: Theory and Practice*. New York: Harcourt, Brace and World.

Part IV

Looking Outward

As admitted at the very beginning of this book educational consultancy is very much in its infancy but will certainly grow into a healthy adulthood over the next few years. Perhaps not surprisingly, there has been more genuine (and conventional) educational consultancy overseas in the developing world. It is easy to see why the educational practices of technologically developed countries should be of interest to countries with the need to develop their own technological structures. But, of course, it does not follow that traditional and national educational systems can be usefully transferred to other cultures and climates. Indeed, in every part of the world there is the danger of emulation rather than the development of indigenous systems. Yet in all situations consultants with the right experience and training can be of immense use; it is all a matter of style and approach.

John Elliott-Kemp (Chapter 14) has wide experience as an educational consultant in the United Kingdom and overseas. He writes with wisdom and respect about approaches to consulting overseas and much of what he says applies within any one country, especially where there are regional differences and a non-standardized pattern. He brings a very personal tone to his writing (in the same way that Robin Snell did in Chapter 4) because it cannot be too strongly emphasized how personal in approach and style consultancy is. It is idle to think that knowledge or experience are enough for a consultant. In fact they can be a disadvantage. The skills of a consultant are personal and intimate; they are about the quality of relationships that are developed with the consultant who has to be seen as concerned, committed, empathetic and non-judgemental. The consultant has the task of helping his clients to hear themselves and to understand what they are saying to one another. It is not the job of the consultant to tell clients what to think but to help them to find out for themselves by a reflective process what they think they think—and then to become clear about what they want to think. As with Stanley Putnam and Steve Murgatroyd (Chapters 10 and 5), for John Elliott-Kemp the skills of the consultant are based on the counsellor's skills of listening, reflecting back and facilitating the client to make sense of his own world.

Mike Milstein (Chapter 15) takes a robust look at consulting and, possibly more than any of the other writers, shows a confidence in what consultants can achieve in the way of positive, material gain. As with Don Musella earlier (Chapter 11), he writes in a context where consultants have an established history and where principals are quite clear about their managerial responsibilities. An interesting difference between UK heads and American principals is that in the United Kingdom heads are being encouraged to teach less and to concentrate more on being managers, while in the United States principals are being encouraged actually to do some teaching so as not to lose touch with the class teacher, and also to help them to avoid the flight from reality that preoccupation with administration can induce. The awareness of need in the United States for consultant help is very much more positive than in Europe. While many of the problems are the same—falling rolls, increased unionization, diminishing funding—the context of solutions is different. American teachers, for one thing, are more self-assured than their British counterparts and are likely to be both politically more experienced in resisting enforced change and more personally committed to improving professional development within school systems.

There can be no question but that consultancy in schools—internationally—has a rosy and much extended future. Perhaps the most important contribution that management approaches to consultancy can make is in underlining the importance of partnership between clients and consultants, working together for the common good of those who use the schools. In the past there has often been a strong reformist and paternalistic approach to school change which appeals to those of a sectarian and political frame of mind. The R, D and D (research, development and diffusion) and 'cascade' approaches to educational change seem to be redolent of such a hierarchic view of educational change which sometimes comes over as 'teacher bashing'. There are lots of 'experts' from outside schools who are only too willing to tell teachers what they ought to be doing and who would willingly go into a school, show teachers how to run them properly and demonstrate how they ought to teach. The forms of consultancy described in this book are nothing like that; they are about a partnership of able, reflective people sharing their perspectives and insights in order to make schools better places for everyone.

Chapter 14

The International Consultant: Some Principles, Problems and Pitfalls

John Elliott-Kemp

INTRODUCTION

What do I gain from doing overseas consultancy? Not just a living, but above all a life. I have the pleasure of feeling useful and appreciated; the unpredictability and risk-taking of working in another land; the stress which challenges and stretches; the humility gained from working often with less privileged people who have little in material terms, but work with passion, joy and commitment to ideals. Above all, I have the thrill of sharing different ways of life, often in exotic places, of learning about and appreciating different traditions, values and ways of seeing. Every time I return home from an overseas consultancy I feel able both to appreciate and question my own culture, and myself, a little better than before.

I propose to begin with a brief, illustrative case of an overseas contract, using this to develop a conceptual framework for overseas consultancy. This framework will then be used to provide a structure for this chapter and some of its main components explored.

In 1985 I led a national workshop conference in Thailand for educational leaders and administrators on the theme of values and moral education. This is a subject which gives me great concern, but one which is seldom discussed in my field of education management. The project was especially interesting for me as it was based within a Buddhist culture and in a country that combines both highly sophisticated metropolitan characteristics with some very remote rural areas which would be classified as 'underdeveloped' in western materialist terms. One of the best schools I have ever encountered, however, in terms of both its humane, collaborative climate and its staff and student commitment and achievement, lies in a wild, jungle area of southern Thailand.

I had been drawn into a discussion on the clash between traditional Buddhist values and the implicit values of 'modernization' the previous year in Bangkok during a workshop seminar on training for group facilitation. This was followed by a lively debate after the seminar and the realization of a need for a national conference on values and moral education. This informal discussion was then followed up through the formal communication channels of government agencies, a draft proposal made, and funding arrangements clarified and agreed. Shortly afterwards, the Thai Ministry of

Education officially invited me to lead the conference organized through the British Council, and supported by the World Bank. My contract and precise terms of reference were negotiated, with the British Council acting as my sponsoring and liaison linkage with Thailand.

For this contract my immediate client and host organization in Thailand was the Institute for Development of Educational Administrators (IDEA) of the Ministry of Education, and my immediate colleagues were the directorate and senior staff of the institute, who would be responsible for the logistics and organization of the conference. The planning of content and inputs to the programme was done jointly between the IDEA conference director and myself, with the British Council facilitating the handling of resource materials and conference papers from its headquarters in London and the Council centre in Bangkok.

The different variables, or elements described in this project can now be used to construct a framework which will be applicable to most overseas consultancy work, and which covers those key issues which typically need to be considered when working internationally (Figure 14.1). The diagram has a vertical division into two halves, which

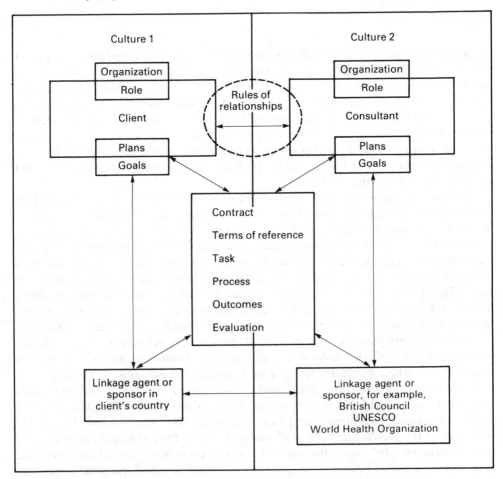

Figure 14.1 A framework for overseas consultancy

represent two cultures which the consultant must be able to bridge in order to be effective. The key 'bridging' areas of concern (contract and task, and the rules of relationships) are situated on the interface between the two cultures. In the process of coming to understand and appreciate the workings of another culture it will be essential to have a grasp of the formal and informal rules of relationships (including non-verbal communication) in that culture, and to be sensitive and skilful enough to respect and work within those rules. The bridging of different cultures will also involve a willingness to modify the concepts and ideas which form the basis of one's expertise.

The trap of unconscious ethnocentricity or cultural imperialism may easily lead one to assume that the process of helping another country is simply a mechanistic act of importing ideas, concepts or technology and attaching them in a 'bolt-on' manner to the country concerned. Nothing could be further from the truth, for the very concepts which help to build the solution to a foreign country's problems, if imported from a different culture, must be seen as problematic rather than taken for granted, and therefore negotiated, not imposed.

At the hub of the framework is the section concerned with the issues of contract negotiation and agreement, the terms of reference within which the consultant will be working and the key concept of 'task': what it is that the consultant is expected to do and achieve. The task and the goals of a project may be achieved in either or both of the cultures—for example, a course or training programme in the consultant's country and a follow-up project in the client's country.

Related to these issues of contract and task are the processes of consultation, teaching and facilitation of learning involved in the project. It will also be important to monitor and evaluate plans, processes and outcomes of the project, including evaluation of the social impact and consequences of new ideas or technology upon the culture.

In addition to these key areas of contract, task and rules of relationships this chapter will be concerned with the consultant himself and personal factors such as expertise, skills, qualities and values. I shall argue that expertise is not enough in international consultancy: the consultant must be able to fulfil successfully two distinctive roles, those of 'agent of change' and 'student of the culture'. In order to combine these roles fruitfully he will need to demonstrate particular attitudes and values if his work is to be successful or effective.

CONTRACTING AND THE CONSULTANCY PROCESS: RELATIONSHIP AND TASK

In this section I shall explore the area of 'contract, task and evaluation' from the model developed earlier, and attempt to integrate these concepts within the consultancy process. The role of the international linkage organization in the contract will also be examined briefly.

There is a considerable literature on consultancy and the part of contracts in consultancy (Alderfer and Brown, 1975; Lippitt and Lippitt, 1978; Lippitt, 1979; Louis, 1981; Louis and Rosenblum, 1981; Havelock, 1981). My personal preference leans towards Ulschak's (1978) analysis in terms of 'client–consultant' and 'client–problem' concerns, although my own terminology differs somewhat from his.

I regard the key concerns of contracting as clarifying and reaching agreement, or

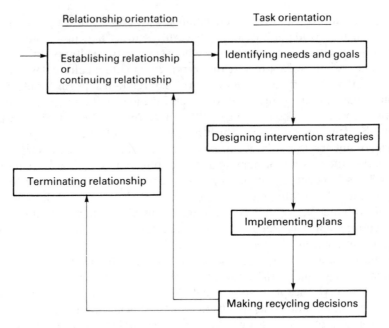

Figure 14.2   Basic consultancy cycle

consensus, on two major issues which I term the 'relationship' dimension and the 'task' dimension. The 'relationship' dimension of contracting is concerned with the negotiation of roles, expectations, mutual benefits, ethics and legality to the satisfaction of both client and consultant. The 'task' dimension has as its focus the determination of goals, the intervention strategies proposed and the criteria for success. The distinction thus hinges on whether the focus is expressive, that is, primarily related to the building or maintenance of the relationship between client and consultant, or whether it is instrumental, that is to say, primarily related to the attaining of the goals of a project or to the completion of tasks. In each of these two areas there will be a number of basic questions to be explored with the client system, and the two dimensions taken together form the basic consultancy cycle (Figure 14.2).

How is evaluation related to contracting? There are appropriate forms of evaluation for each of the stages in the consultancy process, and the practitioner will need to have a broad repertoire of programme evaluation methods and techniques to fit each stage. Evaluation activities in fact tie the different stages of the contracting cycle together. It is, therefore, essential that these are thoroughly thought out and executed in a unified approach to evaluation so that it becomes an integral part of one's work.

Programme evaluation is defined, then, as the systematic investigation of each phase in the cycle of relationship building, needs and goal analysis, implementation of plans and decisions pertaining to recycling. It can be used to improve a programme, for accountability purposes, or to assess the cost-benefit relationship in an innovation or training course. One of the most comprehensive and practical guides to programme evaluation is that of Brinkerhoff *et al.* (1985) which provides resource materials and related case studies to assist the consultant in the production of a complete programme evaluation design.

We are now in a position to set out some of the critical issues or questions in the contracting cycle.

RELATIONSHIP ORIENTATION ISSUES

How is the quality of relationship between client and consultant to be assessed or judged? Who, in fact, is the client? Are there multiple clients, or is there a hierarchy of clients? Do both parties to the contract have an adequate understanding of the agreement, and do their expectations of each other and of the roles and tasks each is to perform coincide? How do we know this? Have issues such as time involvement, costs, methods to be used and possible risks been clarified and agreed? When is the optimum time to make decisions about modifying, recycling or extending the contract? Is there adequate trust and relationship mutuality between client and consultant, so that both parties give and receive all relevant information? 'Relevant information' here includes facts, ideas and feelings, both positive and negative. 'Mutuality' implies mutual trust, shared goals, and a willingness to face any emerging problems together. The achievement of relationship mutuality may on occasion present difficulties in crosscultural consultancy, especially in the following areas:

Goal clarity

People from different cultures will vary in their need for precision in the statement of goals and in their ability to tolerate goal ambiguity.

Information sharing

Some cultures are more 'open' than others in relation to willingness to share information. Where knowledge is equated with power, it may often be shared only on a reciprocal and highly calculative basis.

Self disclosure

In some cultures to admit to a need is tantamount to confessing weakness or failure. If the culture gives a high value to maintaining 'face', or formal status and age earn a high respect in their own right, then the giving and receiving of critical comment must be approached circumspectly.

Participation in decision-making

Some clients may be accustomed to western consultants working solely in an 'expert' mode with a monopoly of expertise. Such clients may then be very reluctant to participate in any decisions pertaining to needs analysis or formulation of solutions.

Consultants should also beware of the scapegoat effect: if the client allows the consultant to take over the diagnostic and problem-solving phases then he can legitimately apportion all the blame to the consultant if things do not go well.

Resources

Client organizations may view the consultant primarily as a resource bearer (the Father Christmas effect), and be reluctant to acknowledge their own part in providing the vital resources of people, time, effort and commitment. My experience has taught me that this is especially pertinent where a 'hardware' approach to the solution of problems is expected by the client. This may occur in distance learning, educational technology, teacher training or almost any aspect of curriculum development.

TASK ORIENTATION ISSUES

Typical problem areas to be evaluated within the task dimension include:

(a) How should needs assessment be designed and executed?
(b) How may one establish the worthiness of different goals, and how may they be given comparative values?
(c) How should a plan or proposal be evaluated for quality, feasibility or logical consistency?
(d) How should programmes or courses be monitored?
(e) Can the components of an in-service workshop be assembled to give the most 'rational' design? Should components sequencing be carried out to follow logical or psychological criteria?
(f) How should the implementation of a course or project be managed?
(g) How can one carry out evaluation of implementation?
(h) Where and how should one look for evidence of worth of a project?
(i) How could an evaluation method be improved?
(j) How can the wider social impact of an intervention be predicted?

This last question is sufficiently important to merit a section in its own right, especially where work in third world countries is concerned.

The social impact of interventions

With the increasing impact of innovation, especially technological innovation, on individuals, organizations and societies there is a growing need for concerted effort directed at research into more comprehensive and deeper assessment of the effects of innovation, not only in its obvious economic and technical consequences but also of its foreseeable individual, social, cultural, political and ecological impact.

Insensitive foreign innovators have turned flourishing cultures into deserts, both figuratively and literally, because of their greed or egotism, their tunnel vision or shortsightedness, or their inability to appreciate the value of cultures very different from their own. The consultant working to assist developing countries to make use of modern educational technology will need to be skilled in the rather esoteric field of social assessment of technology. Most of the thinking and research in this field is done with reference to applied science and technology, but it has great relevance to educational innovation, not solely in relation to the sophisticated hardware and software of new educational technology, but in some of the wider cultural implications of educational innovation.

For example, the introduction of educational strategies such as distance learning involve both new technology and major changes in professional roles, not only on the part of the teacher but also of the student. A role always implies complementarity; therefore, as one role changes or develops, so other roles within the role set are renegotiated.

With the exception of the use of the telephone, audio cassettes and systems such as shared-screen teleconferencing, modern technologies for distance learning will need not only teaching subject expertise but also high levels of skill in application of the relevant technology to the management of learning. The alternative is for the country to obtain the considerable resources needed to establish and maintain specialist educational production organizations or units similar to the BBC–Open University ventures in Britain.

But there may also be fundamental cultural implications of the introduction of a strategy such as distance learning, as I discovered during a project involving a new university degree course in Thailand: the traditional student expectations of a highly valued personal relationship with a revered teacher ran completely counter to the notion in distance learning of the self-reliant, self-managing student who is best able to profit from a degree programme which lays great emphasis on autonomy and self-help.

Technology assessment looks not only at the obvious short-term demands and implications of innovation for a system, but tries to take account of the wider social, political and cultural consequences, and modify or eliminate any which may be harmful or dysfunctional for the people within the system. If the predicted consequences for the system appear too bleak, then the cost of the innovation in human or cultural terms is too high, the technology is not appropriate and the proposed project should be abandoned, or at the very least modified to make use of a more culturally appropriate technology. Technology assessment is not simply an aspect of managerialism, concerned with effective or efficient social management of innovation. It is a systemic approach related to the acceptance of new technology within a culture or society and the cost-benefit relationship in terms of social and cultural consequences of an innovation. This can never be a value-free process, and consequently the consultant and his clients must always be willing to confront what is essentially an ethical–political issue: the issue of who should have the right to assess and judge new technology.

The author has developed a training system for new technology assessment in education, but probably the best information source in technology assessment is UNESCO. The scope and practical use of technology assessment from a Japanese perspective are discussed by Oshima (1975), while strategic problems of evaluation and issues of assessment of changes of social values and norms in systems are featured in Paschen *et al.* (1975).

THE ROLE OF INTERNATIONAL LINKAGE ORGANIZATIONS IN CONTRACTING

Working as an international consultant will inevitably entail a relationship with some of the international agencies which act as linkage agents between the client country and the consultant and which can facilitate one's work by acting as commissioning agents or providing expert support, liaison or advice. Examples of such linking organizations are the British Council, UNESCO, the European Community (EEC), the World Health Organization (WHO), the International Labour Office (ILO), the Commonwealth Institute and Council for Educational Administration, Oxfam and Voluntary Service Overseas (VSO).

Each of these linking organizations will have its own methods, systems and procedures and the consultant will need to familiarize himself with these. A typical pattern of procedure, given the idiosyncratic differences between linking organizations, might be as follows:

(a)   the consultant is placed on the register or panel of consultants of the linking organization;

(b)   a first, tentative, request or proposal is received from a client country and explored;

(c)   a member of staff from the linking organization is assigned to the project as liaison officer;

(d)   if the project is accepted in principle a clear time-scale for the work is negotiated, including any preliminary fact finding visits to the country concerned which may be agreed to be necessary;

(e)   a formal contract is now drawn up, including precise terms of reference for the consultant's work to include the needs of the client, the objectives of the project and what it is that the consultant is expected to provide or do; from these terms of reference would be derived guidelines for evaluation of the project, and the contract would also cover such items as consultant fees and expenses, insurance, accommodation and travel arrangements, provision of resource materials and the logistics of getting these sent to the client organization.

Although one's terms of reference may often specify the actual working hours and working days of a project it has been my experience that one invariably exceeds these by a considerable margin. The enthusiasm and commitment of clients and their need to make the most of the visiting consultant result in many hours of 'overtime', sometimes thinly disguised as social events. Additionally, other organizations in the client country, on learning about the project, will flock to invite the consultant to address community meetings, open festivals, conduct college assemblies or lead university seminars. Often, these gatherings will attract hundreds of participants, especially in the third world. The consultant will need to be aware of his own energy reserves, especially in tropical climates, and manage the problems of negotiating these extracurricular tasks with tact and diplomacy as they arise.

There may sometimes be considerable ambiguity and frustration in the tortuous processes of overseas contracting due to different cultures' interpretations of one's roles and relationships or to the multiple layers of bureaucracy involved in the linking organization, the client organization and the 'target group' for the project. The consultant must be able to manage his own frustration and anxiety and also that of the others involved in the process.

It is not always necessary to have the help of an international linkage organization. Often, where the client organization is autonomous, relatively small or highly entrepreneurial, it will be possible to negotiate consultancy projects directly with the client organization. I have developed overseas contracts directly in this way with universities, colleges, public school systems (in the British sense), professional associations and charity foundations. The advantages of increased freedom and autonomy in working without the resources and expertise of the international linking organization have to be balanced against the increased risk and stress, and the burden of administrative tasks required in managing a project oneself.

THE PROTEAN CONSULTANT

In order to be effective in international consultancy it will be necessary to function in three very distinctive modes. The ability to switch readily from one mode to another I term 'protean', after the ancient Greek god Proteus, the 'Old Man of the Sea', who was able to change his form at will.

These three different modes of working, like different cognitive worlds inhabited by the amphibious consultant, are firstly the field of the consultant's 'content' expertise, for example teacher training or educational technology. This field will undoubtably be the foundation of the consultant's reputation, but his credibility and effectiveness in working crossculturally will hinge on his ability to operate within the other modes of working.

In addition to his expertise in the form or content of innovations in his special field, the consultant will also need to be an expert in the process of planned change. Being an agent of change will necessitate knowledge and skills in the field of management such as situation and needs diagnosis, planning and decision-making techniques, together with interactive skills relevant to negotiation, counselling and conflict management (see Elliott-Kemp, 1982).

Finally, the international consultant must be able to function in an appreciative, learning mode as the student of a foreign culture. This has important implications for the client–consultant relationship, for it will necessitate an essential reciprocity between consultant and client in which each is learning from the other. In this process of 'learning from the culture' the consultant will require a conceptual understanding of, and sensitivity to, such matters as the rules of relationships in different cultures, including such central concerns as 'face' in the Far East, traditional styles of leadership, and concepts of space, time and body language as they differ within other cultures.

As part of the international consultant's information base it will be important to have access to a good library for background data on economic, political, and sociocultural aspects of other countries, and to be able to tap into the valuable background material and expertise of the international educational organizations such as UNESCO, the British Council and the Royal Commonwealth Society.

The concept of the protean consultant and significant aspects of space, time and non-verbal communication in crosscultural settings are explored in Elliott-Kemp

(1987), which also contains a select bibliography of resource materials on other countries, their education systems and their cultures.

While essential foundations for becoming an international consultant include an area or field of expertise, a background resource library and a conceptual grasp of the processes of organizational and personal change, I believe that certain key qualities and attitudes are vital. While not discounting the need for technical competency I feel a higher priority should be placed on interpersonal competence. To achieve this, however, it is necessary first to break out of the prison of one's professional socialization.

Beyond expertise: the consultant and self-transformation

Along the path to becoming an 'expert' in any field there are strong pressures towards intellectual conformity. This conformity is maintained in three ways: through socialization into an academic or professional group, through the exercise of authority, and by means of social exchange (Mulkay, 1972). First of all the student spends several years mastering a body of established knowledge. This is followed by postgraduate work in the subject, which usually involves working under the supervision of a recognized authority or expert in which one learns how to choose and resolve problems defined as legitimate in an appropriate way. This means, in effect, that one's original contribution to knowledge is strictly confined within the bounds of the current cognitive and technical norms.

It is easy to become inured to the rigidly authoritarian nature of this process. Just as the fish is unaware of the water that surrounds it, so the embryo expert is likely to be oblivious of the tunnel vision which his subject expertise gives him. This is especially apparent within the social sciences which are rife with ideology.

The first task of any consultant worth his salt, then, is to break free from his initial socialization, to transcend his training. To develop and temper those qualities most valuable to the consultant it is necessary to have years of experience in which one can test knowledge to destruction, dissolve and reform conceptual categories and question assumptions and beliefs. Above all, there is the necessity to avoid that most deadly and pernicious of professional diseases—certainty. Honest doubt is a quality to be treasured even though it may be painful to live with.

What are the qualities and attitudes which constitute interpersonal competence? Among the key attributes, but not in any order of merit, I believe I can confidently list the following, drawn up partly on the basis of my own experience and values, but also firmly supported by the research and experience of others such as Harrison and Hopkins (1969), and Rogers (1982):

(a)   having a self-awareness permeating one's thoughts, ideas, motives and actions, including a balanced self criticism that is neither too harsh nor too self-indulgent;

(b)   the capacity to generate one's own learning: for no book or resource library can ever prepare one for all the exotic contingencies arising from work in other cultures;

(c)   being comfortable, even when surrounded by ambiguity and uncertainty;

(d)   physical, emotional and intellectual resilience, and the ability to withstand frustration and stress induced by extreme climatic conditions, bureaucratic torpor and incompetence, or seemingly dysfunctional customs or behaviour;

(e)   ability to suspend judgement, including a non-judgemental acceptance of people as they are;

(f)   having an essentially positive, optimistic stance to other people, their motives and their problems;

(g)   empathic understanding of the feelings of others;

(h)   ability to give and inspire trust;

(i)   ability to trust one's own and others' feelings and to be comfortable in working with feelings, attitudes and fears;

(j)   the ability to involve and risk oneself, often at a very deep level, and not having to maintain emotional distance between oneself and other people and their problems and concerns. This involves a refusal to allow the intellectual, the analytical or the formal role-dominated aspects of encounter to have ascendance over the emotional-intuitive. It requires that blend of self-confidence and trust required to immerse oneself in encounter which involves reciprocal influence: encounter in which the self is deeply involved and changed as the client is similarly involved and changed;

(k)   humility, responsibility and the intelligence of feeling: a realization of the awesome potential for good or evil in much of the work one does.

Perhaps this last group of qualities is the most vital. Esteva (1986), for example, has underlined the salutary fact that often those who are bypassed by so-called development are better prepared to survive, or even flourish, in the harsh world of today, for they have not been disabled by the irresponsible efforts of those who seduce with readymade solutions from the 'developed' world. 'Development' only too often may mean starting on a journey that others know better, in a direction that others have chosen. On the way it may mean the sacrifice of values, customs and even cultures. It may promise prosperity and happiness but provide only the poverty of a growing dependence on outside resources, guidance and management. The international consultant bears a heavy responsibility to help temper his pride and haunt his dreams.

REFERENCES AND BIBLIOGRAPHY

Alderfer, C. and Brown, L. (1975) *Learning from Changing*. Beverly Hills: Sage Publications.

Argyle, M. (1983) *The Psychology of Interpersonal Behaviour*. Harmondsworth: Penguin Books.

Argyle, M. and Henderson, M. (1985) *The Anatomy of Relationships*. London: Heinemann.

Bennis, W., Benne, K. D. and Chin, R. (1969) *The Planning of Change*, 2nd edition. New York: Holt, Rinehart and Winston.

Brinkerhoff, R. O., Brethower, D., Hluchj, T. and Nowakowski, J. (1985) *Program Evaluation: A Practitioner's Guide for Trainers and Educators*. Boston and The Hague: Kluwer-Nijhoff.

Elliott-Kemp, J. (1982) *Managing Organisational Change*. Sheffield City Polytechnic: PAVIC Publications.

Elliott-Kemp, J. (1987) *Working in International Consultancy and Teaching—A Resource Guide for Practitioners*. Sheffield City Polytechnic: PAVIC Publications.

Elliott-Kemp, J. and Rogers, C. (1982) *The Effective Teacher: A Person-Centred Development Guide*. Sheffield City Polytechnic: PAVIC Publications.

Esteva, G. (1986) 'Development is dangerous', *Resurgence*, **114, January**.

Harrison, R. and Hopkins, R. (1969) 'The design of cross-cultural training: an alternative to the university model', in Bennis W., Benne K. D. and Chin R., *The Planning of Change*. New York: Holt, Rinehart and Winston.

Havelock, R. (1981) *School–University Collaboration Supporting School Improvement*, vols. I–IV. Ann Arbor, Mich.: Knowledge Transfer Institute, American University.

Lippitt, R. (1979) 'Consultation: traps and potentialities', in Herriott, R. and Gross, N. (eds.), *The Dynamics of Planned Educational Change*. New York: McCutcham.

Lippitt, G. and Lippitt, R. (1978) *The Consulting Process in Action*. La Jolla, Cal.: University Associates Inc.

Louis, K. (1981) 'External agents and knowledge utilisation', in Lehming, R. *et al.* (eds.), *Improving Schools*, Beverly Hills: Sage Publications.

Louis, K. and Rosenblum, S. (1981) *Linking R and D with Schools: A Program and its Implications for Dissemination*. Washington, DC: National Institute of Education.

Morris, D. (1985) *Bodywatching: A Field Guide to the Human Species*. London: Jonathan Cape.

Mulkay, M. J. (1972) *The Social Process of Innovation*. London: Macmillan.

Oshima, K. (1975) 'Practical use of technology assessment' in *Methodological Guidelines for Social Assessment of Technology*. Paris: OECD.

Paschen, H. *et al.* (1975) 'Some problems of evaluation in technology assessment studies', in *Methodological Guidelines for Social Assessment of Technology*. Paris: OECD.

Rogers, C. R. (1982) 'Education—a personal activity' in Elliott-Kemp, J. and Rogers, C. R., *The Effective Teacher: A Person-Centred Development Guide*. Sheffield City Polytechnic: PAVIC Publications.

Ulschak, F. L. (1978) 'Contracting: a process and a tool', in Pfeiffer, J. and Jones, J., *Annual Handbook for Group Facilitators*. La Jolla, Cal.: University Associates Inc.

Chapter 15

What the Future Holds: An American View*

Mike Milstein

INTRODUCTION

What is the future going to look like for consultancy in schools? There are many opposing forces that make it difficult to foretell, but overall the future will likely be a challenge that will try the staying-power of would-be consultants. In the mid-1970s Robert Blake and Jane Mouton concluded that although 'consultation is still in its infancy . . . as greater skills are acquired in helping clients to solve their problems, consultation will become a more and more relied upon means of assistance' (Blake and Mouton, 1976, p. 464). This conclusion shows prescience as we observe current trends in business, but when we look closely at the state of consultation in educational organizations, the accuracy of their forecast becomes problematic.

Because there are so many pushing and pulling forces in education, such as declining student enrollments, demands for accountability, a changing work force composition, a shrinking resource base, and growing demands for educational reform, consultancy in schools is in a state of flux. Inevitably the grinding together of these forces will have a significant impact on school consultation. Prediction of future directions is fraught with risk under circumstances such as those that presently dominate education. One thing does seem clear: consultancy in schools will probably be dramatically different in the future. The intent here is to explore the forces that are pushing and pulling as they relate to present consultancy practices in the United States and draw implications for the future of consultation in school settings. It should be noted, before commencing, that there are considerable variations on the consultancy theme even *within* education. For example, the focus may be upon instructional concerns such as the development of curricular packages and classroom management techniques, or upon organizational issues such as the designing of decision-making structures and the clarification of goals. Consultants might be internal or external and the process might range from highly directive to highly participative. Rather than become mired in a quagmire of definitions within this conjectural paper, consultancy will be treated as a general topic—in other words, as the act of helping others and doing so within the context of elementary and secondary education.

* This chapter is based upon an earlier piece: Milstein (1986) 'The future of consultation in public education', *Urban Education*, **21**(2), 119–68.

CONSULTANCY: FROM YESTERDAY TO TODAY

Consultancy in schools has expanded rapidly over the past several decades in the United States. In large part this is related to the demand for educational innovation. Beginning with the National Defense Education Act in 1958, one of that nation's responses to the Soviet Union's challenge to America's scientific supremacy, the record of federal initiative has been continuous. The emphasis has shifted over time, starting with a concern about the nation's scientific capacity in the late 1950s, turning to a focus on equalization of educational opportunities in the mid-1960s, to the upgrading of education as a profession, along with concern about improving vocational and technical education in the late 1960s, to an effort to bring children with special education needs into the mainstream of public education in the mid-1970s, and, most recently, to concern about overall educational reform in the mid-1980s. To compound the pressure on educational organizations, many states have imitated federal initiatives with categorical aid programs of their own. Further, many school districts have set out to establish locally based innovative programs. Whatever the source of the initiative, the underlying theme remains: *change the educational system.*

The broadly expanded interest in change, and the allocation of resources to bring it about, has led to an upsurge in demands for consultancy in schools. Innovations such as team teaching, ungraded classrooms and open schools have created the need to upgrade skills and modify attitudes of teachers who previously labored under more traditional conditions. Similarly, organizationally based innovations, such as management by objectives, participative decision-making and team management have created a need to upgrade the skills and knowledge, as well as modify the attitudes, of educational administrators.

In short, consultancy, which has long been an accepted organizational practice in government and the private sector, has moved rapidly into the public education sector. As external pressures increase and organizational life grows more complicated, educational practitioners find it increasingly necessary to seek the advice of others to cope effectively. The demands being made on educational organizations and the expanding resources being allocated to cope with them have enabled consultation to gain a secure foothold in schools.

CONSULTANCY AND THE FUTURE: SOME CLOUDS ON THE HORIZON

There are forces that threaten the recently gained legitimacy of consultancy in education in the United States. While these forces may vary in intensity and scope in different school settings, they tend to exist across the educational landscape. Four of these forces seem particularly relevant for the future of consultancy in schools settings: declining enrollments, a tenured work force, the power of teachers' unions, and economic constraints.

Declining enrolments

Most developed countries are experiencing a major reversal of enrollment trends. In the United States, for example, after a steady rise in pupil attendance in public schools which approached 52½ million in 1970, there was a decline to an estimated 51 million students in 1980 and a predicted decrease to between 44 and 45 million in the late 1980s (National Center for Educational Statistics, 1978, p. 11).

As long as enrollments were increasing, there were demands for innovations of all sorts: for example, split-shift school days; novel designs for school facilities; alternative strategies for manpower deployment to maximize the potential for efficient and effective assignment of teachers; curricular modifications to meet the needs of increasingly diverse student populations; and the development of new management systems to coordinate such complex activities. These new ventures called for inputs from consultants. School leaders were generally eager to secure such services.

With declining enrollments a new attitude appears to have set in. This is an attitude that holds that, with fewer students, there is less need to develop and implement alternative approaches to educational and managerial functions. It is also related to what I view as a form of 'bunker mentality'; a mentality that avoids rather than invites new approaches. If personal conversation with school people who have been responsible for overseeing the response to decline is an accurate indicator, there is a shaken self-confidence on the part of educational leaders. It is one thing to manage a growth industry with all the robustness that this implies; it is quite another thing to preside over a declining industry that seems to shrink before your eyes, despite any and all efforts to revitalize the system. School leaders tend to be less enthusiastic about inviting outsiders into the system if they believe that, somehow, the 'problem' reflects badly upon themselves.

A tenured work force

In the United States untenured faculty members tended to outnumber tenured faculty members on most school staffs in the past, but this is not currently true. With declining enrollments there has been less need for a large number of neophyte teachers to enter the system. In fact, in the United States the demand for new teachers declined from 203 000 in 1970, to 161 000 in 1975, and to a low of 100 000 in 1980 (National Center for Educational Statistics, 1978, p. 61). This downward trend has only recently begun to be reversed (National Center for Educational Statistics, 1984, p. 172).

At the same time, with shrinking student enrollments, there have been fewer opportunities for teachers already in place to move from district to district as freely as in the past. For that matter, there are data to support the contention that it is becoming more difficult for senior teachers who are dissatisfied with conditions of employment to leave education. There have been fewer opportunities for employment for dissatisfied teachers in other sectors of our recession-orientated economy. Charters (1970) found that only 35 per cent of the teachers included in his 1962 survey were still teaching after four years. By 1972, Mark and Anderson (1978) found that 59 per cent of the teachers in their study were still teaching after four years. By the mid-1980s, according to a Metropolitan Life Insurance Company study conducted by Lou Harris (1984), the median on-the-job experience of American teachers was 14.7 years. My own recent consultancy work has often been conducted in school settings where the mean-longevity of the staff is 15 or more years. This trend represents a marked increase of 'veterans' on the payroll of American public schools.

This presents a dilemma for consultants. The traditional pool of teachers who are receptive (or at least more vulnerable) to in-service education offerings comes mainly from those who are untenured. These teachers, just out of professional school, tend to be anxious to please, are acutely aware of their limitations, and are seeking curricular ideas and classroom management approaches that can compensate for the pre-service training gaps they discover in their first year or so of teaching. Teachers with greater longevity, on the other hand, tend to be more confident about their mastery of classroom management, are more skeptical about the possibility of improving their schools, and are less susceptible to pressures for attendance at in-service activities.

The same can be said of senior administrators. While there are certainly exceptions, many, especially those who have found continued promotions beyond their grasp because of personal limitations or there being less room at the top, tend to be status quo-oriented. Understandably, few administrators want to take undue risks when they already feel that their careers are stalled. In fact, there are times when it is necessary to wait out the twilight years of senior administrators before schools are 'ready' to implement the advice of consultants.

The resistance on the part of administrators is a critical problem for consultants. In a summary of the massive Rand study on educational change, Berman and McLaughlin (1980) concluded that the active support of building administrators is a vital factor in the implementation of change efforts. Principals who support change projects and participate actively in them give teachers the sense that the efforts are important and that there is a good chance that results of the efforts can be instituted.

With a growing consciousness of the key role of administrators in the facilitation or hindrance of change, a number of school districts are beginning to experiment with schemes that might induce senior administrators who are resisting changes to take early retirement. Some of the impetus for this effort may be based on simple economics— that is, it is less expensive to employ administrators with fewer years of service. However, it is also an attempt to infuse the system with energy, ideas, flexibility and leadership.

The power of teachers' unions

The teachers' union movement has grown rapidly in the United States. The American Federation of Teachers won key battles for representation of teacher groups in several major United States cities during the mid-1960s. Their successes soon pushed the much larger National Education Association to adopt union-type behaviors in order to retain its own members' loyalties. As a result, the vast majority of America's public school teachers are members of local, state and national unions.

The effect of the growing influence of teachers' unions on educational governance and on relationships between teachers and administrators is persuasive. In the past, teachers and administrators could cooperatively explore ways of working together on curricular modifications or school policies. Today it is more likely that there will be formal rules dictating who is to do what, when and how, written directly into the collective negotiations agreements fashioned between boards/administrators and teachers.

The formalization of relationships causes difficulty for the consultation process in at least two ways. First, because teachers' unions usually have veto power over in-service type activities, school district leaders must gain approval and support of union leaders for projects before the rank and file will participate. Getting this approval and support is no easy matter, since union leaders tend to view any new program as a potential threat to the delicate balance of power between the teachers' group and boards/administrators. They are also prone to view these programs as potential threats to their own positions as leaders of teacher groups. The upshot is that they are just as likely to exercise their veto power as they are to support a proposal, as much for reasons of power relations as for questions they may have about the educational soundness of the proposal.

Second, most contracts specify teachers' hours of service and require compensation for any efforts that go beyond that agreement. Consequently it is becoming increasingly difficult for teachers to voluntarily take part in consultant-led efforts without, according to the union, violating the terms of the contract. The rigidity that has set in makes it quite difficult for school leaders to implement any programs that may not have been anticipated at the time the contract was negotiated.

My own experience is that the union's virtual veto position and the rigidity of negotiated contracts make school leaders less than enthusiastic about initiating in-service activities. After all, why put so much energy into activities that will be so widely resisted? Under such circumstances it is safer and much less stressful to abstain from designing educational change and professional growth activities.

Economic constraints

School budgets have come under increasing scrutiny in recent years. One reason is concern about decline in educational outcomes. For example, high school students taking the scholastic aptitude test are getting lower scores than earlier student groups, and prospective employers are lamenting the inability of candidates to score well on basic literacy tests.

Further, communities are upset that, despite declining enrollments, school budget requests continue to rise. In 1970 the annual cost of public elementary and secondary education was about $41 billion (£27 billion). This figure rose to almost $77 billion (£51 billion) by 1977 and to almost $87 billion (£58 billion) by 1980. During the ten years between 1972 and 1982 per pupil costs rose from $990 (£660) to a predicted $2670 (£1780) (National Center for Educational Statistics, 1978). Educators emphasize that larger budgets are due to increasing costs for materials, equipment and services, but most citizens do not give much thought to the effects of inflation; rather they focus on the almost doubling of the educational bill.

Given both the decline in student population and the alleged drop in educational outcomes, there is less willingness to support educators' seemingly ever-increasing budget requests. In fact, today citizens and policy makers are more and more likely to scrutinize proposed budgets line-by-line to look for places to save money. Under such conditions educators tend to be fiscally conservative. They recognize that taxpayers, as well as policy-makers, are more sophisticated and more critical so they excise items from the budget that might be interpreted as 'frills'. Not surprisingly staff development projects are usually among the first items to be dropped while budget items that appear to be related to 'educational basics', that is, reading, writing and arithmetic, tend to be emphasized.

To further complicate the picture, teachers' contracts often include annual conference days. These sessions which, at best, tend to be demonstration efforts that have little or no long-term impact, often capture the few staff development dollars that survive the budgetary review process. In short, there are fewer dollars earmarked for staff development and those dollars that exist are often devoted to less meaningful efforts.

FORCES THAT ENCOURAGE CONSULTANCY

As the above discussion indicates, the present is a time of relative uncertainty concerning consultancy in schools. There are forces that impinge upon further expansion of consultancy and that may well threaten its continued existence. Certainly consultancy as we know it today will be severely tested. There are, however, counter-forces that support the needs for continuing consultancy in school settings. Four of these appear to be particularly relevant and are gaining in momentum: governmental demands, shifts in teacher training programs, increasing community demands, and educator stress.

Demands of governmental bodies

Within the past several years increasing demands have been placed on school districts from the legislative and executive branches of government at all levels of our federal system. These demands have challenged educational leaders to develop effective responses. For example, demands for accountability have encouraged the development of more effective management systems; passage of state legislation requiring that students achieve minimum levels of competency has led to exploration of alternative delivery systems for less able youngsters; the recent push in many states to require teachers to take examinations which ensure that they will be able to perform adequately in the classroom has led the profession to explore alternative approaches to teacher training and the self-policing of its ranks; and the federal government's emphasis on such issues as mainstreaming special children and increasing the focus on the 'basics' has resulted in a debate among teachers and administrators over the best ways to gear up to meet the challenge. The current demand for educational reform (see Adler, 1982; Goodlad, 1983; National Commission on Excellence in Education, 1983; Task Force on Education for Economic Growth, 1983; Sizer, 1984) has fueled the debate even further.

These demands add to workload. Even more important, they also call for different behaviors on the part of educators. New knowledge and skills will be required if educators are to meet demands for modified behaviors. There is some recognition of this reality; with increasing frequency many of the recent state and federal programs, which represent the codification of these demands, include funds for staff development. In fact, consultants are as likely to be employed through such external funding sources as they are through funds generated locally by the school districts in which they conduct their efforts.

Shifting approaches to teacher preparation

Traditionally teacher education has been based on colleges and universities. At present there is much discussion about the effectiveness of this arrangement. In fact, in states as diverse as New York, Massachusetts, Indiana, Kentucky, Georgia and California, an alternative approach is being designed and implemented. Referred to as 'teachers' centers', these new structures are being developed cooperatively by state education agencies, school districts and teachers' unions to provide some of the training that has, until recently, been the exclusive domain of teacher preparation programs in institutions of higher learning. In future, the former monopoly enjoyed by colleges and universities in teacher preparation will be increasingly challenged. As alternative structures such as teachers' centers are developed and put into place, professors will no longer be able to count on passive or captive pre-service and in-service teacher audiences.

Those who sit on the governing bodies of the newly established teachers' centers are beginning to recognize the need to employ resource persons to meet programmatic requirements. These policy-makers are able to identify purposes for the centers but are usually unable, because of insufficient time and/or skills, to deliver the required pre-service and in-service activities.

Those who are interested in working with alternative structures such as teachers' centers will have to be able to deliver practical forms of consultancy that teachers believe are directly relevant to their job performance. This will represent a dramatic change in consultancy contracting in that it will give teachers greater control over the designation of what consultancy services are required and who should provide them. In other words, the sponsor and the client may become one and the same. If and when this occurs, there will be more pressure put on consultants to deliver services that are viewed as immediately relevant by those receiving these services. Often what teachers get today is decided upon by others some distance from the classroom level. Consequently, what is offered is often viewed by teachers as superfluous. Teachers are clear about what they feel they need. As consultants find themselves negotiating directly with representatives of this group, they will have to learn to tailor their offerings to fit these needs.

INCREASING COMMUNITY DEMANDS

Although signals are often confusing, depending upon which community interest group happens to be speaking the loudest at the moment, communities seem to be demanding more of their schools. Better school performance in the traditional academic areas of math, reading, and writing is the current demand, but there are also concerns about such issues as citizenship training, better discipline, racial desegregation, and the moral development of students.

Most educators find themselves severely constrained as they attempt to meet these growing demands. Their pre-service training probably did not prepare them for the variety of roles they are expected to play. Further, for many, expectations may run counter to their own values, as, for example, when they are pressed to play a larger custodial role at the expense of subject matter dissemination. Educational leaders are coming to recognize that they will have to upgrade abilities, as well as modify attitudes, of their professional staffs if schools are going to be able to respond to community demands. More often than not, this will require them to call on specialists for much of the required staff development work.

Educator stress

The professional literature is replete with articles about teacher and administrator 'burnout'. What burnout refers to, in reality, is the phenomenon of excessive stress which occurs when an individual perceives himself or herself unable to function adequately. The stress being felt is related directly to factors already explored, including increasing community demands, lack of career mobility, calls for accountability, and expectations for attainment of at least minimal teacher and student competencies.

While the literature concerning the existence of educator stress is mixed (Hiebert and Farber, 1984), clearly there are behavioral indicators that indicate some negative realities, for example, the early retirement of school administrators, the short tenure of school superintendents and the concern of administrators and school boards that the finest teachers are showing signs of exhaustion and complaining about low morale, lack of participation, and unsupportive leadership. The cost of stress includes high absenteeism, low enthusiasm, declining productivity in the classroom, and hurried retreats from the school building at the end of the day.

There is growing recognition that the problem is real, relevant, and must be addressed. In fact, there are a number of packaged workshops, most of which focus on 'cure thyself' strategies. Inevitably, sophisticated approaches will be developed and it is likely that future consultation activities will focus on organizationally based issues as well as individual symptoms, such as lack of teacher participation in meaningful decision-making and insufficient job enrichment opportunities. Some large school districts have already instituted in-service sessions for school administrators, frequently referring to them as executive seminars or leadership seminars rather than stress management workshops. These districts often select subject matter which is directly related to job stress, such as time management, dealing with pressure groups, and running meetings more effectively, and hire experts in these areas to conduct one or more sessions.

IMPLICATIONS FOR SHIFTS IN THE FOCUS OF CONSULTANCY

Given the forces and counterforces noted, it seems safe to say that consultancy in schools will change in the future. As schools adjust to declining student enrollments, aging work forces, and the demands of hostile environments, requirements for consultancy will inevitably shift. Below are five highly probable modifications in the school–consultant relationship.

Increasing senior work force

An increasing senior work force will force consultants to modify behaviors. The trend over the past decade has been towards tenured school staffs; staffs with increasing mean-years of service. The lingering after-effects of the economic recession will compound this situation, making it more difficult for staff members already in place to leave education. The aging-of-the-work-force trend will continue for the next several years, at least until the enrollment decline and the demand for new teachers change these demographics.

Much of our present consultancy activities tend to focus on neophyte teachers and administrators. Approaches to classroom management, discipline and the development of curriculum content are aimed at newer teachers who are more available because they are still developing their teaching approaches and, as untenured staff members, are more susceptible to pressures to participate. Similarly, newly appointed administrators tend to feel the need and pressure to participate in growth-type activities more than do their more senior colleagues. However, for the near future there will be relatively few of these neophyte teachers and administrators in school districts.

School district leaders are becoming increasingly aware of the fact that many of their present work force members will probably be with them for some time. They cannot count on senior teachers and administrators who have become disillusioned or complacent to leave in great numbers. As a result, there is growing interest in the development of programs that can rekindle enthusiasm and upgrade the ability of these professionals to meet changing role requirements.

For those of us who consult in schools this presents a great challenge. More and more we will be called upon to work with mature professionals who find what has typically been offered up in in-service efforts to be irrelevant and/or who are attached to the current manner in which they conduct their activities. As Berman and McLaughlin's review of teacher implementation of innovations showed,

> the longer a teacher had taught, the less likely was the project to achieve its goals or to improve student performance. Furthermore, teachers with many years on the job were less likely to change their own practices or to continue using project methods . . .
> (Berman and McLaughlin, 1980, p. 60.)

School district leaders and consultants may think that teachers are in need of professional upgrading, but it is unlikely that many highly experienced teachers will agree with this conclusion. It is going to take potent persuasion to convince teachers with much longevity to display new forms of behavior or to modify their educational objectives to meet changing conditions.

The ability to persuade will become all the more important because the status differential between consultants and clients will be significantly reduced. Senior teachers and administrators are less likely than those who are new to the job to take advice and suggestions at face value simply because they come from consultants. Having gone through the steps to reach the top of their professional ladders, they will not be overly impressed by consultants' credentials. As consultants become less able to rely on status, they will have to become more convincing about the goodness of what they have to offer.

Demands

There will be less demand for highly structured consultancy and more demand for consultancy designed for specific school sites. Consultants often develop specific materials with sequenced activities, usually in the form of 'packaged' workshops, which are then applied, *repeatedly*, in many school settings. Examples of highly structured consultancy in the noninstructional area include management by objectives, inter-personal and intergroup communications, human relations, and time management. Examples in the instructional area include new maths effective teaching, mainstream-ing, and student discipline. Teachers and administrators are becoming more critical about such efforts, especially if they are viewed as rituals rather than as events that have the potential to affect classroom performance.

The Rand study findings lend support to this pessimism. Analysis of the outcomes of highly structured activities in a wide sample of school districts led to the following conclusion (Berman and McLaughlin, 1980, p. 62):

> packaged approaches to planned change typically were too inflexible to permit the local adaptation necessary to effective implementation. No matter how comprehensive the 'road maps' provided by educational packages were, they could not anticipate those local conditions or events that require project plans and practices to be modified. . . . Even if packages could increase the efficiency of implementation, they seem to pose a severe problem for continuation, by depriving the staff of a necessary sense of ownership of the materials.

While there will still be an audience for packaged consultancy, it will probably decline in popularity and there will likely be a growing demand for consultancy that is designed specifically to meet the needs of given situations at particular places. This form of consultancy is much more complex. At minimum there will be a necessity to negotiate agreements about the nature and content of the services to be delivered; the design of accurate diagnoses; the provision of survey feedback; and the development of mutual problem identification strategies between consultants and school-based clients.

For many consultants this will mean giving up safe packages and developing a variety of skills in order to respond to diverse needs. In the process they will open themselves to the possibility of criticism and judgements that they are not providing adequate assist-ance. Consultants who are capable of making the necessary adaptations will probably find themselves in increasing demand, while those who cannot or will not adapt will find themselves shunted aside.

Interests

(a) There will be less interest in skill development activities and more interest in long-term, issue-specific efforts. It is less likely that there will be widespread interest in the development of skills such as communications, participative decision-making and approaches to curriculum redesigning. Senior teachers and administrators will have achieved, or at least *they will perceive themselves to have achieved*, these basic skills and will be less open to round after round of such consultation efforts.

However, while there is less enthusiasm for skill development, there is a growing recognition of the need for consultancy regarding a number of problems in education that seem to be less amenable to resolution than in the past. Educators are looking for external help to find more effective approaches for dealing with such complex issues as racial desegregation, declining enrollments, discipline problems, and the adversarial impact of collective negotiations.

Consultants will find more requests for assistance in dealings with such issue-specific problem areas and, probably, fewer requests for 'pure' skill-related assistance. Whether they can actually deliver useful services when it comes to such complex issues is questionable. At best it is uncertain that we are prepared to meet these demands and we should not promise more than we can deliver. Probably under such conditions we ought to be less prescriptive in our approach. Instead, as discussed below, we should foster a consultant–client relationship that encourages those who must live with the outcomes of our efforts to play maximum roles in problem identification, development of alternative responses, and action planning.

(b) There will be growing interest in the development of internal consultancy capabilities. School officials are beginning to turn to their own personnel as potential consultants. This is happening for a number of reasons. First, in this era of severe budgetary constraints there are many districts that find it difficult to gather the resources required to obtain the services of external consultants, especially on a long-term basis. Second, there is growing recognition that the institutionalization of change requires the active and wide participation of organizational members. What better way to insure participation than to enlist staff members as resource persons? Third, this approach can be a means of finding alternative career paths for senior professionals who have much to offer but who might tend to disengage because there is no room for advancement along established promotional routes. Fourth, there is evidence to support the contention that school staffs are more willing to cooperate if projects are managed by their own colleagues than if projects are led by external consultants.

For these reasons it seems reasonable to conclude that there will be a growing interest in the development of internal consultation. In fact, in a small number of school districts this interest has culminated in the development of teams of internal consultants that are on call to help their colleagues. For example, Schmuck and Runkel (1985) have trained internal change teams in two medium-sized school districts, while Milstein (1979) has adapted their approach to a complex urban school district.

Even where external consultants will continue to provide services directly to school staffs, it is more likely that *they will work in cooperation with internal groups* to plan for and conduct activities. School officials are becoming increasingly aware of the need to monitor consultancy efforts and to involve their teachers in order to increase the potential that these efforts will improve the local situation.

Thus consultants will probably find themselves providing less direct services and more training-the-trainer activities; in other words, they will frequently become consultants to internal consultants. They will do more initial training and then be on call when those they have trained require advice or additional training.

Emphasis

There will be more emphasis on long-term consultancy. Disenchantment with highly structured consultancy as well as with the emphasis on skill development, as noted, is growing. There is also an increasing recognition among educators that they should be seeking consultancy that can help them confront the increasingly complex problems that call for long-range programmatic responses. For example, several years ago a survey of school districts in the United States and Canada identified 76 districts that had employed outside consultants for three or more years on a given project (Fullan, Miles, and Taylor, 1980). This is still a minimal response when compared with the number of school districts in these countries, but at least it is a clear recognition on the part of some educational leaders that long-term consultancy is necessary if a lasting impact is to be achieved.

If this trend continues the implications for school-based consultancy are relevant. Consultants will have to be able to respond over a long period of time rather than merely fly in for a day or so and fly out again. Further, they will have to be capable of conducting a variety of activities that include diagnosis, cooperative problem identification, development of alternative prescriptions, designing and managing action plans, monitoring progress, and evaluating outcomes. At the present time few consultants possess such a wide range of skills. While some may become at least minimally proficient in the many facets of long-term consultancy, it is also likely that most will have to develop cooperative efforts by forming resource pools of consultants who can assist at different stages of long-term efforts.

CONCLUSIONS

For better or worse these are one observer's visions of the future of consultancy in educational settings. First, consultants will have to take the changing composition of their client group into account. That is, they will be working with more mature teachers and administrators whose needs and interests will differ from those of newer educational professionals. Second, they will be challenged to create designs that meet the specific needs of particular school settings more often than has been the case in the past. Third, they will find themselves engaged in helping internal resource persons to develop skills and carry out many of the direct consultancy services now being performed by outsiders. Finally, they will be called upon to design and conduct more long-term consultancy efforts, that will test their capacity to respond and will hold them more accountable for results.

Whether the forces and counter-forces that have been explored will result in consultancy of the nature that I foresee is uncertain, but it is highly likely that consultancy as we know it today will be extensively modified. Whatever crystal ball one employs, the future of consultancy in schools should be marked by challenges for those who take on this function. The rapidly shifting context within which public education exists cannot help but have a spillover effect on school-based consultancy.

Predicting the future is a hazardous business at best. When predictions are made in times of uncertainty the probability of being on target is even less. Readers may well argue with the conclusion for the future of consultancy in schools that have been derived herein. In fact, it is my hope that such debates will occur, for without attention to the future, we will become passive responders rather than proactive initiators.

REFERENCES

Adler, M. J. (1982) *The Padeia Proposal*. New York: Macmillan.

Berman, P. and McLaughlin, M. W. (1980) 'Factors affecting the process of change', in Milstein, M. M. (ed.) *Schools, Conflict, and Change*, pp. 57–71. New York: Teachers College Press.

Blake, R. R. and Mouton, J. S. (1976) *Consultation*. Reading, Mass.: Addison-Wesley.

Charters, W. W. Jr. (1970) 'Some factors affecting teacher survival in school districts'. *American Educational Research Journal*, **7**, 1–27.

Fullan, M., Miles, M. B. and Taylor, G. (1980) 'Organization development in schools: the state of the art'. *Review of Educational Research*, **50**, 121–83.

Goodlad, J. I. (1983) *A Place Called School*. New York: McGraw-Hill.

Harris, L. and Associates, Inc. (1984). *The American Teacher*. New York: Metropolitan Life Insurance Company.

Hiebert, B. and Farber, I. (1984) 'Teacher stress: a literature survey with a few surprises'. *Canadian Journal of Education*, **9**, 14–27.

Mark, J. H. and Anderson, B. D. (1978) 'Teacher survival—a current look'. *American Educational Research Journal*, **15**, 379–84.

Milstein, M. M. (1979) 'Developing a renewal team in an urban school district', *Theory Into Practice*, **18**, 106–13.

National Center for Educational Statistics (1978) *Projection of Educational Statistics to 1986–87*. Washington, DC: US Government Printing Office.

National Commission on Excellence in Education (1983) *A Nation At Risk*. Washington, DC: Government Printing Office.

Schmuck, R. A. and Runkel, P. J. (1985) *The Handbook of Organizational Development in Schools*. Palo Alto, Cal.: Mayfield.

Sizer, T. R. (1984) *Horace's Compromise: The Dilemma of the American High School*. Boston: Houghton Mifflin.

Task Force on Education for Economic Growth (1983) *Action for Excellence*. Denver: Education Commission of the States.

Name Index

Subject Index